Critical Studies of the Asia Pacific Series

Series Editor: **Mark Beeson**, Professor of International Politics, Murdoch University, Australia

Critical Studies of the Asia Pacific showcases new research and scholarship on what is arguably the most important region in the world in the twenty-first century. The rise of China and the continuing strategic importance of this dynamic economic area to the United States mean that the Asia Pacific will remain crucially important to policymakers and scholars alike. The unifying theme of the series is a desire to publish the best theoretically informed, original research on the region. Titles in the series cover the politics, economics and security of the region, as well as focussing on its institutional processes, individual countries, issues and leaders.

Titles include:

Thomas Birtchnell
INDOVATION
Innovation and a Global Knowledge Economy in India

Lindsay Black
JAPAN'S MARITIME SECURITY STRATEGY
The Japan Coast Guard and Maritime Outlaws

Aurel Croissant, David Küehn, Philip Lorenz and Paul W. Chambers
DEMOCRATIZATION AND CIVILIAN CONTROL IN ASIA

Giovanna Maria Dora Dore, Jae H. Ku and Karl Jackson (*editors*)
INCOMPLETE DEMOCRACIES IN THE ASIA-PACIFIC
Evidence from Indonesia, Korea, the Philippines and Thailand

Kelly Gerard
ASEAN's ENGAGEMENT OF CIVIL SOCIETY
Regulating Dissent

Felix Heiduk (*editor*)
SECURITY SECTOR REFORM IN SOUTHEAST ASIA
From Policy to Practice

Brendan Howe
THE PROTECTION AND PROMOTION OF HUMAN SECURITY IN EAST ASIA

Jane Hutchison, Wil Hout, Caroline Hughes and Richard Robison
POLITICAL ECONOMY AND THE AID INDUSTRY IN ASIA

Eun Mee Kim and Pil Ho Kim (*editors*)
THE SOUTH KOREAN DEVELOPMENT EXPERIENCE
Beyond Aid

Jikon Lai
FINANCIAL CRISIS AND INSTITUTIONAL CHANGE IN EAST ASIA

Jonathan London (*editor*)
POLITICS IN CONTEMPORARY VIETNAM
Party, State, and Authority Relations

Arndt Michael
INDIA'S FOREIGN POLICY AND REGIONAL MULTILATERALISM

Mohammad Zulfan Tadjoeddin
EXPLAINING COLLECTIVE VIOLENCE IN CONTEMPORARY INDONESIA

Claudia Tazreiter and Siew Yean Tham (*editors*)
GLOBALIZATION AND SOCIAL TRANSFORMATION IN THE ASIA-PACIFIC
The Australian and Malaysian Experience

Sow Keat Tok
MANAGING CHINA'S SOVEREIGNTY IN HONG KONG AND TAIWAN

William Tow and Rikki Kersten (*editors*)
BILATERAL PERSPECTIVES ON REGIONAL SECURITY
Australia, Japan and the Asia-Pacific Region

Barry Wain
MALAYSIAN MAVERICK
Mahathir Mohamad in Turbulent Times

Mikael Weissmann
THE EAST ASIAN PEACE
Conflict Prevention and Informal Peacebuilding

Robert G. Wirsing, Christopher Jasparro and Daniel C. Stoll
INTERNATIONAL CONFLICT OVER WATER RESOURCES IN HIMALAYAN ASIA

Hidetaka Yoshimatsu
COMPARING INSTITUTION-BUILDING IN EAST ASIA
Power Politics, Governance, and Critical Junctures

Critical Studies of the Asia Pacific Series
Series Standing Order ISBN 978–0–230–22896–2 (Hardback)
978–0–230–22897–9 (Paperback)
(*outside North America only*)

You can receive future titles in this series as they are published by placing a standing order. Please contact your bookseller or, in case of difficulty, write to us at the address below with your name and address, the title of the series and the ISBNs quoted above.

Customer Services Department, Macmillan Distribution Ltd, Houndmills, Basingstoke, Hampshire RG21 6XS, England

---

Also by Hidetaka Yoshimatsu (published by Palgrave Macmillan)

INTERNATIONALIZATION, CORPORATE PREFERENCES AND COMMERCIAL POLICY IN JAPAN

JAPAN AND EAST ASIA IN TRANSITION: Trade Policy, Crisis and Evolution, and Regionalism

THE POLITICAL ECONOMY OF REGIONALISM IN EAST ASIA: Integrative Explanation for Dynamics and Challenges

Comparing Institution-Building in East Asia

Power Politics, Governance, and Critical Junctures

Hidetaka Yoshimatsu
Ritsumeikan Asia Pacific University, Japan

palgrave
macmillan

First published 2014 by
PALGRAVE MACMILLAN

Palgrave Macmillan in the UK is an imprint of Macmillan Publishers Limited, registered in England, company number 785998, of Houndmills, Basingstoke, Hampshire RG21 6XS.

Palgrave Macmillan in the US is a division of St Martin's Press LLC, 175 Fifth Avenue, New York, NY 10010.

Palgrave Macmillan is the global academic imprint of the above companies and has companies and representatives throughout the world.

Palgrave® and Macmillan® are registered trademarks in the United States, the United Kingdom, Europe and other countries.

ISBN 978–1–137–37054–9

This book is printed on paper suitable for recycling and made from fully managed and sustained forest sources. Logging, pulping and manufacturing processes are expected to conform to the environmental regulations of the country of origin.

A catalogue record for this book is available from the British Library.

A catalog record for this book is available from the Library of Congress.

Contents

Tables and Figures

Tables

Figures

Preface and Acknowledgements

The international relations of East Asia are multifaceted. On the one hand, major states in the region have achieved steady economic growth, which has led to increasing economic and social linkages among their societies and peoples. This growth has also raised the region's political status, which is typically given prominence in the Group of Twenty (G-20). On the other hand, despite growing economic and social linkages, nationalistic sentiments still remain strong in most of the countries. Moreover, political animosities and security tensions constitute critical issues in international relations of East Asia. While the tensions in the Korean Peninsula remain unresolved, those relating to maritime security are escalating in the East China and South China Seas.

A key factor in promoting regional cooperation is the development of formal institutions. For a long time, initiatives for advancing explicit cooperation through formal institutions remained at a preliminary stage in East Asia. Not only is East Asia's history of regionalist initiatives and projects a short one, but the major countries' propensity to maintain sovereign rights and territorial integrity has also hindered the initiation and development of regional institutions. As a background factor, diversity in terms of political regimes, economic development, and cultural traditions including religion has hindered the formation of a common regional identity. Since the late 1990s, however, countries in East Asia have gradually strengthened their aspirations to advance formal institutions designed to tackle common challenges that the region is facing and to provide regional public goods for collective interests.

The development of regional institutions in East Asia is primarily dependent on the extent to which state actors can coordinate their diverse interests towards long-term collective objectives. At the same time, practical processes of institution-building are influenced by various factors. While overall historical trends on the global scene influence the speed and direction of regional institution-building, the presence and involvement of non-state actors provide particular input for deepening regionalist initiatives and projects. This monograph aims to make some contributions to the study of regionalism in East Asia by linking practical moves towards regional consolidation to key perspectives and concepts in the theories of politics and international relations.

It is a pleasure to acknowledge my debt to those who have provided significant assistance for the completion of this volume. In the process of preparing it for publication, many scholars have become a source of inspiration and support. I am particularly thankful to Purnendra Jain, Glenn

D. Hook, Mark Beeson, Christopher W. Hughes, Seung-Young Kim, Yoichiro Sato, Vyas Utpal, In-Won Hwang, and Min-je Lee. I also wish to express my deep gratitude to the Graduate School of Asia Pacific Studies, Ritsumeikan Asia Pacific University (APU). Although APU is a relatively new university located in a small city in southwestern Japan, its internationally oriented academic environment has provided me with valuable intellectual stimulus through participation in international conferences and daily discussions with other colleagues. I also thank the Centre for Asian Studies, University of Adelaide and the School of East Asian Studies, University of Sheffield. Visiting fellowships at these organisations helped crystallise the thinking that resulted in this book. This work was supported by the Grant-in-Aid for Scientific Research (23530208) from the Ministry of Education, Culture, Sports, Science and Technology, Japan.

Finally, gratitude goes to my wife, Mutsumi, and our son, Satoshi, for their willing sacrifices and continuous support. They have sustained my life as a researcher by allowing me to spend time on research even during weekends. Without their understanding and encouragement, this project would not have been possible.

Abbreviations

ACAP	Asia Centre for Air Pollution Research
ACE	ASEAN Centre for Energy
ACFTA	ASEAN–China Free Trade Area
ACU	Asian Currency Unit
ADB	Asian Development Bank
AEC	ASEAN Economic Community
AEM	ASEAN Economic Ministers
AERR	ASEAN Emergency Rice Reserve
AFSIS	ASEAN Food Security Information System
AFSRB	ASEAN Food Security Reserve Board
AFTA	ASEAN Free Trade Area
AJCEP	ASEAN–Japan Comprehensive Economic Partnership
AMAF	ASEAN Ministers on Agriculture and Forestry
AMEM	ASEAN Ministers on Energy Meeting
AMF	Asian Monetary Fund
AMRO	ASEAN+3 Macroeconomic Research Office
APEC	Asia-Pacific Economic Cooperation
APF	Asian Policy Forum
APSA	ASEAN Petroleum Security Agreement
APTERR	ASEAN+3 Emergency Rice Reserve
ARF	ASEAN Regional Forum
ASEAN	Association of Southeast Asian Nations
ASEAN+3	ASEAN Plus Three
ASEM	Asia–Europe Meeting
BSA	bilateral swap agreement
CASS	Chinese Academy of Social Sciences
CCP	Chinese Communist Party
CDM	Clean Development Mechanism
CEPEA	Comprehensive Economic Partnership Agreement in East Asia
CMI	Chiang Mai Initiative
CMIM	Chiang Mai Initiative Multilateralisation
CNEMC	China National Environmental Monitoring Centre
DPJ	Democratic Party of Japan
DSM	dispute settlement mechanism
EAERR	East Asia Emergency Rice Reserve
EAFTA	East Asia Free Trade Area
EANET	Acid Deposition Monitoring Network in East Asia
EAS	East Asia Summit

EE&C	energy efficiency and conservation
EHP	Early Harvest Programme
EMEP	European Monitoring and Evaluation Programme
EPA	economic partnership agreement
EPGG	Energy Policy Governing Group
ERIA	Economic Research Institute for ASEAN and East Asia
ERPD	Economic Review and Policy Dialogue
EU	European Union
FAO	Food and Agriculture Organization
FDI	foreign direct investment
FTA	free trade agreement
G-7/G-8	Group of Seven/ Group of Eight
G-20	Group of Twenty
GATT	General Agreement on Tariffs and Trade
GDP	gross domestic product
IEA	International Energy Agency
IEEJ	Institute of Energy Economics, Japan
IEF	International Energy Forum
IIMA	Institute for International Monetary Affairs
IMF	International Monetary Fund
JETRO	Japan External Trade Organisation
JICA	Japan International Cooperation Agency
JOGMEC	Japan Oil Gas and Metals National Corporation
JSEPA	Japan–Singapore Economic Partnership Agreement
KEEI	Korea Energy Economics Institute
KIEP	Korea Institute for International Economic Policy
LDP	Liberal Democratic Party
LRTAP	Convention on Long-Range Transboundary Air Pollution
LTP	Long-Range Transboundary Air Pollutants in Northeast Asia
MAFF	Ministry of Agriculture, Forestry and Fisheries
MAV	minimum access volume
METI	Ministry of Economy, Trade and Industry
MOAC	Ministry of Agriculture and Cooperatives
MOE	Ministry of the Environment
MOFA	Ministry of Foreign Affairs
MOFCOM	Ministry of Commerce
MOU	memorandum of understanding
NDRC	National Development and Reform Commission
NEAT	Network of East Asian Think-tanks
NGO	non-governmental organisation
NOC	national oil company
NOx	nitrogen oxides
NRE	new and renewable energy
ODA	official development assistance

OECD	Organisation for Economic Cooperation and Development
OREC	Organisation of Rice Exporting Countries
OSRM	Oil Stockpiling Roadmap
PM	particulate matter
RCEP	Regional Comprehensive Economic Partnership
RIN	Research Institute Network
SAC	Scientific Advisory Committee
SO_2	sulphur dioxide
SOME	Senior Officials Meeting on Energy
TDRI	Thailand Development Research Institute
TPP	Trans-Pacific Partnership Agreement
UNCED	United Nations Conference on Environment and Development
UNEP	United Nations Environmental Programme
UNEP RRC.AP	UNEP Regional Resource Centre for Asia and the Pacific
WFP	World Food Programme
WTO	World Trade Organization

1
Introduction

In the new millennium, East Asia has emerged as an increasingly prominent region in the global economy and in world politics. The region has continuously achieved relatively high economic growth, becoming the world's primary source of manufacturing products with intensive production networks and supply chains. Such growing economic capabilities have led to an enhanced political presence. Not only three core Northeast Asian countries – China, Japan, and South Korea – but also Indonesia gained a seat in the Group of Twenty (G-20), an increasingly important political grouping. The Association of Southeast Asian Nations (ASEAN) has raised its international profile by forming substantial linkages with its neighbouring countries such as India and Australia/New Zealand and by pursuing closer relationships with global players such as the United States and the European Union (EU).

For a long time, initiatives and projects for regional cooperation in East Asia stayed at a preliminary stage especially compared with Europe, where regionalist ideas and projects have been advanced for more than half a century. The East Asian states, which have a strong propensity to pay respect to maintaining sovereignty and domestic regime autonomy, find great difficulties in coordinating their interests for achieving far-reaching, collective goals. Despite such backwardness and difficulties, a regionalist aspiration in East Asia has surely intensified in the new millennium. The states in the region have developed various multilateral frameworks with the expanding scope of issue-areas for cooperation and deepening efforts to institutionalise cooperative initiatives. This book intends to make some contributions to the study of international relations in East Asia by elucidating complicated processes of institution-building in the region.

Evolving regionalism in East Asia

Regional cooperation has evolved and proliferated in East Asia by advancing several multilateral frameworks. The members of ASEAN and the three major Northeast Asian countries have deepened and expanded regionalist ideas and projects under the framework of the ASEAN Plus Three (ASEAN+3). The framework, formed at a summit meeting in December

1997, was positioned as the 'main vehicle' for the building of an East Asian community. The East Asian Summit (EAS) was created in 2005 among the ASEAN+3 members as well as Australia, New Zealand, and India as a regional forum to discuss political, security, and economic issues in East Asia. The EAS became an 18-member institution in 2011 by adding the United States and Russia as new members. In addition to these two frameworks, the East Asian countries have advanced cooperative activities under the economic-oriented Asia-Pacific Economic Cooperation (APEC) and the security-relevant ASEAN Regional Forum (ARF), which hold a larger membership involving several countries in the Americas or South Asia. Thus, multilateral frameworks for regional cooperation in East Asia have developed in the multilayered structure under complicated political configurations involving diverse memberships.

ASEAN members as well as China, Japan, and South Korea have been the key players of institution-building in East Asia, and the ASEAN+3 framework has provided the main locus for their collaboration. The range of cooperative fields under the framework expanded to various functional areas including finance, energy, trade, health, and agriculture. As a consequence of continuous dialogues among participating countries, multilateral institutions for advancing cooperative programmes have gradually developed in several policy areas. While financial ministers achieved the multilateralisation of bilateral swap agreements under the Chiang Mai Initiative (CMI), agricultural ministers reached an agreement to establish the ASEAN+3 Emergency Rice Reserve (APTERR). In the trade field, the East Asian countries are engaging in the formation of the Regional Comprehensive Economic Partnership (RCEP) as an advanced step from the ASEAN+1 free trade agreement (FTA) networks.

In the process of regional cooperation, political leaders in East Asia have confirmed political will and the overall direction of cooperation at the summit meetings, and the building of cooperative institutions has been advanced in specific policy fields. Under the ASEAN+3 framework, ministerial meetings for discussing cooperative initiatives and projects have been organised in individual policy areas. Significantly, there are notable differences in the progress of cooperative initiative and the degree of institutionalisation among different policy areas. While there are areas where the progress of cooperation has led to the relatively tighter institutionalisation of cooperative projects, such as the financial sector, the process for realising cooperative arrangements has been slow and fragmented in other sectors such as trade and energy. Such differences are produced by various factors including political bargaining among participating governments, commitments and pressures from extra-regional states and forces, the creation and development of collective norms and principles sustained by common identity, consideration of domestic political and economic interests, the range and involvement of non-state actors, and so on.

This research explores the causes and implications of the diverse degree of institution-building in different policy areas in East Asia by examining two processes of initiating and developing multilateral institutions in five policy areas: trade, finance, agriculture, energy, and the environment. It pays particular attention to political interactions among China, Japan, South Korea, and ASEAN – the four major parties in East Asia – in realising their specific interests and preferences in the process of institutional creation and evolution.

Reviewing research on regionalism in East Asia

The main objective of this book is to examine the process of regional institution-building by shedding light on the genesis, evolution, and design of concrete institutions in specific policy fields. Such an examination is designed to make contributions to the study of regionalism in East Asia. Importantly, regionalism in East Asia incorporates specific features of an emphasis on informality, consultation, and voluntarism largely because ASEAN, the driver of regional institution-building, has paid respect to these norms. Moreover, regionalism in East Asia has developed in seemingly contradictory political economic conditions: lingering political tensions and dynamic economic interdependence. These factors have encouraged the students of international relations, area studies, and comparative politics to explore the origin, development, and effects of regionalism in East Asia from various theoretical angles.

The first set of studies highlights the influence of power politics on the evolution and management of regional affairs. Quite a few studies have demonstrated that the predominance of the United States and its bilateral links with regional states (the so-called hub-and-spokes system) were the major reasons why the development of regional institutions among East Asian states and political will to sustain such a development have been weak and fragmented (Grieco 1999; Beeson and Berger 2003; Beeson and Higgott 2005; Katzenstein 2005; Sutter 2008). In this respect, Katzenstein's research needs particular attention. Katzenstein (2005) explains the evolution of regional institutions in Asia (and Europe) in terms of the American imperium and the presence of the regional core state. The American imperium through preponderant material and ideational capabilities has established specific interactions with Asia such as cross-fertilisation, co-evolution, and blowback. Japan, which held specific historical experience and evolution in the American imperium, played a role as the core state in creating an institutional order in Asia. While some scholars have applied the neorealist perspective to an analysis of regional cooperation in specific functional areas, others have analysed the cases where the US veto power disturbed the development of cooperative initiatives in East Asia.[1]

The second set of studies sheds light on domestic politics as the main source of constraint in regional affairs in East Asia. Solingen (2008) argues that while the nature of dominant domestic coalition often explains the genesis of regional institutions, it is underdetermining in accounting for their design, and that the nature of domestic coalitions matters when the consequences of creating or designing institutions for relative power distribution, transaction costs, or normative convergence are negligible. Stubbs (2011) applies the domestic coalition model to the relationships between the responses of the East Asian governments to the global financial crisis and domestic battles of state-interventionist and neo-liberal coalitions. Other studies also focus on domestic elements such as the adherence to domestic political legitimacy (Narine 2004) and domestic regulatory capacity (Hamilton-Hart 2003) as the most critical factors disturbing the creation of effective multilateral mechanisms in East Asia. These studies posit that preferences of dominant domestic actors and their coalitions or the state's political capabilities and shared beliefs are crucial factors conditioning the genesis and design of regionalism in East Asia.

The third set of studies explains regional affairs in East Asia by employing constructivist concepts such as identity and norms. Several scholars account for growing momentum to regional cooperation in East Asia in terms of gradually developed collective identity. They hold that the Asian financial crisis in 1997–98 played a catalytic role in consolidating the East Asian identity by strengthening policymakers' perception of living in a common destiny and the image of a region in adversity besieged by outsiders (Nabers 2003; Terada 2003; Yu 2003). Other scholars have paid attention to ASEAN and its shared norms as variables that have promoted regional cooperation and integration in East Asia (Acharya 1997; 2001; 2003; 2004; Khong and Nesadurai 2007). The development of ASEAN became possible in search of a common identity through shared norms and socialisation. ASEAN members have developed, through diplomatic interactions and practices, the so-called 'ASEAN Way', a set of norms that include the non-interference principle, informal consultation, pragmatic expediency, consensus-building, and flexible incrementalism (Acharya 1997: 329–33; Liu 2003: 20–22).[2] According to Acharya (2003: 211), regional leaders have asserted that their non-legalistic, consensual, and process-centric ASEAN Way is a distinctive and workable alternative to a European-style multilateralism. The cumulative and social process has played a critical role in making Southeast Asia a stable, cooperative, and coherent region. ASEAN has distinctive founding ideas on regional resilience for 'One Southeast Asia', which was bounded by the members' nationalism. ASEAN's elites have, then, reaffirmed, maintained, or renegotiated ASEAN ideas through dynamic dialogue-driven social processes such as argument, consensus-seeking, and social reinforcement (Ba 2009).

The brief overview of the past research reveals complex causal factors that affect regionalism and regional affairs in East Asia. Although I categorised the studies of regionalism in East Asia into the three groups, quite a few studies have sought to synthesise certain theories and approaches and build an integrated analytical framework (Katzenstein and Sil 2004; Aggarwal and Koo 2008; He 2009; Rathus 2011). In reality, an approach that relies on one or two theoretical angles or conceptual frames is not enough to elucidate regional cooperation in East Asia, especially the complicated process of institution-building. This study also adopts an integrative approach to look into evolving and complex political processes for the initiation and development of specific regional institutions. A critical issue is what factors are considered as variables that have significant effects on progress or regress in the building process of the institutions.

Four factors influencing regional institution-building

This research takes up four key variables that are assumed to bring about diverse institutional designs and processes in different policy areas. The first is political interactions among involved parties. In East Asia, distribution of capabilities among great powers has constituted the basic framework for international affairs, and the states have a strong adherence to maintaining national interests and sovereignty. This neorealist perspective is considered the first variable that influences the process of institution-building in East Asia. The second is policymakers' preferences in the domestic political process. The great powers can reflect domestic political elements in pursuing specific goals in external policies. In particular, policymakers' preferences in relation to political legitimacy are regarded as influencing the states' external commitments and policies. The third is the involvement of non-state actors in the policy formation process. State actors do indeed remain vital and active participants in regional public affairs, but they are no longer the only players who initiate regional policies, nor do they control the entire process of policy development. The non-state actors can provide specific information and expertise that state actors require in making decisions in a wide range of issue-areas such as the economy, technology, social development, and the environment. In other words, the governance perspective on sustaining coordination and coherence among a wide variety of actors is crucial for understanding public policy formation in the current world. The fourth is critical junctures in historical trajectory. Regional affairs including institutional arrangements follow the overall historical sequence. The historical sequence is not smooth and even, and some contingent shocks and events create critical junctures in the trajectory. Such critical incidents and crises have profound influences on the subsequent track, changing patterns in the path of institutional development.

The main argument of this book is fourfold. First, regional power transition casts significant shadows on the development of institution-building in East Asia. Japan initiates regional institutions in major policy areas, but the key actor who conditions the progress of these institutions is China. The degree of commitment that China makes to regional cooperation directly influences the degree of institutional development. Second, the configuration of policymakers' preferences for political legitimacy is different between Japan and China: Japanese government officials seek to pursue political legitimacy of their own ministries through regional commitments, while the ruling party's aspiration for maintaining its political legitimacy has strong influences on Chinese behaviour and policies towards East Asian cooperation. Third, governance elements in regional institution-building remain underdeveloped in East Asia. The non-state actors represented by research institutes can be involved in the policy formation process, but their real influences on policy development are limited largely because of weak internal cohesion and the states' dominance of policy networks involving non-state actors. Fourth, the building of regional institutions proceeds under the marked influence of critical events. The critical events represented by global/regional crises play a catalytic role in revealing the dysfunction of the existing institutions and making policymakers recognise the need to hold effective regional mechanisms, resultantly elevating the institutional path to a new level at which it is impossible to return to the previous point.

The values of the research

This research has four diverse values and significances. First, it contributes to developing the theoretical study of regionalism in East Asia by synthesising theoretical perspectives of politics and international relations. The dominant theoretical approach that explains international relations in East Asia is neorealism, and liberal and constructivist approaches provide alternative theoretical foundations. This study gives priority to political interactions over power and interests, but seeks to go beyond the neorealist paradigm by incorporating three additional theory-oriented perspectives – domestic politics, regional governance, and critical juncture. The influence of the variables that derive from the perspectives is woven into power-based interactions among the states.

Second, this study contributes to deepening the study of regionalism in East Asia by expanding the scope of empirical research. The growing importance of East Asia in international politics and the global economy has encouraged the study of the political economy of regionalism in East Asia. These studies have surely made valuable contributions to regionalism in East Asia, but representative studies have dealt with major empirical cases, typically security, trade, and finance. Comprehensive and comparative research on other policy areas has been limited although multilateral cooperation has gradually developed in these areas. This study can fill in the gap in research by examining the development of regional institutions in two cases in the economics field, two in the non-traditional security field, and one in the environmental field.

Third, this research can reveal the complicated political process of regionalism in East Asia. It highlights specific policy fields, and traces scrupulously the initiation and development of major institutions mostly formed under the ASEAN+3 framework. The development of institutions and political interactions among state actors are carefully examined by paying attention to their interests and preferences. Such a process-tracing method enables this study to elucidate forward and backward forces in the construction of institutions and changes in the forces in the evolving historical context.

Fourth, this research can provide perspectives on the maintenance of a contemporary regional order in East Asia. While the gradual formation of cooperative institutions is seen in East Asia, various challenges are also emerging in the region. Representative of such challenges is the rise of China in an accelerated regional power transition. While China's rise surely provides economic and social benefits for the entire region, its rising economic power and resultant assertive diplomacy tend to provoke political concerns among its neighbouring countries, which search for various strategies including balancing and hedging. This research is expected to elucidate how the rise of China occurred in the practical context of policy evolution and to provide some insights on the management of the Chinese ascendency in East Asia.

The structure of the book

The main objective of this study is to describe how processes in regional institution-building are different in diverse policy areas and explain why such differences have been produced in the institutions' developmental path. In order to achieve this objective, this book sets up an analytical framework on the basis of independent and dependent variables, and traces the creation and development of particular institutions in five policy areas.

Chapter 2 presents analytical frameworks that comprise primary and supplementary pillars. The primary pillar is based on the neorealist perspective that highlights political interactions among states with an interest in initiating and developing multilateral institutions for regional cooperation. The supplementary pillars consist of three variables: state policymakers' policy preferences for pursuing political legitimacy; non-state actors' involvements in the policy formation process; and a contingent crisis or critical event in historical trajectory. On the basis of the frameworks, I will undertake empirical analyses regarding institutional creation and evolution in specific policy fields.

In chapters 3–7 empirical analyses are conducted in five policy fields. In Chapter 3, the development of FTAs in East Asia is examined. Although major states in East Asia engaged in the formation of bilateral or minilateral FTAs after the late 1990s, it took a long time to develop these bilateral, line-based FTAs into a multilateral, square-based FTA. Chapter 3 examines the political process towards the launching of negotiations on the RCEP in 2013. The focus of Chapter 4 is financial cooperation. In 2000, ASEAN+3 finance ministers agreed on bilateral swap agreements for liquidity provision – the CMI – and the Economic Review and Policy Dialogue (ERPD) system to underpin the CMI. Afterwards, financial officials engaged in continuous talks on the multilateralisation of the CMI. The main interest of this chapter is to investigate the political process towards achieving this objective by establishing a new institution with joint decision-making methods. In Chapter 5, our focus turns to institution-building for regional food security in general and a rice reserve system in particular. In the early 2000s, an initiative to set up a rice reserve system in East Asia was launched, and this initiative was realised in 2012 with the formation of the APTERR. I will analyse the political process towards the launching of this collective institution to respond to common challenges in food security. Chapter 6 examines the development of ASEAN+3 cooperation on energy security. In 2003, the Energy Policy Governance Group was formed, and concrete projects for energy security have been advanced through dialogues at forums targeting specific policy issues such as oil stockpiling, energy security, oil market, renewable energy, and so on. The main interest of this chapter is to explore processes and challenges for deepening cooperation on energy security through the formulation of regional institutions. In Chapter 7, the Acid Deposition Monitoring Network in East Asia (EANET) is highlighted as a representative of regional environmental institution. EANET was launched in 2001 in order to resolve transboundary air pollution problems in East Asia. The network, which was formed among 13 countries in Northeast and Southeast Asia, began its activities after sufficient preparatory phases, and holds organisational bodies involving the Secretariat and the Network Centre. Chapter 7 analyses EANET's development process to become an autonomous institution by resolving financial burden sharing problems and establishing tighter institutional frameworks.

Chapter 8 evaluates evidence in regional institution-building in East Asia in the previous five cases. It identifies common features in the process of institution-building and institutional design. It also examines causal mechanisms between the institutional processes and factors that influence the processes. The particularly important factors are the parties' commitments to institutions, their underlying interests, and their political interactions. Chapter 8 also takes into account other factors such as policymakers' preferences for pursuing political legitimacy in the domestic political process, the involvement and influence of non-state actors in the policymaking process, and critical junctures in historical trajectory.

2
Frameworks for Analysing Institution-Building in East Asia

This research aims to examine institution-building for regional cooperation in specific policy fields that East Asian states have gradually developed since the early 2000s. In making a meaningful analysis of the development of regional cooperation in East Asia, it is necessary to be mindful of major features of the region and establish an analytical framework by linking them to theoretical perspectives and concepts that have developed in the study of international relations.

The analytical framework of this research comprises two pillars. The primary pillar is based on the neorealist perspective that puts stress on power politics among states that pursue national interests. The secondary pillar incorporates three elements that supplement the neorealist perspective: preferences of state policymakers in the domestic political process; the meaningful involvement of non-state actors in the policy formation process; and the historical trajectory that underpins the development of institutional paths.

Before presenting the analytical framework, it is necessary to define the most important concept: institution. In this research, 'institution' is considered as 'explicit arrangements, negotiated among international actors, that prescribe, proscribe, and/or authorize behavior' (Koremenos et al. 2001a: 762). This definition is relatively narrow in scope compared with other definitions that include conventions that are 'informal institutions, with implicit rules and understandings, that shape the expectations of actors' (Keohane 1989: 4). The main objectives of this research are to describe the initiation and development of institutions for regional cooperation and analyse political interactions among actors over the design and direction of such institutions. The focus on explicit arrangements contributes to taking hold of the essence of states' political interactions in a deliberative manner to solve specific problems (Koremenos and Snidal 2003: 433).

The primary framework: Power politics over national interests

Power politics in East Asia

In the post-World War II period, great power politics has provided the basic configuration of international affairs in East Asia. The US foreign policy established the principal form of international relations in the region. The United States adopted a bilateral-oriented foreign policy, forging the 'hub-and-spokes' structure through security partnerships with Japan, South Korea, the Philippines, and Thailand.[1] Japan gradually emerged as a regional power, but its neighbouring states were not willing to promote regional cooperation with it because of the memories of the Pacific War and the fear of dominance by an economically resurgent Japan (Grieco 1999: 338–40). Although the US-centred networks of security partnership were formed at the early stage of the Cold War, they have remained political and military links for most states even after the end of the war. Furthermore, interplays among the United States, China, and Japan have determined the degree of conflict and cooperation in East Asia, and actions and policies of other smaller states were regarded as strategic responses to great power politics (Mols 2000: 20–23; Ikenberry and Mastanduno 2003). The smaller states have indeed provided initiatives in launching major regional institutions, but they have been forced to adopt discrete strategies varying from bandwagoning and accommodating to hedging and balancing to secure their interests in complicated regional politics manipulated by great powers.

Great power politics has been apparent in the process of institution-building in East Asia in the post-Cold War period. In the 1990s, partly driven by intensive moves towards regionalism in other parts of the world, East Asian states began to exhibit explicit interest in the construction of regional institutions. Such interest led to the establishment of several formal institutions: the ASEAN Regional Forum (ARF) in 1994, the Asia-Europe Meeting (ASEM) in 1996, the ASEAN Plus Three (ASEAN+3) in 1997, and, later, the East Asia Summit (EAS) in 2005. Great power politics had a strong impact on the development of concrete regional institutions. Japan's initiative in establishing the Asian Monetary Fund during the Asian financial crisis in 1997–98 was shot down by adamant opposition from the United States and China (Grimes 2009). When the EAS was newly established in 2005, Japan and China disagreed over its membership and basic character. China considered that the EAS should be composed of ASEAN+3 members, and the ASEAN+3 would remain the main body for discussing the future East Asian community (Malik 2006). In contrast, Japan asserted the expansion of the EAS members beyond the ASEAN+3, and supported the idea that the EAS should become a venue to discuss the East Asian community as well.

The conflictual nature of East Asian politics has been underpinned by regional states' strong preferences for maintaining national interests and sovereignty. Since most East Asian states are relatively 'young', gaining independence after World War II, residual social, ethnic, and religious differences have stood as formidable barriers against any collective national identity, and consequently the establishment of national unity still remains a major political goal for national leaders (Pempel 2005b: 257). The political leaders of these states have paid particular attention to preserving sovereignty, largely because of their desire to maintain and strengthen national unity and collective national identity. Indeed, the East Asian economies showed rapid growth with expanding trade and investment linkages. Yet, such moves were not accompanied by the rapid eclipse of national self-interest and sovereignty (Pempel 2005a: 12). Furthermore, most states in East Asia have a strong sense of nationalism. The history of colonisation has stimulated the development of nationalism in populations. If the emergent independent states in East Asia were to amount to notional claims to jurisdictional authority, political leaders needed the support of the populations they claimed to represent and the populations needed to recognise themselves as part of the same collectivity (Beeson 2007: 104–05).

The neorealist relevance to regional affairs in East Asia

In East Asia, distribution of capabilities among great powers has provided the basic framework for international affairs, and regional states retain strong adherence to sovereignty. Given these regional features, the neorealist logic is supposed to have strong validity in explaining regional games that East Asian states play. The neorealist theory, which has been the dominant paradigm in international relations, highlights the relative distribution of material capabilities in the international system as the main factor explaining international affairs (Waltz 1979). The neorealists assume that the states, not multilateral institutions or domestic actors, are the key organising agents of international affairs, and the states struggle for power and survival. The international system can account for recurring international affairs and commonalities in the state's external commitments because its foreign policy behaviour is constrained by the anarchical nature of the international system. Under the anarchical system, the state, a unitary and rational egoist, pays due attention to the maximisation of power and national interest in playing international games.

The state calculates, through a cost–benefit analysis, positive and negative effects that intra-regional and extra-regional forces have on national interest. The state is capable of identifying diplomatic goals and strategies to attain them, and determining the relative importance of such goals and strategies. Although the state recognises the need to engage in various forms of arrangements for international cooperation, it seeks to draw maximum benefits from such arrangements by carefully avoiding the surrender of its sovereignty to external forces. In so doing, the state's concern is with relative gains rather than absolute gains. States give serious attention to the gains of partners because they 'worry that today's friend may be tomorrow's enemy in war, and fear that achievements of joint gains that advantage a friend in the present might produce a more dangerous *potential* foe in the future' (Grieco 1988: 487).

The neorealists assume that a state's motivation in external behaviour is a given: to maximise its power. However, its position in the distribution of political and economic power has a significant impact on the state's diplomatic goal of maintaining influence on the management of regional affairs. The state needs to respond strategically to changes in the international power structure and global/regional economic crises, which will impinge on its political and economic capabilities and its relations with other states. In particular, the states' adherence to national interests becomes intensive when one state emerges as a regional pre-eminent power with accumulated political and economic capabilities. In such a power transition period, the existing balance of power is likely to transform and destabilise. The neighbouring states of the pre-eminent power are forced to avoid a situation where the latter exercises unilateral and arbitrary use of power, which will pose a serious threat to their sovereignty and national autonomy.

Diplomatic goals and strategies of the four parties

In the development of regional institution-building in the new millennium, Japan, China, and to a lesser extent South Korea had capabilities to provide political leadership in overall regional cooperation or specific policy areas and prepare for material resources to sustain such leadership. ASEAN played a pivotal role in initiating multilateral institutions for regional cooperation and providing wider opportunities for dialogues among East Asian states. The four parties have different diplomatic goals in response to the evolving distribution of political and economic power in the region. China as an emerging power seeks to consolidate its steady economic growth by creating a stable regional environment and to elevate its international profile to match its political and economic power. The other three parties are forced to maintain self-interests in the evolving regional environments. In particular, their regional diplomatic policies are directed towards the maintenance of individual interests in the face of the military and economic rise of China (Ross 2006).

China: History constitutes the foundation for considering China's diplomatic goals. In much of its history, China occupied a dominant position on the globe, and the China-centred, vertical order was maintained in East Asia before the intrusion of the western powers in the 19th century. This hierarchal, suzerain system created between China and its neighbouring peripheral states provided relatively stable regional order for many centuries

(Kang 2003/04; 2005). This historical fact indicates that Sino-centric regional order is normal, and a weak China after the mid-19th century was abnormal in the long history of East Asia.

Given China's special historical record, the Chinese people have a strong aspiration to regain honour and respect for their country globally. Such an aspiration casts a long shadow on China's diplomatic goals. Chinese political leaders need to satisfy the people's nationalistic sentiment through its diplomatic policies and relations. Consequently, China's primary diplomatic goal is to cultivate legitimate recognition as a strong and significant power in the international society including East Asia (Deng 2008; Larson and Shevchenko 2010).

In order to attain its diplomatic goal, China adopts specific foreign policy strategies. China makes efforts to increase its presence and influence *vis-à-vis* the United States, the global power, challenging the western-dominated international order. It advocates the possibility of developing international norms, principles, or models, which might become alternatives to western-oriented ones. In East Asia, China seeks to take the lead in constructing regional cooperative frameworks particularly through proactive engagement in the development of ASEAN+3 (Wang 2005). In this context, China attempts to raise its relative position in East Asia by reducing the influence of Japan, another regional power that has the willingness and capabilities to lead the development of regional institutions. Complicated historical memories and Japan's strategic position as an ally of Washington and a member of the western bloc increase Beijing's rival mentality against Tokyo.

In examining China's diplomatic policies, it is important to take into account its equivocal nature. Shih and Yin (2013) hold that two discourses are derived from Chinese self-role conceptions: core national interest and harmonious world. The pragmatic calculation coupled with these two discourses has produced two approaches in Chinese regional diplomacy. On the one hand, China seeks to maintain its principle of non-negotiability on affairs pertinent to its core national interests. The Taiwan Strait issue and territorial claims in the South China Sea and the East China Sea belong to such core national interests. In order to protect its interests, China does not hesitate to adopt offensive diplomatic postures. On the other hand, China seeks to avoid creating an unfavourable image among its neighbouring countries. In order to mitigate concern about the negative effects of its economic rise, China stresses its 'peaceful rise' and shows willingness to behave as 'a responsible country' by adopting cooperative diplomatic postures (Zheng 2005; Qin 2008). China also adopts the soft-power approach in cultural and language promotion in order to foster a positive image in and improve friendly relations with other countries (Kurlantzick 2007). China's harmonious postures are particularly apparent in its diplomatic relationship with ASEAN because Southeast Asia has become increasingly important for its economic development, especially in its south-western provinces, and for creating its own sphere of influence in the Asia-Pacific region.

Japan: For a long time, Japan assumed a specific position in East Asia. As the Japanese economy achieved the dominant position in East Asia with its remarkable economic growth in the 1960s and 1970s, Japan gradually came to play an important role in regional economic affairs. It sustained the economic growth of its neighbouring countries by providing official development assistance (ODA) for the development of infrastructure for industrialisation and foreign direct investment (FDI) in the manufacturing sector. Japan also played a leading role in advancing regional institutions after the late 1980s. The Japanese government took the lead in launching the Asia-Pacific Economic Cooperation (APEC) behind the scenes (Funabashi 1995). During the Asian financial crisis in 1997–98, Japan provided huge amounts of money under the New Miyazawa initiative, and strove to develop regional financial architectures in order to prevent the recurrence of the financial crisis. Furthermore, Japan, which had been the sole advanced nation in East Asia for a long time, played a distinctive role in expressing an Asian voice at the advanced nation clubs.

Japan's dominant economic position in East Asia gradually eroded after the late 1990s. While Japan's economic capabilities declined due to long-term stagnations after the bursting of the bubble economy, other Asian countries have raised industrial prowess by integrating their economies into the global market. The gap in economic power between Japan and other East Asian countries has narrowed, leading to an economic power shift with Japan's decline and China's rise in the new millennium. China has achieved nearly two-digit economic growth since the early 1990s, and consequently superseded Japan as the second largest economic power in the world and the regional trading hub. Given this power transition, Japan pursues a diplomatic goal to secure its political and economic position and influence in East Asia by taking into account China's growing influence.

This external policy goal encourages Japan to pursue a soft balancing strategy.[2] 'Soft balancing' means a balancing strategy involving non-military tools such as international institutions, economic statecraft and other diplomatic arrangements in order to delay, complicate, or increase the costs of using extraordinary power by a preponderant state (Pape 2005: 17). In order to meet pressures from China's growing economic power, Japan needs to pursue internal balancing to regain its economic might through effective economic policies designed to revitalise its industrial sectors and stimulate technological innovations. Equally importantly, Japan is willing to strengthen external balancing through political and security linkages with the United States, the most critical extra-regional state that can counter China's influence. In the regional context, Japan needs to tighten political and economic linkages with Southeast Asian countries to forge a counterbalance against China. Southeast Asia has been an important region for

Japan because Japanese companies have accumulated economic assets in the region through massive amounts of FDI and the Japanese government has forged tight political partnerships with ASEAN in accordance with such economic linkages. Balancing through close alignment with ASEAN is an effective and feasible strategy to retain its regional influence *vis-à-vis* China.

In addition to a soft balancing strategy, Japan, the old regional power, seeks to maintain its influence by exhibiting a clearer leadership in power transition. Japan has experience of membership in international institutions such as General Agreement on Tariffs and Trade (GATT)/ World Trade Organization (WTO), International Monetary Fund (IMF), Organisation for Economic Cooperation and Development (OECD), and Group of Eight (G-8), and know-how in effective management of multilateral institutions. Japan also possesses long experience and domestic institutions for economic and social stability and technological development. Accordingly, Japan is supposed to take the lead in promoting regional cooperation in East Asia through the development of formal institutions whose objectives are to improve economic and social conditions, to facilitate policy coordination among states, and to contribute to the stable regional order. Such leadership for providing regional public goods to sustain economic and social development and thereby create a stable regional order is conducive to the maintenance of Japan's influence in East Asia.

South Korea: The geopolitical location has imposed significant constraints on South Korea's diplomatic goals. South Korea is in a unique environment, surrounded by 'four great powers, each of which considers itself in the tops rank and entitled to an assertive regional policy' (Rozman 2007: 199). Accordingly, how to maintain its political and economic presence in such an environment has been a critical diplomatic challenge for Seoul. Moreover, South Korea has been in intensive military confrontation with North Korea. This security confrontation on the Korean Peninsula has required Seoul to establish stable international relations in Northeast Asia by gaining support from other great powers. In the economic domain, South Korea achieved outstanding industrial and economic advancements with the growth of the *chaebol*, large conglomerated companies. The Korean companies have had a strong global orientation in business operations because limited domestic market size and scarce natural resources have forced them to rely on linkages with external markets. The maintenance of steady economic growth has required the expansion of economic linkages in the form of trade, investment, and financial transactions. Given these security and economic conditions, South Korea has shown the unstable capture of the 'region' among East Asia, Northeast Asia, or Pacific, and has a relatively weak aspiration for East Asian regionalism compared with China and Japan (Hundt and Kim 2011).

The primary diplomatic goal in South Korea's East Asian diplomacy is directed towards the issue of establishing a stable political and security order in Northeast Asia and maintaining its presence as an intermediary power between China and Japan. The stable political order in Northeast Asia is indispensable for South Korea, and its government seeks to take an initiative in promoting political and economic cooperation in this geographical area. South Korea has middle-power weight to promote institutionalised cooperative projects in East Asia, and has sometimes provided initiatives in promoting regional community-building processes.[3] However, Seoul's ability to lead regional projects singlehandedly between its giant neighbours is very limited (Bluth and Dent 2008: 265). It closely checks implications of regional initiatives provided by China or Japan and accommodates to them to maintain its position in East Asia. Seoul's primary concern is that the two great powers' initiatives for creating cooperative frameworks will weaken its presence and interests in East Asia.

In South Korea's East Asian diplomacy, a particularly important factor is the rise of China. The rise of China brings about substantial economic opportunities, which encourage Seoul to adopt accommodating diplomacy towards Beijing through increased trade and investment linkages (Kang 2009). At the same time, the Chinese ascendency poses various challenges for Seoul, from increasing commercial frictions and clashes of values and norms to complicated triangular relationships involving the United States (Chung 2012). Seoul keeps a cautious eye on the security implications of Chinese military build-up and its influence on tensions at the Korean Peninsula.

ASEAN: ASEAN has been regarded as the core of regionalism in East Asia (Severino 2007). Major multilateral institutions in the region such as the ARF, ASEM, and ASEAN+3 have developed under ASEAN's explicit initiatives and involvements. Moreover, ASEAN has developed an ASEAN+1 framework with its major neighbouring countries through continuous political dialogue. Successful commitments through this framework have led to the formation of ASEAN-centred free trade agreement (FTA) networks in the Indo-Pacific, and most states in the region including China and Japan have paid respect to ASEAN's special status as the driver of regional cooperation.

The political and economic environments surrounding Southeast Asia began to exhibit significant evolutions after the mid 2000s. China and India, two of the newly emerging economies, exhibited outstanding economic performance, developing as major production bases and huge consumer markets. In particular, the Chinese economy has shown robust growth, raising a possibility that the prosperity of the Southeast Asian economies depends on Chinese industry and markets. Moreover, moves to strengthen regional institutions have gained momentum and such moves have led to strengthened institutionalisation of financial cooperation under the initiative of states in Northeast Asia. Given these evolutions surrounding Southeast Asia, ASEAN needs to pursue a strategic goal to retain its central position in managing regional affairs in East Asia.

In order to realise the diplomatic goal to maintain centrality in regional affairs, ASEAN adopts two strategies. The first is the indirect balancing strategy. The modifier 'indirect' indicates that the strategy is not directed at a specific great power explicitly as the clear and present threat, and aims to gain balancing effects from strategies directed towards other great powers as well (Kuik 2008: 170–71). ASEAN involves regional great powers in regional strategic discourses and makes them compete with each other in order to avoid one state's gaining preponderant influence in Southeast Asia. In particular, it adopts complex measures for balancing a great power's influence, including military, economic, institutional, and ideational, by inviting other great powers to become involved in the region's political, economic, and diplomatic matters (Ciorciari 2009). This indirect balancing strategy enables ASEAN members to secure alternative sources of goods, investment, and aid, and thereby reduce the potential risk of vulnerability posed by a pre-eminent state. Moreover, a pre-eminent state is likely to make concessions in economic arrangements with ASEAN in order to secure influence against its rival states.

The second strategy is the asset-accumulation strategy. ASEAN has, since its foundation in 1967, accumulated diplomatic assets in establishing and developing norms and principles that facilitate internal coordination among its members. In particular, ASEAN has, through multilateral negotiations, developed a wide range of institutions, including rules of implementation and operational guidelines for economic integration (Davidson 2002). ASEAN is likely to take advantage of its own norms and principles as well as experience in institution-building, seeking to make other great powers respect such ideational assets. For instance, ASEAN provides 'honest brokerage' to coordinate political and economic affairs in a region where the greater powers are suspicious of each other (Goh 2011; Shekhar 2012). A purposeful strategy that takes advantage of its various assets is used to maintain its diplomatic position among the neighbouring states.

In brief, the primary pillar of the analytical framework is provided by the neorealist theory that stresses systemic power politics and state-centrism. The circumstances of power politics and adherence to maintaining national interests constitute fundamental constraints on the diplomatic behaviour of East Asian states. Their relative positions in the region encourage the states to formulate different diplomatic goals and adopt specific strategies to realise them in response to the evolving regional configuration of political and economic power.

The supplementary frameworks: Domestic politics, governance, and critical juncture

Neorealist power politics provides the fundamental framework for analysing institution-building in specific policy areas in East Asia. However, the neorealist perspective alone is inadequate to explain the complexity of the real process of regional institution-building. The initiation and development of regional institutions imply that self-motivated states can overcome collective action problems regarding relative power maximisation, and an analysis of such state behaviour needs to be made in the broader and more comprehensive framework. What domestic factors do the states take into account in shaping external policies regarding regional affairs? What external conditions motivate state policymakers to consider the building of regional cooperation seriously? And how can non-state actors be involved in the development of cooperative institutions? Additional variables need to be examined to address these questions.

A state's external policy and domestic politics

The neorealist theory is useful in explaining broad policy outcomes across time in different states or general trends in the overall international system. Yet, the theory's parsimonious epistemology imposes serious constraints on the explanation of major aspects in international affairs. Namely, the neorealist theory has intrinsic limitations in accounting adequately for why different kinds of external policies are adopted by the states under similar international conditions or why the same state adopts diverse external policies in different policy fields or different time periods. In order to address these questions, it is necessary to highlight interest formation at the state's domestic political level. The constraints and opportunities that the international environments create are transmitted to the state's external policy through the filter of domestic interest formation.

Domestic politics has a significant influence on the formation of external policy for every state. However, domestic political factors of all states do not matter in real interactions at the systemic level and the evolution of international affairs. In this regard, it is appropriate to take into consideration the neorealist's insight that international relations are politics of material capabilities among great powers. The states with preponderant political and economic power have the capabilities to reflect their domestic political conditions on the development and outcomes of political interactions at the international level. In the East Asian context, China and Japan are two great powers that have sufficient material capabilities to affect the development of regional cooperation. Their domestic political factors have a direct impact on the genesis, evolution, and design of regional institutions.

The domestic political factors include various elements such as domestic political institutions and demands from and interests of societal actors. The domestic political institutions constitute the filter through which demands from domestic societal groups are transformed into policies, and their political behaviour responds to the opportunities and constraints created by these institutions (Goldstein 1988; Garrett and Lange 1996). They privilege specific political actors' preferences, and determine how such preferences are aggregated and changed into actual policies. Public policy often reflects specific interests of major societal groups that are closely linked to political actors. According to this view, the government is the place for interactions among demands from societal groups and their coalitions, and the public policy is a function of interests and capabilities of societal groups that compete with each other for higher benefits or incomes and form political coalitions to attain these objectives (Milner 1997; Frieden 1999).

Policymakers' preferences and political legitimacy

Certainly, domestic political institutions and demands from major societal groups influence a state's external policy. However, this study highlights preferences and behaviour of state policymakers as main variables in explaining a state's external policy and commitment. The external environments in general and relative power capabilities in particular provide broad contours that lead a state in particular policy directions. However, state policymakers' perceptions and preferences have significant influence on the ways through which pressures and opportunities of the international environments are translated into a state's external policy. As Rose (1998: 147) argues, 'foreign policy choices are made by actual political leaders and elites, and so it is their perceptions of relative power that matter'. In the domestic political context, state policymakers have capabilities to set up their own policy goals and use various tools to achieve these goals such as budgets, regulatory rules, and legitimacy to enforce measures. They are autonomous players, resisting pressure from societal groups in achieving their determined policy objectives. They are capable of pursuing national interests or their own private interests, independent of the myopic interests and concerns of societal interest groups.

The importance for this research of policymakers' preferences and behaviour derives from historical developmental trends and political cultures in East Asia. Japan is the country that inspired the concept of the 'developmental state', which became the model of economic development in East Asia (Johnson 1982; 1995). In Japan, capable and disciplined state bureaucrats, being motivated to pursue export-led economic development, implemented efficient and coherent industrial policies by targeting specific strategic sectors. Moreover, these bureaucrats retained relative autonomy to decide on their policy objectives and pursue them with various policy tools. This relative autonomy enabled the state bureaucrats to avoid being captured by any dominant social class (Wong 2004: 352). The implicit division of labour within the polity between politicians in charge of reigning and bureaucrats in charge of ruling enabled the latter to hold off special interest claimants and to legitimise their decisions (Onis 1991: 115). In the 1990s, the Japanese government sought to revitalise its depressed economy by adopting neoliberal reform programmes. It pursued successive deregulation and privatisation measures, reducing the scope of state intervention in the market and creating more transparent business–government relations. This was because undue state intervention and a close relationship with the government impeded the private sector from displaying the vigour needed for new innovation and breakthrough ideas in the matured economies like Japan. Despite such reforms in state–market relations, Japan still held residues of state developmentalism in response to demands and pressures from liberalisation (Pekkanen and Tsai 2005).

The People's Republic of China has, since its foundation in 1949, advanced state construction under the reign of the Chinese Communist Party (CCP). The state-party dominance has created the statist policymaking in which the state has played the dominant role in formulating public policies for every segment of the society. The fragmented political system gradually provided peripheral officials, non-governmental organisations (NGOs), and the media with greater access to the central policymaking process (Mertha 2009). In the external policy field, the continuing pluralisation of Chinese society and China's growing interdependence with the international society allowed non-state actors such as state-owned enterprises, financial institutions, and the media to be involved in the policymaking process (Jakobson and Knox 2010). Notwithstanding such developments, the party-state regime still retains the top-down decision-making system to manage political, economic, and social affairs partly by institutionalising the pluralistic society as a means to respond to its rising interests and demands (Dickson 2008). Equally important is that the Chinese government has been aware of the success of the developmental state in Japan and South Korea. It has shown a strong aspiration to emulate their developmental styles, as these are helpful for maintaining an authoritarian regime, and has studied their past patterns of state-initiated policy.[4]

Japan and China are very different in terms of political and economic systems. While the former is an advanced country with an open democratic regime and a matured capitalist system, the latter is a newly industrialising developing country with a party-dominant authoritarian regime and a reforming socialist market economy. Despite such differences, the two states have significant similarities in the history of statism in which they 'built a dominant state apparatus that was designed to promote national economic well-being' (Pekkanen and Tsai 2005: 18).

The history of statism in both Japan and China certainly provides state policymakers with relatively high freedom to extract and direct national resources for foreign policy goals. However, there is an imperative factor that influences the preferences of policymakers: political legitimacy. Political legitimacy implies that the existing government is perceived by the nation as holding legitimate rights to govern the state because their reign and policies contribute to the enhancement of its well-being. The existing government is dependent on the public's perception that it is legitimate. Accordingly, the ruling elite need to meet expectations and demands from the public, and thereby convince them that the existing government has the legitimacy to maintain and exercise power. The maintenance of political legitimacy is generally a critical issue for policymakers in a democratic political regime that has intensively competitive party systems and strong social inputs from influential societal groups. Even in the one-party dominant political system, policymakers are required to pay attention to demands from the nation. This is because positive responses to such demands guarantee continuous support for and consolidate the political foundation of the ruling group.

As the state has increased economic and social interdependence, international factors are more likely to influence the public's economic and social well-being. The ruling group is required to consider seriously the impact that an external policy will have on the domestic society. For instance, a trade policy to open up national borders to goods and services from the outside can bring greater benefits to competitive industrial groups while it can cause the ruin of uncompetitive producers. Accordingly, trade policy is particularly susceptible to accusations of illegitimacy (Meunier 2003: 76). Political leaders, vulnerable ones in particular, are disinclined to adopt a risky external policy that will invite an apparent opposition from major political and social groups. Political leaders with weak support from the public have less policy capacity to mobilise domestic resources to pursue an external policy. On the contrary, they seek to take advantage of external policies or relations as a means to enhance the legitimacy of the regime or to deflect attention away from divisive domestic problems (Hagan 1993: 7).

Given that this study highlights the development of regional institutions in specific policy fields, it is appropriate to consider policymakers' preferences for political legitimacy at two levels. The first is the government level. The government as a whole seeks to maintain political legitimacy in formulating its external policy. The government shapes and undertakes external policies with due consideration to how these policies affect the domestic society and to the political support of the people. The second is the government agency level. The concrete policy in specific policy fields is formulated and implemented by individual government agencies. The government agencies as the state's administrative organs take into account national interests in formulating external policies. At the same time, government bureaucrats pursue specific interests that are pertinent to power, prestige, or security of their own agencies (Downs 1967; Buchanan 1977). The government agencies seek to maintain political legitimacy in order to increase narrow interests under their jurisdiction and autonomy in relation to other agencies within the government.

Globalisation, governance, and non-state actors

Neorealist theory has contributed to the study of international relations by providing parsimonious assumptions with a limited number of variables for feasible comparison in various affairs of international relations. In particular, it has stressed state-centrism in the international system. Under the anarchical international system, the state seeks to protect its national interest, sovereignty, and ultimately survival in self-help conditions. However, evolving international phenomena represented by globalisation have imposed serious qualifications on state-centrism.

Globalisation challenges increase the relative importance of collaboration with non-state actors in managing global public affairs. Globalisation is best regarded as a multifaceted structural phenomenon generating multiple pressures and incentives arising from the complex interplay of its material, institutional, and cognitive dimensions (Higgott 2000: 70). The complicated dimensions of globalisation challenges imply significant impacts on various segments of society that state actors alone cannot respond to effectively. The state actors need to draw on specific knowledge and expertise held by various non-state actors such as NGOs, private economic actors, international media, or transnational movements. Under such conditions, the non-state actors have unprecedented opportunities to participate both in discussing international affairs and in proposing agendas of global public policies (Ivanov 2013: 50). This background explains why the concept of 'governance' has emerged as a critical notion for analysing the development of regionalism since the 1990s.

A distinctive feature of governance is sustaining coordination and coherence among a wide variety of actors with different purposes and objectives. What previously were indisputably roles of government have been increasingly seen as issues of the 'commons' that involve commitments by both state and non-state actors (Pierre and Peters 2000: 4–5). Thus, governance goes beyond traditional notions of government or formal public authority by relaxing the boundaries between the state and society or between the public and private sectors. Indeed, states remain vital and active participants in regional public affairs, but they are no longer the only actors who initiate policies nor do they necessarily dominate the resulting processes of public affairs. Various non-state actors that hold specific knowledge, assets, and networks have the potential to play an important role in creating governance structures at the regional level.

In East Asia, the presence of NGOs in policymaking has remained weak. In China, a social organisation has existed as a state-authorised mass organisation, which provides a means for interest groups to express their views on policy affairs within strict limits. This is because the party-state authority tried to avoid the formation of autonomous social groups and movements. There has been an outstanding increase in the number of NGOs since the late 1990s, but their activities are highly regulated by the government. The operations and influences of NGOs are more prominent in Japan and South Korea, two democratic states. However, the representation of NGOs in policymaking has been weak even in these two states largely because the government's primacy over society hampered the development of an independent and vibrant non-profit sector. In Southeast Asia, region-wide NGOs have been formed in various policy areas, gaining access to participating in the ASEAN policymaking. However, such access is limited to a miniscule segment of the growing NGO community in the region (Rüland 2012).

The states in East Asia have a strong developmental orientation. The business actors are the players who conduct the games to increase the state's industrial capability and economic welfare. Accordingly, they have enjoyed privileged access to the policymaking process via formal and informal routes. The business actors formally influence policymaking as members of the state's deliberative councils or submit policy recommendations regarding specific policy areas. They can also deliver their preferences and demands through informal policy dialogues and study groups with government bureaucrats and political parties.

Notwithstanding their privileged access to the policymaking process at the domestic level, the business groups' influence at the regional level is still underdeveloped in East Asia. This point becomes apparent in comparison with Europe. In the European integration process, pan-European business groups such as the European Round Table of Industrialists and Union of Industrial and Employers' Confederations of Europe played significant roles in providing the European Union (EU) organs and European governments with valuable information used to promote market integration in general and the promotion of the Single Market Programme in particular (Cowles 1995). In Southeast Asia, a region-wide association – the ASEAN Chamber of Commerce and Industry – has offered meaningful inputs to regional integration schemes represented by the ASEAN Free Trade Area (AFTA) (Yoshimatsu 2007). In Northeast Asia, a business summit of China–Japan–Korea was formed in 2009, and its meetings have been held in conjunction with governmental summit meetings.[5] Furthermore, the first meeting of the Asian Business Summit was held in March 2010 with participation of 13 business associations from 11 Asian economies. These transnational business networks play a role in identifying common challenges the business groups in East Asia are facing and confirming common stances on desirable public policies to be considered by the state actors. However, their direct influence on policy formation is still limited because they have neither created solid internal cohesion nor established sufficient connections to the policymaking process at the regional level, largely due to a rather short history of operations.

Research institutes as non-state actors

This study focuses on research institutes as crucial non-state actors influencing institution-building in East Asia. A group of researchers or experts has distinctive characteristics compared with other groups in that they pursue the truth about the real world on the basis of shared beliefs and consensual knowledge. The group of researchers and experts can form a so-called epistemic community, which is defined as 'a network of professionals with recognized expertise and competence in a particular domain and an authoritative claim to policy-relevant knowledge within that domain or issue-area' (Haas 1992: 3). The epistemic community is a community of experts in specific issue-areas and these experts seek to persuade others by developing shared principles, causal beliefs, and shared notion of validity. In particular, the experts define their policy goals in terms of expertise and knowledge, and thereby maintain knowledge authority in social discourse and social practice (Antoniades 2003: 26; Cross 2013: 142).

The research institutes perform several distinctive functions of policy development including the evolution of regional institutions. First, they can offer professional interpretation and advice on important public affairs. In general, research institutes can help policymakers to formulate feasible public policy by providing objective interpretation of facts in their research areas and advice on a set of technical solutions to problems in the areas. Since their interpretation and advice are authorised by their professional knowledge and insights, policymakers who need policy input and legitimacy pay attention to suggestions from research institutes. In particular, the interpretation and advice from research institutes are crucial for international policy agendas that are accompanied by a high degree of uncertainty regarding transnational issue-linkages and policy effects. Such uncertainty is a major factor that motivates policymakers to solicit and use advice from researchers, especially when a crisis or shock occurs (Haas 1992: 14–16).

Second, research institutes can establish a transnational networking of professionals and experts. Indeed, various actors can form transnational networks to construct the rules and norms of the international system.[6] But research institutes can become the key actors of such networks by forming a transnational epistemic community that can undertake broad research on the phenomenon of transnational governance. Rapid developments in communication methods and the free flow of information have enabled researchers to convey and discuss issues within a network operating transnationally (Hasenclever et al. 1996: 209). The researchers in transnational networks develop a common worldview that involves beliefs about how causal relationships unfold in a given area, agreed methods for assessing the relationships, and normative beliefs about policy implications (Zito 2001a: 588). The researchers involved in transnational networks have intensive arguments on new ideas and policy innovations, and develop a 'social relationality' that leads to the fostering of common identity to pursue shared objectives. The researchers can contribute to proposing ideas and methodologies to resolve problems on the basis of shared scientific beliefs as well as the creation and maintenance of social institutions that deal with responses to problems and establish patterns of cooperation (Haas 1992: 4).

Third, research institutes can provide a venue to promote 'social learning'. Social learning is defined as a deliberative 'process whereby agent interests and identities are shaped through and during interaction' (Checkel 2001: 561). The research institutes organise informal conventions and meetings where non-governmental professionals and governmental officials exchange views and opinions in a frank manner. This kind of unofficial (or semi-official) setting outside the formal government structure can serve as a channel for defusing potentially volatile issues and as a venue for depersonalising policy initiatives (Sohn 2012: 600). Moreover, researchers can, with shared causal beliefs and shared professional knowledge, create collective understandings on even politically sensitive issues and redefine state interests by framing facts and solutions objectively from the scientific and technocratic standpoint. Such objective policy goals and fact evaluation facilitate social learning that 'involves reinterpretations of national and elite interests on the basis of new knowledge that affects fundamental beliefs and ideas behind policy' (Stone 2002: 6). Thus, the researchers' involvement in social learning contributes to state actors' definition of problems and search for solutions to them beyond political considerations by helping them to shift their policy orientation from 'the logic of consequentialism' to 'the logic of appropriateness'.[7]

In this study, I employ the presence and influence of research institutes and researchers in the process of institution-building in East Asia. 'Research institutes' generally means the private institutes that hold independent operational funds and undertake research activities according to their funding objectives. Some research institutes in East Asia deal with regional political and economic affairs and have played meaningful roles in establishing regional research linkages.[8] In addition to these private research institutes, this study highlights government-affiliated research institutes. In East Asia, the cabinet or government agencies have set up a number of government-affiliated think-tanks in order to conduct surveys and research on specific policy areas.[9] These think-tanks have weak features in terms of flexibility and autonomy, critical elements in the function of non-state actors. They might not be regarded as track II frameworks but 'track 1.5' or an informal track I channel with government officials acting as a representative of their agencies (Capie and Evans 2002).[10] At the same time, government-affiliated think-tanks can perform the core functions of research institutes such as the provision of professional knowledge and insights as well as the formation of a transnational network. This research pays attention to such functions, which the government-affiliated think-tanks perform in relation to institution-building in East Asia.

Critical juncture in historical trajectory

Regional affairs including institutional arrangements develop in the overall historical sequence. The historical sequence is not smooth and even, and some contingencies produce punctuated phases in the trajectory. Such phases have profound influences on the subsequent path, changing the pattern of the development trajectory. Scholars call such a pivotal historical turning point a critical juncture.

A critical juncture is defined as 'a period of significant change, which typically occurs in distinct ways in different countries (or in other units of analysis) and which is hypothesized to produce distinct legacies' (Collier and Collier 1991: 29). The critical juncture is a period of time that is qualitatively different from the 'normal' historical development because the probability that agents' choices will affect the outcome of interest is high relative to that probability before and after the period (Capoccia and Kelemen 2007: 348). A crisis or other critical event calls the legitimacy of existing institutional arrangements into serious question, and opens a window of opportunity for change, which then generates a demand for establishing new institutional forms, powers, and precedents. While the crisis convinces policymakers that they can remain in office only by pursuing a new course of action, it weakens society's resistance to change by producing urgency for taking some action. Critical junctures are important because they place institutional arrangements on developmental paths or trajectories, which are then very difficult to alter (Pierson 2004: 135).

The concept of the critical juncture is in line with the historical institutionalist perspective. The historical institutionalists focus on mechanisms for institutional continuity, and articulate the determining role of pre-existing institutional structures. This interest produces the concept of path dependence, which is defined as 'the constraints on the choice set in the present that are derived from historical experiences of the past' (North 2005: 52). Path dependence is a dynamic social process in that once a particular trajectory is initiated, certain institutional arrangements are entrenched, which obstructs an easy reversal of the initial choice (Thelen 1999; Pierson 2004). The relative benefits of the current achievement compared with once-possible options increase, while the costs of switching to some previously plausible alternative or even a more efficient alternative rise. Researchers in historical institutionalism have presented four main mechanisms to explain why developments along a particular institutional path reinforce: lock-in, positive feedback, increasing returns, and self-reinforcing (Fioretos 2011: 377).[11] The critical juncture explains a historical breakpoint of institutional change in which a path-dependent institutional structure cannot resist and absorb shocks from crises or critical events and lead to the establishment of a new institutional path. Thus, historical institutionalism presents 'a dual model of institutional development' characterised by relatively long periods of path-dependent institutional stability and reproduction that are punctuated by critical junctures during which more dramatic change is possible (Capoccia and Kelemen 2007: 341).

Critical junctures have several distinctive features. First, critical junctures provoke significant changes in possible courses before and after them. Since there is a lack of determined, pre-ordained outcomes from the events, a wide range of outcomes may be possible before the junctures. 'Once a particular option is selected, it becomes progressively more difficult to return to the initial point when multiple alternatives were still available' (Mahoney 2001: 113). Second, critical junctures are highly dependent on contingency.[12] Pempel (2012: 195) explains this point as follows: 'we cannot determine *in advance* what kinds of historical events will in fact prove to be critical junctures nor can we determine whether or what kind of institutional response might follow any particular critical juncture'. Third, the duration of the juncture is not fixed. Revolutions, economic crises, and electoral landslides are typical examples of critical junctures, and these events occur in short periods of time. However, long periods of trajectories in national development or national regime change are also regarded as constituting critical junctures (Collier and Collier 1991; Mahoney 2001). Accordingly, the time frame of the juncture is relative, implying 'that the duration of the juncture must be brief relative to the duration of the path-dependent process it initiates' (Capoccia and Kelemen 2007: 350). Fourth, critical junctures often accompany substantial changes in ideational structures. An ideational change – extant ideational collapse and new ideational consolidation – differentiates critical junctures from those that lead to less significant policy change (Hogan and Doyle 2007). Put in a different way, during a critical juncture actors undertake 'complex learning' from a crisis or other critical event, not 'simple learning'.[13]

Critical junctures and regional institution-building

In terms of the concept of critical juncture, past studies have analysed domestic public policies, examining how political leaders' decisions and political interactions at critical decision points have influenced the subsequent development of political-economic institutions and their forms and functions (Gal and Bargal 2002; Lynch 2006). If national institution-building follows a crisis and sequence pattern, similar logic may be at work in a region where states have developed highly interdependent relationships (Calder and Ye 2010: 42). The development of multilateral institutions in a particular region should be influenced by political or economic upheavals at critical historical points.

Several scholars have applied critical juncture or similar concepts to institution-building in East Asia. Calder and Ye (2004; 2010) seek to provide an explanation for Northeast Asia's organisation gap – the lack of multilateral coordination structures needed for meeting financial and security challenges – highlighting individual decision-making at critical historical points as central factors shaping the ultimate institutional product. They hold that while the 1950 Korean War became a critical juncture in developing the hub-and-spokes relationship between the United States and its allies in East Asia, the 1997 Asian financial crisis became a critical juncture in encouraging Asian states to get together to confront a common economic challenge. MacIntyre et al. (2008) also regard the Asian financial crisis as a catalyst to create changes across political, economic and social arenas both in crisis-hit countries and in the region as a whole. They argue that the crisis became a watershed by producing a strong preference for reducing domestic economic vulnerability, a shifting policy for social insurance, an ideational change regarding development, and a changing approach to regionalism. In a similar vein, Katada (2011) holds that the global financial crisis in 2008 became a catalyst in changing the focus of solving regional economic vulnerability from regional arrangements to national and global commitments. A study of the ASEAN–China Free Trade Area (ACFTA) by Chin and Stubbs (2011) regards the period from the Asian financial crisis in 1997 to China's entry into the WTO in 2001 as a historical critical juncture in China's ASEAN policy. During this period, China was motivated to respond to the China threat perception, deal with the result of the WTO membership, and offset Japan's regional influence, and such motivations led to a proposal for the ACFTA.

In this book, a critical juncture is regarded as creating the crucial conditions that encourage states to adopt a new policy for regional cooperation. As states in a given region deepen economic and social interdependence, they accentuate the need to establish some forms of institutions to promote collective interests and address common challenges. However, in reality it is not easy to coordinate diverse interests among states and lead their behaviour in a certain concerted direction. A pressing and manifest necessity resulting from crucial exogenous shocks and events becomes a catalyst in guiding state policymakers to respond to such shocks and events in a concerted manner. The policymakers raise incentives to give priority to a regionalist aspiration and seek to generate new institutional innovations for realising the aspiration.

The critical juncture is particularly important for regional cooperation in East Asia. The states in the region have increased market-driven interdependence since the mid-1990s, creating a condition when cross-regional collective actions are required to address common challenges and advance shared interests. Although the state policymakers recognise the need for establishing new institutions and policy patterns to achieve these objectives, it takes a long time to change such recognition into tangible initiatives in launching multilateral institutions. A critical juncture might become a turning point in encouraging policymakers in East Asia to begin a new institutional path. Even when the states in East Asia launch multilateral institutions, these are often primitive and fragile with weak authority and underdeveloped administrative functions. The underdeveloped multilateralism in the region often derives from the regional states' propensity to give priority to myopic self-interest rather than long-term collective interests. A critical juncture might become a catalyst in overcoming collective action problems by shifting a state's policy priority from the maintenance of self-interest to policy coordination to advance a regionalist aspiration.

The summary of the analytical frameworks

The previous sections present the frameworks for analysing institution-building in specific policy areas in East Asia. The independent and dependent variables in the analytical frameworks are shown in Figure 2.1. The primary independent variable is based on the neorealist perspective that highlights relative power distribution among states. This perspective provides critical insights on analysing political interactions among states with interests in initiating and developing institutions for regional cooperation. It is assumed that the major states' pursuit of specific diplomatic goals under systemic constraints and the undertaking of political interactions to realise them are the primary variables in qualifying the initiation and development of regional institutions. However, the state-centric perspective alone is insufficient to account for complicated processes of institution-building.

This research is mindful of three additional independent variables. The first concerns the domestic political process. Indeed, a state pursues specific diplomatic goals with the rational calculation of national interest under international constraints. However, concrete policies to realise these goals

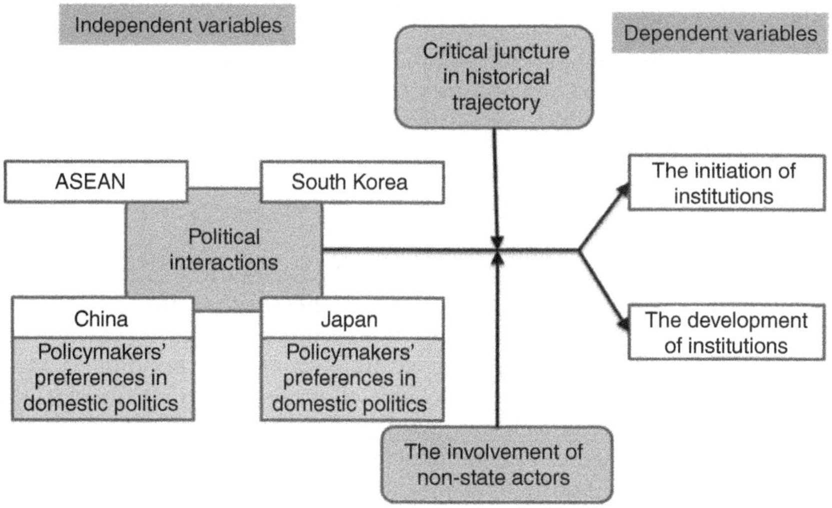

Figure 2.1 Independent/dependent variables in analytical frameworks

are formulated and implemented through interest formation in the domestic political arena. In particular, state policymakers' policy preferences have a decisive influence on how the state reconciles tension between external pressure and domestic conditions and how it formulates external policies and measures. Such policy preferences are then influenced by policymakers' desires to maintain and increase their legitimacy in the domestic political arena.

The second variable is relevant to the policy formation process. In the policy formation process, state actors are primary players who have the authority to determine specific goals of public policies and hold resources to realise them. At the same time, there is a possibility that non-state actors have meaningful influence on the policy formation process. This is particularly the case in functional areas where non-state actors retain information and expertise that become the foundation for appropriate policies. Accordingly, it is crucial to investigate the issues of what relationships state and non-state actors form in initiating and developing regional institution and how their expertise and knowledge are communicated in the policy formation process. This study considers researchers and research institutes as the representative non-state actors involved in debates on the creation of cooperative institutions in East Asia.

The third variable is pertinent to the historical trajectory. All social phenomena including international relations take place in the historical sequence that provides the environments to which agents concerned are forced to adapt. The overall historical trajectory has a decisive impact on the evolution of international relations, going beyond the self-interest of individual states. In particular, a contingent crisis or critical event becomes a turning point: the beginning of a new historical path that is quantitatively different from the previous development. During such a critical period of time, the states seek to create a new institutional arrangement by changing the perception of the external world and adopting new ideas through complex learning.

The selection of policy fields

This research takes up individual policy areas as empirical cases, and analyses political interactions among parties concerned in the genesis and evolution of cooperative institutions. The focus on individual policy areas contributes to elucidating the concrete trajectory in the building of institutions and major factors that influence the trajectory. In particular, the policy area-oriented approach can reveal involved actors' self-interest in policy development, their mutual interactions over realising them, and the nuanced influence of pertinent events and phenomena.

In addition to the above general factors, the examination of individual policy areas has specific value in the context of regional cooperation in

East Asia. The European model of regional integration aims to establish multilateral institutions that lead to sovereignty constraint or sovereignty pooling. In East Asia, the experience of colonisation made the regional states adhere to a strong sense of nationalism and intense commitment to the ideals of Westphalian sovereignty (Moon and Chun 2003: 111). The states are extremely reluctant to promote regional integration that would bring about negative connotations for sovereignty and domestic regime autonomy. Accordingly, regionalism in East Asia tends to pursue closer integration through common national regulation and policy coordination, which carry fewer negative connotations for sovereignty and regime autonomy (Higgott 2005: 35–36). The strength of a more interlinked economy requires the increasing regularisation and harmonisation of domestic governance and standards such as corporate governance, transparency standards, and broad macro- and micro-economic policies (Jayasuriya 2004). In response to such requirements, state actors develop selective, issue-specific strategies to enhance regional stability and competitiveness in the face of recognised limitations in the institutional structures of global economic and political management (Higgott and Timmermann 2008: 52).

This research selects specific policy areas through the two-step process. The first is relevant to the selection of overall frameworks. In East Asia, functional cooperation in various policy fields has been advanced under various frameworks. For instance, cooperation in a wide range of policy areas has been discussed at the Committee on Trade and Investment as well as the Senior Officials' Meeting (SOM) Committee on Economic and Technical Cooperation under the APEC, while the EAS has promoted regional cooperation in energy, education, finance, disaster management, and measures against avian flu. However, the ASEAN+3 framework has provided the main locus for promoting substantial cooperation in various functional areas, largely because it is positioned as the main vehicle for the building of an East Asian community. In fact, ministerial meetings, senior officials' meetings, and meetings of directors general have been organised in various policy areas under this framework.

The second process concerns the selection of individual policy fields under the ASEAN+3 framework. I select the policy fields according to the degree to which concrete institutions have been created and have evolved through discussions at ministerial meetings. This approach implies the selection of cases on the dependent variable, which has been severely criticised as a cause of inviting selection bias (King et al. 1994: 129–37). Indeed, such a criticism is reasonable for quantitative research, but is not totally valid for qualitative research in which the selection of cases on the dependent variable could be acceptable under certain conditions such as large within-case variance and an availability of data rich enough to permit process tracing (Van Evera1997: 46–47; Collier et al. 2004: 209–13). In particular, when researchers make causal inferences by focusing attention centrally on processes and decisions, the selection of cases where the overall outcomes being explained—for instance, war or evolution—have occurred could make a key contribution to the research process by generating the kind of insights into causal mechanisms without which the analysis of covariation is incomplete (Munck 2004: 114).[14] Given that the main interest of this research is not to examine and compare differences in the creation of institutions per se but to elucidate and compare factors that generate variations in the initiation and development of institutions in diverse policy areas, the cases in which particular forms of cooperative institutions are developed need to be selected.

Cooperative initiatives and projects have been advanced in numerous policy fields since ASEAN+3 members held the first summit meeting in 1997. Among various policy areas, particularly important are those in which annual ministerial meetings have been institutionalised because the cooperative initiatives and projects in these areas could gain high political support and their progress is examined regularly at working-level talks among senior officials and directors-general. This research takes up the development of regional institution-building in finance and agriculture. The financial sector is regarded as the most successful area of regional cooperation in East Asia (Haggard 2011: 17). ASEAN+3 members have, through talks at finance ministers' meetings, advanced several financial architectures such as bilateral swap agreements for liquidity provision – the Chiang Mai Initiative (CMI) –, regional surveillance mechanisms, and Asian bond markets. They have developed the cooperative process in an incremental manner, reaching an agreement on the CMI Multilateralisation (CMIM) in December 2009. The CMIM provides for clauses regarding the individual country's contributions, borrowing accessibility, common decision-making methods, and so on. The development process towards the CMIM will be a valuable case in the analysis of factors that have conditioned the development of regional cooperation to advance specific institutions in response to collective regional challenges.

In the agricultural sector, a similar development of regional institutions for food security in general and a rice reserve system in particular has been seen. In the early 2000s, ASEAN+3 agricultural ministers began to deliberate on regional cooperation to enhance food security and alleviate poverty in rural areas, and launched the pilot project for the East Asian Emergency Rice Reserve (EAERR) in 2004. After the project was implemented for six years, an initiative to institutionalise the regional rice reserve system was realised in 2012 with an agreement on the formation of the ASEAN Plus Three Emergency Rice Reserve (APTERR), a collective mechanism to respond to common challenges in food security. The examination of the development process from an initiative in the EAERR to an agreement on the APTERR will provide an important case for analysing the genesis and evolution of cooperative institutions in East Asia.

As the third and fourth cases, this research focuses on institution-building in the trade and energy fields, where it is more complicated than in the financial and agricultural sectors. In the late 1990s, major states in East Asia began to engage in bilateral or minilateral FTAs. The creation of the FTA networks proceeded relatively smoothly, completing the formation of ASEAN+1 FTA networks by 2010. Yet, it took a long time to develop from the bilateral, line-based FTAs into a multilateral, square-based FTA in East Asia. The expert group's study of an FTA among ASEAN+3 members began in 2005 according to China's proposal. A similar study of an FTA among ASEAN+6 members also started two years later, and after that the two ideas of a region-wide FTA came into existence simultaneously. It was in 2011 that China and Japan jointly proposed the formation of a region-wide FTA in East Asia, and ASEAN transformed the proposal into its initiated Regional Comprehensive Economic Partnership (RCEP). In such a complicated development process, China, Japan, South Korea, and ASEAN remained the core participants, playing the key role in initiating and designing trade arrangements in East Asia.

In the energy sector, ASEAN+3 energy ministers' meetings began in 2004, and senior officials' meetings and policy-specific forums were organised to promote cooperation on oil stockpiling, natural gas, new and renewable energy, and so on. The ASEAN+3 energy cooperation expanded the scope of issues to civilian nuclear energy and Clean Development Mechanism (CDM), and concrete projects such as the Oil Stockpiling Roadmap (OSRM) were produced in the cooperative process. At the same time, the growing importance of energy security is likely to make the parties' perception of regional energy collaboration more complicated, producing nuanced commitments by each party.

In addition to the above four policy fields, this study examines one particular institution in the environmental sector. The preservation of the environment has emerged as one of the most crucial international agenda, and various institutions have been formed in global and regional settings. Although ASEAN+3 members have discussed a wide range of environmental affairs since they launched an environmental ministers' meeting in 2002, prominent institutions for East Asian cooperation have not developed yet. However, there is a unique institution that highlights an environmental issue in East Asia: the Acid Deposition Monitoring Network in East Asia (EANET). EANET was formally launched in 2001 as the main institution to tackle acid deposition problem in East Asia. While the network consists of 13 members, two ASEAN members – Singapore and Brunei – are not included. Instead of these the network includes two Northeast Asian countries: Russia and Mongolia. In addition to the merits of including a case from the increasingly important area of environmental affairs, focus on the EANET development has two benefits for advancing this research. First, the process of regional cooperation in this case is very similar to other four cases. The cooperative institution was launched in the early 2000s, and an initiative to advance the institution was realised around ten years later. In this development process, political interactions among China, Japan, South Korea, and Southeast Asian countries should have played a significant role. The second and more specific value is relevant to the presence of ASEAN in institution-building in East Asia. One of the key characteristics of this case is the non-relevance of ASEAN as an entity. The examination of implications from this fact will contribute to the comparative evaluation of ASEAN's presence and role in regional institution-building and a better understanding of regionalism in East Asia. Thus, the incorporation of this air pollution case is appropriate for broadening the scope of issues with valuable policy relevance and enriching research on the creation of regional institutions in East Asia.

3

Promoting Trade Liberalisation through Free Trade Agreements

International trade has been an important vehicle for promoting economic development and economic integration. International division of labour and exchange of goods and services stimulate manufacturing and service activities among countries involving trade. The expansion of transactions beyond national borders requires the removal of cross-boundary barriers, and accordingly trade is a major area where regional integration takes place as Bela Balassa's five-stage economic integration model indicates.

In East Asia, foreign direct investment (FDI) in the manufacturing sector has sustained industrialisation and economic growth, forming regional production networks. The regional production networks have stimulated intra-regional trade by promoting transboundary exchange of intermediate goods and final products. The expansion of intra-regional trade has functioned as an engine of steady economic growth and a driver of regional integration. International trade has contributed greatly to the advancement of market-driven regionalisation in East Asia.

After the early 1990s, a growing number of states showed interest in regional trade arrangements because of slow progress in market liberalisation under multilateralism. The global trend towards the formation of free trade agreements (FTAs) had a significant impact on economic integration in East Asia. Several states in the region began to search for the FTA formation in the late 1990s, and such moves proliferated to the entire region in the new millennium. The states engaged in bilateral FTAs with intra- and extra-regional trade partners, forming minilateral FTA networks with the Association of Southeast Asian Nations (ASEAN) as the hub. Then, they gradually envisioned the formation of an East Asia-wide FTA.

The central objective of this chapter is to examine how major states in East Asia have committed to the development of regional trade arrangements. It analyses political interactions among East Asian countries over trade cooperation and policymakers' interests underpinning the interactions. The chapter also explores possible effects that specific incidents and events had on the development of regional trade arrangements, and the involvement of research institutes in the development process.

The initiation of bilateral/minilateral FTAs

The launching of FTA policies in East Asia

In the late 1990s, the wave of market liberalisation through FTAs reached East Asia. Most countries in the region gradually showed an interest in forming FTAs with intra- and extra-regional countries. Southeast Asian countries had proceeded with start on FTA formation in East Asia. In 1992, ASEAN leaders launched an initiative for creating the ASEAN Free Trade Area (AFTA) by 2008. Afterwards, ASEAN members accelerated the schedule of trade liberalisation under the AFTA and expanded the scope of economic integration, targeting investment areas, services sectors and procedures for goods movements. ASEAN as an entity concluded FTAs with its major dialogue partners. In 2002, ASEAN concluded the Framework Agreement on the ASEAN–China Free Trade Area (ACFTA), followed by similar agreements with South Korea and Japan. ASEAN also forged FTAs with India and Australia/New Zealand. Individual ASEAN members also engaged in bilateral FTAs, and Singapore and Thailand led such a move (Table 3.1).

New moves in trade policy emerged among Northeast Asian states. In the late 1990s, Japan began to shift its relative emphasis on trade liberalisation from multilateralism to regionalism and bilateralism. In line with this shift, Tokyo signed the Japan–Singapore Economic Partnership Agreement (JSEPA)

Table 3.1 FTAs among countries in the wider East Asia (as of April 2013)

Name	Effective date	Name	Effective date
Australia–New Zealand	1/1/1983	Japan–Indonesia	7/1/2008
AFTA	1/28/1992	Japan–Brunei	7/31/2008
New Zealand–Singapore	1/1/2001	China–New Zealand	10/1/2008
Japan–Singapore	11/30/2002	Japan–ASEAN	12/1/2008
Singapore–Australia	7/28/2003	Japan–Philippines	12/11/2008
ASEAN–China	1/1/2004	China–Singapore	1/1/2009
China–Macao	1/1/2004	Japan–Vietnam	10/1/2009
China–Hong Kong	1/1/2004	ASEAN–Australia/NZ	1/1/2010
Thailand–Australia	1/1/2005	ASEAN–India	1/1/1010
Thailand–New Zealand	7/1/2005	India–Korea	1/1/2010
India–Singapore	8/1/2005	Malaysia–New Zealand	8/1/2010
Korea–Singapore	3/2/2006	Hong Kong–New Zealand	1/1/2011
Japan–Malaysia	7/13/2006	India–Malaya	7/1/2011
Korea–ASEAN	6/1/2007	Japan–India	8/1/2011
Japan–Thailand	11/1/2007	Malaysia–Australia	1/1/2013

Source: Compiled by the author from data on the WTO website.

in January 2002. Japan then entered into formal negotiations on FTAs with Mexico in November 2002 and South Korea in December 2003. Afterwards, Japan directed its focus to Southeast Asia, launching FTA negotiations with ASEAN and its individual members after January 2004.

For a long time, the main agenda for Chinese economic diplomacy was accession to the World Trade Organization (WTO). After the conclusion of negotiations on this agenda in November 2001, the Chinese government turned its interest to the FTA policy. China stirred regional FTA moves by signing the Framework Agreement on the ACFTA in 2002, which marked the official launching of a process that would establish the free trade area by 2010 for the old ASEAN members and 2015 for the new members. Afterwards, China engaged in bilateral FTAs with Chile, Pakistan, New Zealand, and so on.

In the same manner as Japan, South Korea put emphasis on multilateralism as a means to promote trade liberalisation. The stance on trade policy changed with the start of the reform-minded Kim Dae-jung administration in February 1998. South Korea began negotiations on its first FTA with Chile in December 1999 and reached a signature in February 2003. The Roh Moo-hyun administration, which started in February 2003, changed the previous administration's still cautious FTA policy into a proactive one. In August 2003 the administration's Ministers' Meeting for External Economic Affairs adopted the FTA Promotion Roadmap. Japan became the primary target in this step, and negotiations with the country began in December 2003. However, negotiations stalled just 11 months later in November 2004. Afterwards, South Korea signed FTAs with small countries and their groups: Singapore in August 2005, the European Free Trade Association (EFTA) in December 2005, and ASEAN in August 2006.

The initiation of FTAs in East Asia incorporated two critical features. The first is relevant to the selection of FTA partners. East Asian countries often chose to negotiate FTAs with medium and small trading partners (Searight 2009: 205–07). This was the case for Japan, China, and ASEAN, as well as South Korea at the initial stage. Equally importantly, unlike Europe and North America, some states in East Asia did not select their neighbours but chose distant trade partners in their initial FTA commitments – Japan–Mexico, South Korea–Chile, and Singapore–New Zealand. This outward orientation derived from reliance on the extra-regional markets to sustain export-oriented growth and the existence of significant obstacles to deeper internal integration in East Asia (Solís 2011: 324). The second feature is pertinent to the degree of liberalisation. Compared with FTAs in other regions, those in East Asia are generally low-quality in terms of liberalisation ratio and the coverage of WTO-plus measures. Since East Asia contains many developing countries, these concluded FTAs under the generalised system of preferences (GSP). Equally important is that government officials adopted a strategy of 'liberalisation without political pain' (Ravenhill 2003).

They sought to exclude market liberalisation in sensitive sectors and issues that may invite strong opposition from the domestic political and social circles.

1997–99 as a critical juncture

The major states in East Asia achieved steady economic growth in the 1980s and the first half of the 1990s. The inflow of FDI sustained the growth of manufacturing bases in the region, and the expansion of manufacturing bases led to growing exports of final products to the markets in Europe and North America. The multilateral institutions under the General Agreement on Tariffs and Trade (GATT) provided the foundation that underpinned trade expansion in the region.

In the late 1990s there occurred a series of incidents that had significant effects on trade policy in East Asia. The first was the Asian financial crisis in 1997–98. The crisis began in Thailand in July 1997 and caused serious damage to the economies of East Asia due to contagion effects. In 1998, per capita gross domestic product (GDP) fell 26 per cent in Thailand, 29 per cent in Malaysia, 57 per cent in Indonesia, and 22 per cent in the Philippines (ICSEAD 2000: 4). The crisis had negative effects on states in Northeast Asia, reducing South Korea's GDP growth rate from 5.0 per cent in 1997 to minus 6.7 per cent in 1998. The crisis was caused directly by monetary and financial turmoil, but a crucial background factor was a balance of payment problem. The crisis-hit countries represented by Thailand incurred huge trade deficits before the outbreak of the crisis.

The second was an expanding gap in regionalism between East Asia on the one hand, and Europe and the Americas on the other. The members of the European Union (EU), which was formed in 1992, steadily advanced the formation of the Economic and Monetary Union, aiming at the introduction of a single currency and the integrated monetary policy under the European System of Central Banks. In North America, the North American Free Trade Agreement (NAFTA) was signed among the United States, Mexico and Canada in 1992 and came into force in 1994. NAFTA urged major Latin American countries to pursue bilateral FTAs, and Chile and Mexico aggressively pursued FTAs with quite a few countries. In contrast, regional trade liberalisation faced great difficulty in East Asia due to the failure of the Early Voluntary Sectoral Liberalisation (EVSL) programme at the Asia-Pacific Economic Cooperation (APEC). At the Vancouver meeting in November 1997, APEC members agreed to take steps to liberalise trade in 15 sectors under the EVSL programme, and nine out of the 15 sectors were identified as 'priority' sectors.[1] However, Japan and several other Asian countries, which were not prepared to accept liberalisation in sensitive sectors, strongly opposed the EVSL programme. Eventually, APEC ministers agreed to refer the programme to the WTO, where they would try to persuade other countries to sign up and reach a WTO-level agreement on trade liberalisation in those nine sectors by the end of 1999. After this incident, expectations of the APEC as a driver of trade liberalisation went down.

The third was the regression of the WTO as a promoter of market liberalisation. The WTO ministerial conference in Seattle in 1999 failed to launch a new millennial round of trade negotiations. Not only did advanced and developing countries differ sharply on the degree and direction of market liberalisation but the United States, the EU, and Japan also exhibited conflicts over major issues such as agriculture, labour, and anti-dumping. Eventually, the conference was closed without launching a ministerial declaration.

The above incidents had profound effects on the basic direction of trade policy pursued by major East Asian countries. The Asian financial crisis articulated the risks of being heavily dependent on the external market. ASEAN members, which had engaged in the AFTA formation, reconfirmed an initiative in fostering a unified regional market in order to alleviate possible shocks from economic slumps in the external market. At the sixth summit in December 1998, ASEAN leaders issued the 'Statement on Bold Measures', which spelled out urgent measures to advance the AFTA.[2] The six original signatories to the AFTA agreed to accelerate its implementation by one year to 2002, and to achieve a minimum of 90 per cent of their total tariff lines with tariffs of 0–5 per cent by the year 2000, which would account for 90 per cent of intra-ASEAN trade.

Among ASEAN members, Singapore was unique in its response to the incidents in the late 1990s. Given that its economy was heavily dependent on external economic linkages, it was necessary for the country to maintain its position as an entrepôt point and to attract FDI. In this policy need, an FTA emerged as a feasible option to strengthen economic linkages with major trading partners and diversify trade connections (Rajan et al. 2001: 7–10). Singapore also recognised the strategic value of FTAs in response to the rise of regionalism in the Americas and Europe. FTAs were regarded as effective means to promote market liberalisation with trading partners that had similar interests. The country agreed to promote an FTA with New Zealand at the 1999 APEC summit, and proposed bilateral FTAs with Chile, Mexico and South Korea (Munakata 2001: 105). During this year, Singapore agreed with New Zealand and Chile to create a broader free trade zone in the Asia-Pacific. This agreement was important in that it sowed the seeds of the Trans-Pacific Partnership Agreement (TPP).

A series of incidents in 1997–99 influenced Japan's trade policy. Japan, as an economy with an unusually diverse range of export markets, had long been cautious about discriminatory regional trade arrangements. However, Japanese trade officials gradually fostered a new idea about trade policy. They deepened a concern that while Japan adhered to trade liberalisation under multilateralism, Europe and North America went to a reverse direction to pursue regional trade arrangements in addition to the WTO. They judged that the new trade policy in these regions contributed to market expansion and economic growth as well as an advantageous position in multilateral negotiations on trade liberalisation. They drew attention to the delay of FTA formation in East Asia, noting that among the world's top 30 economies in terms of GDP, those that have not concluded an FTA were Japan, China, South Korea, Taiwan, and Hong Kong (Hatakeyama 2002).

The shift in trade policy began in summer 1998 when the International Trade Policy Bureau of the Ministry of Economy, Trade and Industry (METI) commenced to investigate the worldwide trends of regional economic integration, its merits and demerits, and possible policy options for Japan (Munakata 2001: 100). The bureau formulated an internal document entitled 'The Promotion of Strategic Trade Policy: The Significance of Regional Economic Arrangements', which spelled out the values of regional economic arrangements and raised the possible target of arrangements – South Korea, ASEAN, and the United States – (Oyane 2012: 205–07). The new policy stance was officially announced in METI's *White Paper on International Trade*. The 1999 edition appreciated positive aspects of regional trade arrangements such as the provision of models of rule-making for multilateral forums and the advancement of multilateral trade negotiations in deadlock by enabling multiple countries to form one voice (METI 1999: 293–94).

South Korea changed its basic idea about trade policy in the late 1990s. The Korean government tilted towards a realistic view that the majority of its trading partners began to commit to multi-track strategies and that a stubborn adherence to exclusive support for multilateralism might invite a serious risk of being left out. More crucially, the Asian financial crisis had a direct impact on South Korea's trade policy. The Korean economy suffered devastating damages from the contagion of the crisis, experiencing minus 6.7 per cent GDP growth in 1998. The country was able to improve trade balancing quickly after 1999, largely due to liberalisation measures under the International Monetary Fund (IMF) conditionality and currency devaluation. However, the securing of the stable export market was a major concern and the collapse of the 1999 WTO ministerial conference deepened this concern (Koo 2006: 142). FTAs were recognised as a feasible policy option to expand the export market by creating alternative trade channels. South Korea's global orientation in its FTA policy was originally fostered as a response to a series of incidents in 1997–99.

The stance on trade policy changed with the start of the reform-minded Kim Dae-jung administration in February 1998. In November 1998, the Korean government formally announced that South Korea would start FTA negotiations with Chile, while conducting feasibility studies with other prospective FTA partners such as the United States, Japan, New Zealand, and Thailand (Lee and Moon 2009: 47). During the APEC summit in November 1998, South Korea agreed with Chile to deliberate on the possibility of an FTA, and proposed undertaking a joint study with Japan of the strength of bilateral economic relations, which contained the possibility of concluding an FTA (Munakata 2001: 101).

The incidents in 1997–99 called the past trade policy into question by accentuating the risk of trade diversion effects and the importance of securing the export market. The major states in East Asia began to pursue new institutional architectures to sustain international trade as a source of stable economic growth. Importantly, Singapore, Japan, and South Korea shifted their policy ideas from multilateralism to regionalism and this shift allowed them to pursue a discriminatory FTA policy. As Oyane (2004) confirmed in the Japanese case, policymakers undertook complex learning about a desirable trade policy during this period. Thus, the period 1997–99 became a critical juncture when the long-established policy pattern was abandoned, and a new enduring policy pattern was fostered and proliferated.

The East Asian states' FTA strategies

In the new millennium, major states in East Asia made the FTA formation a main pillar of their economic diplomacy. Since the conclusion of an FTA brought about significant economic and political impact, the governments in the region formulated the FTA policy with in-depth calculations. ASEAN members hoped to be the pivotal force in economic integration in East Asia. ASEAN proceeded with regional economic integration from the AFTA initiative in 1992, ASEAN Framework Agreement on Services (AFAS) in 1995, and ASEAN Investment Area (AIA) in 1998. After the completion of the AFTA in 2002, ASEAN leaders launched the formation of the ASEAN Economic Community (AEC) by 2020. ASEAN sought to lead economic integration in East Asia by launching new initiatives in succession. Moreover, ASEAN members sought to avoid a situation where one state would have a dominant influence in Southeast Asia. ASEAN, a gathering of small states with significant internal and external insecurity, shared two overwhelming strategic imperatives: anti-hegemony and diversification (Goh 2009: 167). In the trade field, ASEAN formed ASEAN+1 FTAs with major dialogue partners, following the imperatives. According to the economic logic, a state with a large market size becomes the hub of FTA networks and attracts numerous FTA partners (Solís 2011: 324). In East Asia, the 'reverse hub-and-spokes' structure was formed, in which a group of relatively small states with a small market size becomes the hub, setting up spoke relations with large states (Yamamoto 2007: 322–24).

Japan became an initiator of bilateral FTAs in East Asia by concluding the JSEPA, and this initiative was urged by intensive moves towards FTAs in the Americas and Europe. Importantly, rivalry sentiment against China gradually cast a long shadow over its regional FTA policy. When China first proposed the formation of an FTA with ASEAN in November 2000, many of the Japanese viewed the proposal as unrealistic lip service and paid little attention to it (Taniguchi 2004: 26). However, China's pre-emptive moves towards the FTA astonished Japanese policymakers, who were forced to adopt counter-measures. After China and ASEAN began to consider the ACFTA seriously, Japan traced the route formed by China and ASEAN by advancing talks on the ASEAN–Japan Comprehensive Economic Partnership (AJCEP). When Prime Minister Koizumi made a formal visit to Southeast Asia in January 2002, he proposed an initiative for the AJCEP. The leaders of Japan and ASEAN issued the Joint Declaration on the Comprehensive Economic Partnership on November 5, 2002, just one day after the signing of the ACFTA.[3] If there had not been quick moves towards the ACFTA, it is unlikely that Japan would have moved as quickly to develop an initiative for economic partnership with ASEAN (Chia 2006: 119–20).

Japan's rivalry sentiment was revealed in two additional aspects of its FTA policy. The first is the targeting of FTA partners. Japan established bilateral FTA networks with individual ASEAN members in addition to ASEAN as an entity. It began FTA negotiations with ASEAN members in succession: Malaysia in January 2004, Thailand and the Philippines in February 2004, and Indonesia in July 2005. Such a bilateral orientation was sustained by a soft balancing against China's commitment to stronger trade linkages with Southeast Asia (Munakata 2006: 117, 121; Ravenhill 2010). The second is its approach to FTAs. The Japanese government labels its trade arrangements economic partnership agreements (EPAs) rather than FTAs, not only because several tariff lines are not liberalised, but also because they contain commercial regulatory measures such as investment, intellectual property, and competition policy as well as economic cooperation (Dent 2008: 198). The government officials believed that EPAs were superior to conventional FTAs as they would serve to promote the overall reform of economic structures by targeting broad areas from investment and intellectual property rules, competition policy, and economic cooperation (Oike 2006). At the same time, the government utilised this EPA approach, differentiating it from China's FTA approach to ASEAN by stressing that EPAs work comprehensively, not applying only to border measures such as tariffs and investment regulations; aiming to create the environments that are conducive to both Japan and ASEAN incorporating cooperative elements (MOFA 2007: 16; Solís 2009: 207).

Competition between Japan and China was fierce in the trade field, and China also embraced rivalry sentiment against Japan in promoting the FTA policy. Since China had engaged intensively in negotiations on the WTO accession, it was a latecomer to the FTA race. However, it quickly caught up with Japan, which took the lead in regional FTA formation through the JSEPA. When Noboru Hatakeyama, Chairman of the Japan External Trade Organisation (JETRO), had a meeting with Shi Guangsheng, Chinese Minister of Foreign Trade and Economic Cooperation, in August 2000, Hatakeyama explained the implications of FTAs to Chinese officials

(Yamada 2002: 19). Although their direct responses were not enthusiastic, the Chinese government proposed the formation of an FTA with ASEAN only three month later. China feared that Japan's attempts at FTAs with Singapore and South Korea would strengthen their political relations, which could dilute China's regional leadership potential (Yang 2009: 223–24). Rivalry sentiment influenced concrete programmes in the ACFTA. China offered the Early Harvest Programme (EHP), early trade liberalisation in the agricultural sector.[4] It calculated that Japan would not make a similar kind of proposal by opening the agricultural market for ASEAN products. The market liberalisation in the agricultural sector was a valuable card for attracting ASEAN members, most of whom were exporters of agricultural products. Clearly, China aimed to establish new political and economic linkages with ASEAN ahead of Japan by accommodating the group's preferences flexibly.

An additional calculation in China's FTA policy was a strategic use of FTAs as tools to maintain stable political relations with Southeast Asian countries. In November 2000, Chinese Premier Zhu proposed a feasibility study of the ACFTA, which surprised the ASEAN side. This unilateral proposal was based on rational calculations of economic diplomacy formed by senior policymakers (Chin and Stubbs 2011: 285–86). In the ACFTA negotiation process, China accepted various formats developed by ASEAN. ASEAN had adopted the format of the 'framework agreement plus protocol plus annexes' in concluding various agreements on economic cooperation, including the AFTA and AIA.[5] The ACFTA also adopted this format, first concluding the Framework Agreement and then subsequent agreements. The subsequent specific agreements also followed the ASEAN format. The Agreement on Trade in Goods provides the dual track of tariff concessions and abolishment (the normal track and the sensitive track), special and differential treatment and flexibility to new ASEAN members, and gradual tariff reduction according to tariff ratios (Ishikawa 2005: 45). These measures reflected the format adopted in the Common Effective Preferential Tariff (CEPT) of the AFTA. Moreover, China embedded its FTA policy into the integrative diplomatic strategy towards Southeast Asia. When China and ASEAN signed the Framework Agreement in November 2002, they concurrently issued the Declaration on the Conduct of Parties in the South China Sea and the Joint Declaration on Cooperation in the Field of Non-Traditional Security Issues. The FTA policy was one pillar of benign postures that China strategically adopted towards Southeast Asia.

China's accommodation to ASEAN's preferences was a response to the China threat. The rapid rise of the Chinese economy provoked the China threat concern among its neighbouring countries. Beijing paid attention to such concern among Southeast Asian countries in particular. China gradually realised that the simple denial of aggressive intent was unpersuasive and its statements of non-aggressive intent should be made more credible by practical actions. It sought to gain a reputation as a peacefully rising power by proposing concrete initiatives that would produce practical benefits, and to hold back the hostile perception of its growing power and influence. In other words, China sought to incorporate an element of 'charm offensive' in its FTA policy towards Southeast Asia (Kurlantzick 2007).

Close economic linkages with ASEAN through the ACFTA also contributed to raising the Chinese government's domestic political legitimacy. In the new millennium, the Chinese authorities raised the development of south-western provinces as one of the most crucial policy objectives. Although China exhibited robust economic growth after the early 1990s, its southern part – the Yunnan Province and Guangxi Zhuang Autonomous Region – remained relatively underdeveloped.[6] The government sought to stimulate growth and development in the southern provinces through close economic linkages with ASEAN, and implemented various policies such as positive commitments to the Greater Mekong Sub-region (GMS) Programme and the holding of the China–ASEAN Expo since 2004.[7] Close trade linkages with Southeast Asia and the expansion of outward FDI on the basis of the ACFTA were important vehicles for attaining an important domestic economic agenda and thereby strengthen Chinese leaders' political legitimacy.

In South Korea, the Kim Dae-jung administration began to pursue the FTA policy. However, the administration did not find sufficient strategic values in FTA promotion. Accordingly, it sought to negotiate as many FTAs as possible with little concern about sequencing (Koo 2009: 187). The subsequent Roh Moo-hyun administration adopted a more strategic FTA policy. As mentioned before, the Roh administration formulated the FTA Promotion Roadmap in August 2003. The roadmap emphasised the value of FTAs as part of Korea's goal to become an 'open trading state' and a strategy for pursuing simultaneous negotiations. The roadmap also classified possible FTA partners into three groups: immediate FTA partners such as Chile, Singapore, the EFTA, and Japan; medium-term FTA partners such as Mexico, Canada, ASEAN, and China; and long-term FTA partners such as the United States, the EU, and India (Lee and Moon 2009: 51). During the Roh administration, South Korea intensified a global FTA strategy targeting trading partners in various regions in the world.

In brief, the four parties in East Asia incorporated strategic calculations in advancing FTA policies. ASEAN sought to secure the hub status in FTA formation in East Asia, establishing ASEAN+1 FTA networks. After China entered into the regional FTA race, political rivalry between China and Japan intensified over attracting ASEAN as the main partner. South Korea located the FTA policy in the broader perspective, showing interest in FTAs with major trading partners including the United States. Importantly, the FTA formation until the mid 2000s was line-based, bilateral networks. In order to promote regional trade cooperation further, it was necessary to change them into a square-based, multilateral FTA.

Research institutes and the initiation of FTAs

A decision on whether or not a state engages in negotiations on an FTA with a particular partner depends on economic analyses of welfare benefits that the agreement will produce. Such analyses cover short- and long-term effects on GDP, trade, investment, employment, industrial sectors, and so on. Researchers and research institutes provide the most fundamental data used for making decisions on the initiation of an FTA.

Research institutes and researchers were involved in the initiation process of FTAs in East Asia. In Japan, researchers who had close connections with the government influenced its external economic policy. In 1999, Prime Minister Keizo Obuchi commissioned the Mission for Revitalisation of the Asian Economy to conduct a broad evaluation of Japan's aid programmes in East Asia.[8] Four out of eight members came from academia. The report of the mission emphasised the formation of FTAs with East Asian countries represented by South Korea and ASEAN, and stressed 'an opening to Asia on the many different levels of people, goods, money, and information, an opening that is commensurate to the growing desire for reform in Asia'. The mission's idea to promote cross-border flows of people, goods, capital, and information was incorporated into the JSEPA, which became a comprehensive EPA going beyond a conventional FTA (Munakata 2001: 110–12). Moreover, the report made bold proposals on the acceptance of nurses and care workers, which would become one of the most controversial issues regarding Japan's FTA policy. The report provided the unbiased perspective on politically sensitive issues with causal beliefs that market opening measures including the acceptance of human resources would provide Japan with substantial benefits from a long-term perspective.

In China and ASEAN, research institutes undertook surveys and analyses regarding external economic policies including FTAs, and presented directions and principles for them. When China began talks on its first FTA – ACFTA – the Ministry of Foreign Affairs invited the Chinese Academy of Social Sciences (CASS) and the Institute of Foreign Trade and Economic Cooperation (IFTEC) to participate in the feasibility study. While the two institutes did not find the large market potential in ASEAN for Chinese products, they rationally judged that the FTA would serve as a first step in regional integration in East Asia. Accordingly, the resulting feasibility study stressed potential mutual merits without specific prediction of the implications for domestic sectors (Jiang 2010a: 112). The research institutes redefined Chinese interests in the evolving regional environments with the broad, long-term perspective on the basis of objective and professional insights. The Chinese government's proposal on the ACFTA was underpinned by a rational judgement by the research institutes that desired long-term stability in the relationship between China and ASEAN.

In Southeast Asia, the Institute of Southeast Asian Studies (ISEAS) prepared a concept paper on the AEC in February 2003. The paper contained various recommendations to promote regional economic integration (Hew and Soesastro 2003; Severino 2006: 345–46). Some of its important recommendations were not accepted by the High-Level Task Force on ASEAN Economic Integration, a body that was in charge of drafting the concept of the AEC. For instance, the task force did not accept an idea to establish suitable institutions with supranational power to facilitate economic integration. However, other ideas such as the 'AFTA-plus approach' and the scorecard system to check the progress of agreements became the principal guidelines for promoting the AEC.

In summary, research institutes and individual researchers contributed to the development of the FTA formation by providing basic data on welfare benefits resulting from the conclusion of FTAs. Furthermore, they presented professional and objective perspectives on the feasibility of the FTA promotion and ideas about concrete approaches and guidelines, which became important references for policymakers.

Weak moves towards an East Asia-wide FTA

The stagnation of talks on a regional FTA

By the mid 2000s, East Asian states concluded bilateral and ASEAN-centred minilateral FTAs. The formation of an East Asia-wide FTA was recognised as the subsequent step. This was because such an FTA would yield various economic benefits: increasing market access to goods and services, and thereby facilitating regional production networks and supply chains; creating a larger and integrated market, and thereby stimulating the entry of more FDI; countering the so-called 'noodle bowl phenomenon'; and reducing vulnerability to extra-regional shocks more effectively (Chia 2010: 33–34). In particular, the noodle bowl phenomenon led to the low utilisation of preferential concessions by private actors because they had to undertake complicated and bothersome paperwork by paying attention to different rules of different FTAs.[9]

An initiative in forming an East Asia-wide FTA was first launched in 2003. At the seventh ASEAN Plus Three (ASEAN+3) summit in October 2003, Chinese Premier Wen Jiabao proposed studying the feasibility of a free trade area in East Asia. On the basis of Wen's proposal, the ASEAN+3 economic ministers agreed in September 2004 to set up an expert group to conduct a feasibility study of the East Asia Free Trade Area (EAFTA). The group held four rounds of meetings from April 2005 to July 2006, and submitted a report to an ASEAN+3 economic ministers' meeting in August 2006 (ASEAN 2009c: 12). The report proposed that the EAFTA be negotiated among ASEAN+3 countries first and membership be open to other East Asian economies, and that an independent process to form the EAFTA be launched in 2007.[10] At the tenth ASEAN+3 summit in January 2007, leaders welcomed the outcome of the group's study, but did not accept the start of the independent process of the EAFTA. Instead, they approved South Korea's proposal to conduct the phase II study involving the in-depth, sector-by-sector analysis of the EAFTA. The first meeting of the EAFTA phase II study was held in Seoul in May 2007 (ASEAN 2009: 53).

The rationale for the EAFTA – an FTA among ASEAN+3 members – was that production networks and supply chains had been developed most significantly among the ASEAN+3 members and harmonising rules of origin (ROOs) among these countries could produce tangible benefits (Kawai and Wignaraja 2011: 14). Furthermore, the ASEAN+3 framework had developed as the most feasible regional framework in East Asia. Since this framework provided ministerial processes for regional cooperation in various policy areas, it could be considered the most plausible basis for cooperation and integration in the trade sector.

In addition to the China-initiated EAFTA, Japan proposed an idea for an East Asia-wide FTA: the Comprehensive Economic Partnership Agreement in East Asia (CEPEA) (See Figure 3.1). This concept, proposed formally in the Japanese METI's report called *Global Economic Strategy* in April 2006, intended to create an EPA among ASEAN+3+3 including India, Australia and New Zealand. This report proposed starting negotiations on this EPA in 2008 after all FTA negotiations centred on ASEAN would likely be concluded in 2007 (METI 2006). At the second EAS meeting in January 2007, Japanese Prime Minister Shinzo Abe formally proposed the idea of seeking

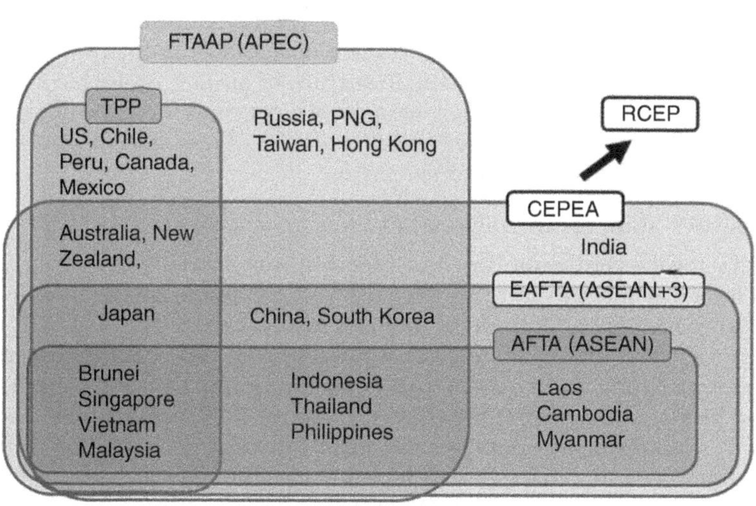

Figure 3.1 Various FTA frameworks in the Asia-Pacific region
Source: Created by the author using data on government reports.

this 16-nation EPA, and leaders endorsed an agreement to begin a private-level study to explore the idea. The private-level study began in June 2007. In August 2008, the result of the study was reported at the EAS economic ministers' working lunch meeting, and the ministers agreed to begin the phase-II, private-level study.

The rationale for the CEPEA was that economic gains from the FTA formation were projected to be larger in the CEPEA scenario than in the EAFTA one. For instance, one computable general equilibrium (CGE) analysis shows that the CEPEA scenario creates US$260 billion gains to world income while the EAFTA scenario does US$214 billion as simulated changes from the 2017 baseline (Kawai and Wignaraja 2008: 133). Moreover, the incorporation of resource-rich Australia and fast-growing India was expected to provide substantial benefits to sustain economic development in East Asia.

The two trade architectures were put in parallel development. In August 2009, economic ministers received the phase-II study reports of the EAFTA and CEPEA, and envisioned the establishment of four working groups on ROOs, tariff nomenclature, customs-related issues, and economic cooperation.[11] Two months later, leaders formally agreed that the EAFTA and CEPEA 'could be examined and considered in parallel'.[12] The economic ministers had agreed in 2009 that ASEAN would take the initiative in establishing the four working groups and discuss matters with partner members after ASEAN completed internal coordination. However, some working groups took a long time to advance discussions involving partner members. For instance, the working group on customs-related issues was first held in May 2011 (Sukekawa 2012: 257–58).

Stallings and Katada (2009: 250) argue that 'coherent regional integration is by no means a logical or natural consequence of FTA proliferation' in the Pacific Rim. In reality, talks on the formation of an East Asia-wide FTA did not make smooth progress largely because two concepts for realising the formation were proposed, and the feasibility studies of the concepts proceeded without any initiative to harmonise them.

The parties' stances on a regional FTA

China's engagement in an East Asia-wide FTA was generally weak compared with its engagement in an FTA with ASEAN. The Chinese government recognised that ASEAN had important interests in advancing ASEAN+1 FTAs and the process of forming these FTAs was underway. Moreover, talks on an FTA among China, Japan, and South Korea did not make any progress after China proposed this FTA at the trilateral summit in November 2002. Given these conditions, it was not easy to launch formal negotiations on an East Asia-wide FTA. China hoped to achieve the formation of the EAFTA through a gradual and long-term process. What the Chinese government intended in proposing the EAFTA was to take the lead in the formation of FTA networks in East Asia. Therefore, the Chinese government did not necessarily intend to speed up the formation of the EAFTA.

An additional factor that influenced China's commitment to an East Asia-wide FTA concerned growing constraints from domestic policymaking. Changes in power configuration within the government impinged on China's FTA policies. During China's WTO accession negotiations, the Ministry of Trade and Economic Cooperation (MOFTEC) promoted domestic reforms and market liberalisation, and a 'Central Leading Group' composed of a premier and representatives from different ministries helped to overcome opposition to trade liberalisation and to break the policy logjam (Zeng 2010: 651). The 2003 administrative reform changed the MOFTEC into a new Ministry of Commerce (MOFCOM) that would oversee many aspects of both foreign and domestic commerce. The MOFCOM became more subject to expectations from interested parties, such as industrial sectors as represented by their related bureaus. This was because the ministry did not possess the formal authority to settle conflicts among domestic interests as its political rank was the same as that of other industrial ministries and even lower than that of some national commissions, and its operations were not helped by a leading small group (Pearson 2010: 626–27; Song and Yuan 2012: 115). The 2003 administrative reform also produced the National Development and Reform Commission (NDRC), which raised its profile during Wen Jiabao's premiership with particular responsibility for industrial policies and investment policies. The commission holds a higher political position than the ministries and inherited a conservative position on reform and opening from its former body, the State Development Planning Commission. The NDRC's conservative position gave substantial support to the protectionist voices of some domestic industries such as large-staple agricultural products and major services industries (Jiang 2010b: 246–47). The autonomy of the government agency in charge of FTA negotiations declined due to increasingly fragmented and porous policymaking and the relative rise of protectionist forces inside and outside the government.

As for the Japan-proposed CEPEA, an increase in participants with different policy preferences and development levels was deemed to make its conclusion difficult. India, a latecomer to economic reforms, had relatively high import tariffs and a longer time required for import to take place than the average for other East Asian countries (Kawai and Wignaraja 2008: 134). The prolonged negotiations of the Japan–Australia EPA and the China–Australia FTA indicated difficulty in conducting an FTA with Australia, which had a strong orientation towards market liberalisation. Despite such apparent challenges, Japan pushed forward the CEPEA concept as a means of soft balancing. The CEPEA had a strategic objective to reduce the relative influence of China, which advocated the EAFTA. Since China presented a clear concept for an FTA for wider East Asia, Japan needed to present a counter-concept in order to block a situation where an important new step in economic integration would follow the Chinese initiative. A senior METI official clearly referred to this point, stating that 'China will take the lead in +3 negotiations. We should promote +6 negations ahead of the curve.'[13]

METI presented the CEPEA concept as a diplomatic card, but other government agencies did not necessarily give support to it. In launching the CEPEA, METI did not undertake due prior consultation with the Ministry of Foreign Affairs (MOFA), the Ministry of Agriculture, Forestry and Fisheries (MAFF), and Ministry of Finance. Accordingly, other ministries gave it a chilly reception. Just after the announcement of the concept in April 2006, MAFF Minister Shoichi Nakagawa stated at the press conference that 'we heard about the CEPEA from newspaper reports', and commented that 'it is reasonable to make prior consultation before proposing at the formal governmental venue'.[14] MAFF was concerned about the unfavourable effects of the CEPEA involving Australia and New Zealand in the agricultural sector. Even MOFA, which adopted the common stance on the FTA promotion, was initially sceptical about the CEPEA concept. The ministry was apprehensive about the negative influence on the political relationship with the United States, which was excluded from the concept, and difficulty in coordinating with ongoing bilateral FTA negotiations (Yoshimatsu 2008: 156). The CEPEA concept was expected to raise METI's political legitimacy as a promoter of FTAs within the government in general and an agent of manufacturing industries that hoped to strengthen regional production networks in particular. But other ministries were both critical of the procedure for presenting the concept and sceptical about its feasibility.

South Korea did not wish to be seen siding with either Japan or China, but had a favourable assessment of the EAFTA rather than the CEPEA. The formation of an EAFTA was originally proposed in two reports issued by the East Asia Vision Group (EAVG) and the East Asia Study Group (EASG), and these groups had been established following a proposal by Korean President Kim Dae-jung. South Korea also made a proposal to conduct the phase II study involving an in-depth, sector-by-sector analysis of the EAFTA. Seoul assisted the development of the EAFTA, and thereby favoured the EAFTA rather than the completely Japan-initiated CEPEA.

However, South Korea did not necessarily have a keen interest in the formation of a regional FTA in East Asia. As already explained, the Korean FTA policy had a strong global orientation. Given its relatively small domestic market size compared with its rivals in industrial competition, the steady expansion of major industrial sectors were dependent on international trade. In particular, South Korea's competitive industrial sectors such as electronics and automobiles were heavily dependent on exports to the global market. Accordingly, the Korean government considered FTA partners from a practical, utilitarian standpoint, selecting trading partners that would produce substantial economic benefits. The Korean government confirmed its willingness to embark on an FTA with the United States, and held the first prior practical meeting on the Korea–US (KORUS) FTA in February 2005. After ten rounds of negotiations from June 2006 to March 2007, the two governments signed the agreement in June 2007.[15] After concluding negotiation on the KORUS, South Korea began negotiations on an FTA with the EU in May 2007.[16] Thus, Seoul adopted a pragmatic FTA strategy to select partners for FTAs that would produce substantial economic gains. This strategy led to South Korea having weak interest in an East Asia-wide FTA.

ASEAN concluded FTAs with China, Japan, South Korea, India, Australia, and New Zealand. Accordingly, the transformation of these ASEAN+1 FTAs into a free trade zone in East Asia seemed to be a feasible strategy for ASEAN. However, ASEAN had two difficulties in pushing forward the formation of an East Asia-wide FTA. First, ASEAN was apprehensive that the formation of a broader free trade area involving China and India would shift the centre of gravity of FDI from Southeast Asia to these emerging economic giants. The line-based network of ASEAN+1 FTAs contributed to raising the attractiveness of ASEAN as an investment destination and the hub of regional production networks. While ASEAN-made products could be exported to all the markets of ASEAN+1 FTA partners, products from the partners were unable to enter each other's markets due to restrictions on the ROOs. The formation of the square-based FTA linkages would divest ASEAN of this advantage, encouraging foreign investors to make direct inroads in China and India. Accordingly, ASEAN members except for Singapore were not necessarily enthusiastic about an East Asia-wide FTA (Sukekawa 2012: 256–57). Second, ASEAN did not have the willingness and capabilities to coordinate the two concepts for a regional FTA suggested by China and Japan. It was difficult for ASEAN to opt for one of China-supported EAFTA and Japan-initiated CEPEA as a feasible trade architecture for East Asia. The rivalry and mutual balancing between China and Japan were basically beneficial to ASEAN in some senses because each of the two great powers provided incentives with ASEAN in exchange for gaining support for its stance. Insofar as the rivalry did not produce direct political and economic disadvantages, ASEAN did not dare to coordinate sharp confrontation between China and Japan.

The launching of the RCEP in intensive moves towards the TPP

Renewed drive for an East Asia-wide FTA

In August 2011, China and Japan jointly proposed the formation of a regional FTA in East Asia at the ASEAN+3 and EAS economic ministers' meetings. The proposal contained the establishment of three new working groups on trade in goods, trade in services, and investment within 2011, and further deliberations on the result of discussions in the working groups at economic ministers' meetings in 2012. At the ASEAN+3 and EAS summits in November 2011, leaders welcomed the constructive joint proposal of China and Japan to establish three working groups for trade and investment liberalisation. The joint proposal was integrated into the ASEAN Framework on Regional Comprehensive Economic Partnership (RCEP), which was agreed among ASEAN leaders. The main objective of the framework was to articulate general principles for the FTA formation process in terms of coverage, process, accession, cooperation, and so on. At the same time, the framework indicated commitment to negotiations in the areas of trade in goods, trade in services, and investment.

In June 2012, the first round of the RCEP Working Group on Trade in Goods was held, and the first ASEAN economic ministers' plus ASEAN FTA partners' consultations took place two months later. The economic ministers from ASEAN and its six FTA partners (ASEAN+6 members) discussed guiding principles for negotiating the RCEP. Some controversies on the principles occurred in relation to the scope of special and differential treatment raised by ASEAN, the protection of sensitive products by Japan, and the inclusion of government procurement and labour/environmental regulations by Australia and New Zealand.[17] Political tensions among the three Northeast Asian states intensified in the mid 2012 due to resurgent territorial disputes. However, ministers adhered to promoting economic initiatives irrespective of political tensions. In November 2012 leaders endorsed the Guiding Principles and Objectives for Negotiating the RCEP. The guiding document spelled out eight principles such as consistency with the WTO, and flexible and differentiated treatment, as well as consideration to individual and diverse circumstances. Some of the principles reflected past FTA practices in East Asia, particularly a prudent approach to unconditional market liberalisation. In terms of the targeted scope of negotiations, the guiding document covers trade in goods, trade in services, investment, economic and technical cooperation, intellectual property, competition, dispute settlement, and other issues. There is room for the expansion of scope through the category of other issues, but this list is not so comprehensive compared with other FTAs.[18] The first round of negotiations on the RCEP took place in May 2013.

The TPP that created a critical juncture

A critical factor that had a significant impact on a renewed drive for an East Asia-wide FTA was the TPP. The TPP, an FTA covering many economies in the Asia-Pacific region, developed from the Trans-Pacific Strategic Economic Partnership Agreement – P4 – between Brunei, Chile, New Zealand, and Singapore, which came into force in May 2006. The TPP negotiation group includes the original P4 members and eight additional participants – the United States, Australia, Vietnam, Malaysia, Peru, Canada, Mexico, and

Japan. The TPP is set to serve as 'the 21st-century's trade accord' with high-quality and comprehensiveness: it targets high-standard liberalisation aiming to abolish 100 per cent of tariff, and facilitates a large area of agendas including services, investment, intellectual property rights, government procurement, labour and environment, and so on. Singapore, New Zealand, and Chile first met to discuss a possible trade arrangement on the sidelines of the 2002 APEC summit in Los Cabos, Mexico, and subsequent meetings were organised at the occasions of APEC meetings. Being reflected in this process, the TPP is regarded as a pathfinder for the Free Trade Area of the Asia-Pacific (FTAAP), an APEC initiative.

A clue that a tiny FTA – P4 – changed into a significant trade arrangement in the Asia-Pacific region was the US participation. In March 2008, the United States joined TPP negotiations to conclude investment and financial services provisions. Half a year later, the Bush administration formally announced that the US government would begin negotiations on comprehensive participation in the TPP. The US action became a catalyst for other Asia-Pacific states, and Australia, Vietnam, and Peru decided to join TPP negotiations in November 2008. Afterwards, forces to advance negotiations were lost due to the global financial crisis, and it was in November 2009 that the subsequent Obama administration expressed a policy to join TPP negotiations in accordance with the APEC summit. Formal negotiations on the TPP began in March 2010, and Malaysia joined negotiations at the third round in October 2010. At the Honolulu APEC summit in November 2011, the participants reached the broad outlines of the agreement, and continued negotiations on sensitive issues that varied for each country. Mexico and Canada were accepted as new members in October 2012, and as a result the three NAFTA members were incorporated into the broader FTA architecture.

The TPP had a significant impact on Japan's trade policy. The Japanese government began the investigation into TPP participation in autumn 2010, but could not make the decision to participate in TPP negotiations for more than two and half years. It was in March 2013 that the returned Liberal Democratic Party (LDP) government under Prime Minister Shinzo Abe formally announced that Japan would join TPP negotiations. Japan was originally cautious about the participation because it would have a negative impact on the development of its proposed regional FTA concept – CEPEA – and because it would invite strong opposition in domestic political and social circles (Terada 2011: 97–98). However, strategic calculations helped to change this stance. During the Democratic Party of Japan's (DPJ) period of government under Prime Minister Hatoyama in 2009–10, US–Japan diplomatic relations deteriorated due to the Futenma US base issue in Okinawa and Hatoyama's using of fairly neutral rhetoric about a new Asian community (Godement 2011: 14). The following DPJ cabinets sought to restore stable political linkages with its ally by exhibiting willingness to engage in the US-inspired TPP. The strengthened tie with Washington was also necessary because China gradually intensified its proactive diplomacy over maritime security, which led to political confrontation after an incident between a Chinese trawler and Japanese Coast Guard vessels in the East China Sea in September 2010. Some government officials clearly admitted this economic-security linkage. Akihisa Nagashima, an assistant to the prime minister, stated that Japan needed to develop strategic environments that China would regard as formidable through participation in negotiations on the TPP.[19]

The TPP policy had a nuanced influence on Japan's approach to a regional FTA in East Asia. Economic costs and benefits differed between the TPP and an East Asia-wide FTA. Economic benefits from an FTA involving dynamic economies such as China and India would be larger than those from the TPP.[20] Since the TPP aimed to achieve high-standard market liberalisation in a wide range of policy areas, participation in it would impose significant burdens on structural reforms at least in the short term. In contrast, an East Asia-wide FTA was deemed to be more flexible by allowing exceptions for market liberalisation. In addition to such economic effects, TPP participation had significant political implications. TPP participation could be used as a diplomatic card to draw diplomatic concessions from China, which hoped to attract Japan to its side by strengthening moves towards a regional FTA in East Asia.

The development of the TPP had significant effects on China's trade strategy. Since the TPP is an open and inclusive trade arrangement, China was able to become a candidate to participate in TPP negotiations. Some think-tank researchers stressed the need to join TPP negotiations. For instance, Wang Li, a researcher at the Chinese Academy of International Trade and Economic Cooperation (CAITEC), asserted that participation in the TPP would enable China to gain an advantage in economic development in the world and raise its voice in the international economy and politics.[21] However, most Chinese researchers were sceptical about the US's authentic intention to push TPP negotiations, accentuating its geopolitical motivation to dilute and reduce China's influence in the Asia-Pacific region (Zhang and Shen 2013: 47). The Chinese government was cautious about considering positively joining TPP negotiations. This was largely because the TPP pursues high-standard market liberalisation that constitutes high hurdles for the Chinese economy in terms of tariff reduction, intellectual property right, and labour/environmental regulations. Moreover, the government regarded the TPP as Washington's strategic card to achieve a crucial diplomatic objective of 'pivot to Asia'.

Equally important was that the TPP contained an ideational challenge to China. The United States gradually raised its concern that China's 'state capitalism' runs counter to the liberal economic system and undermines US business interests. For instance, US Secretary of State Hillary Clinton, in a speech at the Group of 20 (G-20) ministerial meeting in February 2012, referred to 'the challenges countries face from the emergence of what has been called "state capitalism" – the rise of sovereign wealth and the growing presence and influence of state-owned and state-controlled enterprises that operate globally'.[22] The TPP could be a vehicle for imposing rules and regulations regarding state-owned enterprises (SOEs). At the ninth round of TPP negotiations in October 2011, the US government made a new proposal on clauses regarding SOEs, which addressed distortions to trade and competition that result from unfair advantages the government offered to these enterprises.[23] This proposal was directed primarily at Vietnam, and to a lesser extent Singapore and Malaysia. However, China would be affected the most as the TPP could become a template for a larger Asia-Pacific FTA or future WTO negotiations (Fergusson et al. 2013: 42).

The Chinese authorities regarded the formation of the US-inspired TPP as a potential political risk that might undermine its political and economic influence in East Asia. Accordingly, China sought to hedge against this move by promoting the formation of an East Asia-wide FTA that excludes the United States. The re-engineering of talks on the regional FTA was initiated by an unprecedented joint proposal by China and Japan in August 2011.[24] It was China that encouraged Japan to consider the formation of the regional FTA. At the 14th ASEAN+3 summit in November 2011, Chinese Premier Wen Jiabao encouraged the acceleration of the building of the EAFTA and the CEPEA 'in a pragmatic way on the basis of fully respecting ASEAN's centrality'.[25] This implied that China would not adhere to its previous advocacy of an FTA among ASEAN+3 members, but would agree to give ASEAN a mandate to select possible participants in an East Asia-wide FTA. In fact, the ASEAN-initiated RCEP virtually became the 'ASEAN+6' trade framework that Japan had advocated. The US-inspired TPP forced China to shift the base of the geographical scope of the FTA formation from East Asia to the Asia-Pacific, encouraging it to accept the narrower East Asian initiative in order to defend its political stake in moves on the FTA formation in the wider Asia-Pacific. The TPP eroded political confrontation between China and Japan over the FTA initiative, and produced a path to create a new trade institution – the RCEP.

The TPP has had complicated effects on ASEAN members' trade policy and trade relations. Singapore and Brunei were the original TPP members, and Malaysia and Vietnam joined TPP negotiations at the later stage. Cambodia, Laos, and Myanmar – non-members of the APEC – are unlikely to be members of the TPP due to their underdeveloped economic conditions. Some members who have not joined TPP negotiations were worried about the negative impact that the TPP participation would likely bring about on the domestic industry. For instance, Indonesian Trade Minister Gita Wirjawan stated that 'we may review [the TPP] in the medium-term. If we can develop the parameters measuring the readiness of our industries, if we can check off the box, then I think we can be open-minded about entering discussions and negotiations. Until then, no.'[26] Thai Prime Minister Yingluck Shinawatra stated to US President Obama that her country would like to consider joining TPP negotiations during a meeting on the sidelines of the EAS in November 2011. Her hope was not realised in the short term, largely because the Thai government had to examine carefully the TPP's conditions and details that would affect the domestic economy and society. Thus, ASEAN members' position on TPP participation was divided, which potentially risked undermining ASEAN's collective will in regional FTA formation. Moreover, some ASEAN members feared the TPP's negative effects on ASEAN's regional initiative. The TPP formation accompanied a risk that an initiative in regional trade integration might shift from ASEAN to the United States. Accordingly, ASEAN members needed to advance a new trade initiative for showing ASEAN's centrality in promoting regional economic integration.

Unlike critical incidents in 1997–99, the TPP move did not influence the basic ideals of trade policy in East Asia. However, the US-supported trade arrangement provoked various reactions from states in East Asia, one of which was a positive commitment to the formation of a regional FTA. China was concerned about a potential rise in US influence in East Asia through the TPP. ASEAN members were apprehensive about the decline of ASEAN as the central body to initiate and coordinate regional trade policy. These concerns paved the way for creating a new institutional path that overcame 'institutional inertia' under the parallel existence of the two concepts for a regional FTA in East Asia.

The parties' strategies for an East Asia-wide FTA

As already explained, the development of the US-inspired TPP had a significant impact on Chinese trade policy towards East Asia. In addition to positive commitments to an East Asia-wide FTA, China increased its interest in the China–Japan–Korea FTA, a critical condition for forming a regional FTA. Japan asserted the conclusion of a trilateral investment agreement before the trilateral FTA, but negotiations on the agreement lasted for five years from March 2007 largely due to China's reluctance to accept 'national treatment' to handle national and foreign companies equally in government regulations. Later, though, China changed its attitudes towards the trilateral commercial arrangements. When Chinese Premier Wen Jiabao attended the trilateral summit in May 2011, he stated that 'China is ready to do its best and work with Japan and the ROK for concluding the negotiations [on the trilateral investment agreement] before the end of the year'. Wen also referred to the trilateral FTA, proposing that the joint study of the trilateral FTA be concluded within 2011 ahead of the original schedule and formal negotiations would be launched the following year.[27] At the following year's summit, three leaders signed the trilateral investment agreement as the first legal document on trilateral cooperation in the economic field, and agreed to launch negotiations on the trilateral FTA within 2012. The consolidation of formal trade arrangements in both Northeast Asia and East Asia clearly became an important pillar of China's economic diplomacy.

China's renewed interest in FTAs with its neighbouring countries derived primarily from its strategic intention to hedge against intensive moves towards the US-inspired TPP. At the same time, there were two additional factors. First, China increased its willingness to play a substantial role in regional trade integration and institution-building against a background of growing economic power in East Asia (Zhang and Shen 2013: 45). Second, China deepened the recognition of the need for strengthening economic ties with East Asian countries after experiencing shrinking markets in Europe and the United States due to the global financial crisis and facing intensified protectionism against Chinese products in these markets.

Japan hoped to promote the formation of an East Asia-wide FTA with three motivations. The first was to strengthen linkages with ASEAN through a regional FTA. In April 2012, economic ministers of ASEAN made a visit to Japan and held a meeting with their Japanese counterpart. The ministers stressed the need to promote ASEAN's integration efforts such as the AEC and the Master Plan on ASEAN Connectivity, as well as support for fostering small and medium enterprises. Positive engagement in the RCEP also became a major pillar of ASEAN–Japan collaboration.[28] The second was the maintenance of commercial interests in competition against South Korea. The Korean government pursued the proactive FTA policy under the banner of 'Global Korea', and the ratio of trade with FTA partners to total trade reached 35.8 per cent by the end of 2010 compared with 17.6 per cent for Japan (METI 2011: 246).[29] Japan and South Korea are internationally competitive in similar industrial sectors represented by electronics and automobiles. Since South Korea's main FTA partners – the EU and the United States – provide crucial markets for the Japanese manufacturing sectors, differences in tariff imposition were deemed to be serious handicaps to Japanese industry. Therefore, while Japan searched for FTAs with the EU and the United States (through the TPP), it needed to raise the efficiency of production networks and supply chains in East Asia through an East Asia-wide FTA. Third, the formation of a regional FTA in East Asia was necessary to secure benefits from production networks in East Asia involving India and China. In addition to China, India was gradually integrated into production networks formed by Japanese manufacturing firms. India and China maintained relatively high import restriction measures such as high tariffs and complicated customs procedures. Even if Japanese firms were involved in difficulties in relation to products exported from ASEAN to China or India through ASEAN+1 FTAs, the Japanese government could not engage in resolving such difficulties. The formation of a broad FTA was expected to overcome such constraints.

In South Korea, the Lee Myung-bak administration began in February 2008. His ruling party, the Grand National Party, had its supporting base in big business and the relatively rich class that would draw benefits from FTAs. President Lee named 'Global Korea' and pragmatism as two key concepts for his administration. Accordingly, the administration pursued pragmatic and practical FTAs, expanding the number of partners for bilateral FTAs. Particularly important was that South Korea brought an FTA with China into view. South Korea was originally cautious about an FTA with China due to concern about negative effects on domestic industries. However, it began to consider the FTA positively after China and Taiwan concluded the Economic Cooperation Framework Agreement (ECFA) in June 2010. The ECFA had the potential to divert trade from South Korea to Taiwan because the two economies competed in the electronics sector in the Chinese market. Accordingly, the Korean government began to search for the conclusion of an FTA with China. When Korean President made a formal visit to Beijing in January 2012, leaders of both governments agreed to begin negotiations on an FTA, and the first round of negotiations began in May 2012.

South Korea's FTA strategy had negative effects on the formation of the trilateral FTA. As already explained, China encouraged the two states to promote the trilateral FTA and Japan became eager to promote it. However, South Korea preferred a bilateral FTA with China to the trilateral FTA.[30] When the trilateral summit was held in May 2012, the participants were originally expected to launch FTA negotiations within a couple of months after making a formal agreement at the meeting because they had already reached a preliminary agreement on the early start of negotiations. At working-level talks for the summit, South Korea opposed including a specific time to begin negotiations in a joint statement for the summit.[31] Eventually, the joint statement contained the phrase 'the trilateral FTA negotiation would be launched within this year', taking into account Seoul's preferences. South Korea's reluctance to enter into the trilateral FTA derived from its industrial rivalry against Japan. Seoul's vital commercial interest lies in securing an advantageous position for its manufacturing companies against their Japanese rivals. The attainment of the upper hand in the huge Chinese market through the formation of the bilateral FTA before the trilateral one will surely contribute to this commercial interest.

ASEAN's major interest in FTA networks is to maintain its central position in moves towards economic integration in East Asia. While Northeast Asia increased its economic prowess with China's rapid growth, the relative economic power of Southeast Asia still remained weak, partly because of the continuous two-tier ASEAN problem. Under such conditions, the three Northeast Asian states gradually intensified economic integration through the conclusion of the trilateral investment pact and the pursuit of the trilateral FTA. ASEAN members were worried that the centre of gravity of trade integration in East Asia might shift from Southeast Asia to Northeast Asia. Accordingly, ASEAN under the leadership of Indonesia proposed the RCEP framework in response to the joint proposal by China and Japan. The

RCEP's guiding document explicitly states that 'negotiation for the RCEP will recognize ASEAN Centrality in the emerging regional architecture'. In particular, ASEAN had a strong preference for maintaining flexible and equitable treatment for countries at the different development level. The RCEP's guiding principles reflect this element, and its objective is to increase economic and technical cooperation to narrow development gaps.

Research institutes and the development of FTAs

In some countries, researchers played a critical role in propelling the FTA policy, by being directly involved in the policymaking process. During the Koizumi government's term of office in Japan, the Council on Economic and Fiscal Policy (CEFP) gradually played an important role in leading FTA promotion and agricultural reforms.[32] In particular, the four expert members of the council – two business representatives and two economists – pushed forwards the promotion of FTAs. They submitted independent reports that encouraged the government to advance the pro-FTA policy and presented concrete measures to realise it. For instance, the expert members submitted a report entitled the Basic Directions in Promoting FTAs at a CEFP's meeting in April 2005. The report emphasised the acceleration of FTA negotiations, proposing that the government adopt an objective of making the ratio of trade with FTA partners in total trade more than 25 per cent in the coming five years, and more than 50 per cent in the long term. In July 2006, the Koizumi cabinet adopted the cabinet decision, the Basic Policies for Economic and Fiscal Management and Structural Reform 2006. The decision contained the phrase 'the value of trade with countries having concluded EPAs with Japan is expected to account for 25 per cent or more of Japan's total trade value by the year 2010'.[33] This decision adopted a numerical target for FTA policy for the first time. The expert members recognised that Japan's FTA policy had not advanced smoothly in previous years, and such stagnation stemmed largely from political considerations to industrial sectors that would suffer from the FTA conclusions. Accordingly, they raised the objective numerical target in the fixed time frame and thereby narrowed the scope of political considerations.

As the Chinese government deepened its commitment to FTAs, a growing number of academic institutions were involved in feasibility studies. In addition to the CASS and IFTEC, the Development Study Centre of the State Council and the Institute of International Economic Relations at the NDRC carried out the studies. Moreover, Nankai University, Chinese Agriculture University, and the University of International Business and Economics were also involved in the domestic consultation process (Jiang 2010a: 113). The Chinese government recognised that FTAs were directly linked to national interests, which required the consideration of long-term political effects. At the same time, it was necessary to have objective evaluations of the economic costs and benefits that an FTA conclusion would produce. The academic institutes could offer professional data and interpretations that were not biased by narrow interests of specific sectors or provinces, and the Chinese government took advantage of such strength in research activities by academic institutes.

In the process of forging an FTA in East Asia, one research institute was involved in policy development: the Economic Research Institute for ASEAN and East Asia (ERIA). The ERIA, an East Asian version of the Organisation for Economic Cooperation and Development (OECD), was established in June 2008 under Japan's initiative.[34] The ERIA aims to assist the promotion of economic integration in East Asia through survey analyses and policy proposals targeting policy research areas such as deepening economic integration, narrowing development gaps, and sustainable development (METI 2008: 438). Its Governing Board comprises 17 members that include representatives of EAS members and Secretary General of ASEAN. Since the ERIA was established under Japan's initiative and has been managed with funds mostly provided by the Japanese government, its activities have been directed towards enhancing the function of the EAS. For instance, the ERIA's executive director has attended EAS ministerial meetings and ministerial consultations in energy, economic cooperation, and foreign affairs. At the same time, as its name indicates, the ERIA has paid attention to assisting economic integration of East Asia with special attention to ASEAN.

The ERIA has assisted the deepening of talks on a regional FTA in East Asia. The ASEAN Secretariat commissioned the ERIA to provide the comprehensive mapping of existing ASEAN+1 FTAs, and the ERIA created a comparable and quantitatively analysable database of five ASEAN+1 FTAs on four components: tariff component, ROOs, trade in services, and investment rule. On the basis of the dataset, the institute conducted the analyses of similarity and convergence among the FTAs at the disaggregated commodity/sector level, and challenges and solutions towards the creation of an FTA in East Asia. In particular, tariff elimination coverage and commonality of ROOs in ASEAN+1 FTAs were deeply analysed (Nishimura 2013). These research outcomes helped ASEAN to progress activities of working groups that ASEAN established for discussing an FTA in East Asia (Sukekawa 2012: 258). In November 2011, ASEAN leaders launched a new trade initiative of the RCEP, and this initiative was sustained by the ERIA's scientific and technocratic research activities. A major hurdle to the formation of a regional FTA in East Asia was how to coordinate the diverse contents of the existing ASEAN+1 FTAs into a unified FTA. The ERIA assumed the role of overcoming this hurdle with its scientific and professional capabilities. It delivered the outcome of research to the policymaking process through ASEAN, which made it easy for the outcome to be accepted by other parties.

The ERIA also made efforts to create transboundary networks for regional trade policy. In February 2009, the ERIA organised the Research Institute

Network (RIN), which consists of research organisations from the original 16 EAS members.[35] The ERIA-RIN aims to assist the ERIA by providing country information and research findings from individual countries and giving advice to the ERIA's research themes and policy recommendations. The network has issued the ERIA-RIN Statement, which addresses major challenges and problems pertinent to regional economic integration. While the statement is drafted by one economist of the member institutes, its final text reflects views and perspectives provided by various economists. The second statement, issued in November 2012, was relevant to the RCEP. This statement spelled out the desirable designs of the RCEP as a user-friendly, open arrangement to develop and deepen an integrated production base in East Asia by showing theoretical backgrounds to sustain such designs.

The formation of a regional FTA in East Asia was advanced under political interactions among member governments with strategic calculations. Given such complicated political interactions, the ERIA did not necessarily play a distinctive role in paving the way for the smooth development of a regional FTA in East Asia by harmonising the member governments' interests in a certain direction. However, the institute provided objective data that were conducive to the substantiation of discussions on policy directions. The policymakers paid respect to sophisticated, scientific research outcomes and took advantage of them in order to authorise desirable policy directions.

Conclusion

After the late 1990s, states in East Asia intensified their commitments to FTAs as an engine for market liberalisation and economic integration. This chapter examined the development of institutions for trade liberalisation in East Asia including the process towards the formation of an East Asia-wide FTA. It identified major factors that qualified this development by focusing on the trade strategies pursued by China, Japan, South Korea, and ASEAN, and on the involvement of research interests as well as external events and forces.

This chapter confirmed the two-step development of the FTA formation in East Asia. The first was the bilateral or minilateral FTA formation that began in the early 2000s. The states in East Asia shifted emphasis on market liberalisation from multilateralism to bilateralism and regionalism, and intensified their commitments to bilateral FTAs and ASEAN+1 FTAs. This step was triggered by a series of incidents in 1997–99 including the Asian financial crisis and deteriorating multilateralism. The second step was a multilateral FTA initiative that converged into a uniform format in 2011. The states in East Asia advanced talks to coordinate diverse ideas on an East Asia-wide FTA, and this move was urged by the US-inspired TPP formation. Thus, institutions for trade cooperation were created in the developmental path with two critical junctures.

The shift from the first to the second step took a long time, largely because of complicated political interactions among four parties. China surprised ASEAN members by proposing the ACFTA in 2000, and this proposal derived from strategic intentions to counter Japan's regional trade initiatives and mitigate the China threat perception among Southeast Asian countries. China's swift move towards closer economic and political ties with Southeast Asia forced Japan to take soft-balancing counter-measures. Japan approached both individual ASEAN members and ASEAN as an entity, pursuing a conclusion of an EPA that incorporated economic cooperation and other cooperative measures in addition to reduction in tariffs. In the mid 2000s, China and Japan competed for an initiative to form an East Asia-wide FTA by pushing forward the EAFTA and CEPEA, respectively.

Importantly, domestic political processes had significant effects on China and Japan's FTA policies. The Chinese government was able to show cohesive postures towards FTA promotion under strong premiership, which led to the ACFTA proposal. However, protectionist groups gradually increased relative influence within the government. In particular, the NDRC gained power as an administrative body to check the negative impact of market liberalisation on the domestic society and economy. The fragmented domestic political institution distracted the Japanese government from setting up a bold and cohesive FTA policy in a swift manner. Furthermore, the existence of disputes between advocates and detractors of FTAs within the government restricted the political freedom of the Japanese government in the FTA engagement.

ASEAN and South Korea pursued their own interests in promoting regional trade cooperation. ASEAN sought to maintain its central status in the formation of a regional FTA and to reflect its own preferences and agendas in the formation process. South Korea, which selected FTA partners in terms of pragmatic economic benefits, found little incentive to promote an East Asia-wide FTA. The motivations underpinning ASEAN and South Korea's FTA approaches indicate that the convergence of diverse interests among the parties into a unified direction to create a regional FTA in East Asia is a challenging task.

A decision to conclude an FTA requires numerous data and comprehensive analyses of its effects on political, economic, and social dimensions. Political actors make final decisions on an FTA but researchers and research institutes can sustain the promotion of the FTA policy by providing data on and analyses of economic effects that the conclusion of FTAs will produce. Such roles played by researchers and research institutes were seen in the development of FTAs in East Asia. The academic institutes provided objective perspectives and concrete guidelines for promoting FTAs in China, Japan, and ASEAN. Equally importantly, the ERIA assisted the formation of a regional FTA in East Asia by searching for routes to coordinate contents of the existing ASEAN+1 FTAs towards the creation of a new regional FTA.

Lastly, this chapter identified three features in institution-building in the trade field in East Asia. The first is strong politicisation of the FTA formation process. Moves to form FTAs emerged in the late 1990s, but it took a long time to shift from a bilateral-based 'fragmented regionalism' to a region-wide 'unified regionalism'. Japan and China, both of which retained strong economic capabilities and intensive trade linkages, competed for greater influence, and the US involvement through the TPP made regional trade politics more complicated. The second is direct and significant impact of trade on the society. Political leaders paid due attention to the character of trade, whose liberalisation would have significant effects on various segments of society, and this made coordination on regional cooperation more complicated. The third is the effect of linkages with extra-regional states. Close economic and political linkages with extra-regional partners encouraged some states in East Asia to forge trade arrangements with them, and such moves had significant effects on the building of trade institutions in East Asia.

4
Developing Institutions for Regional Financial Stability

The world economy has been hit by sporadic financial crises such as the Asian financial crisis in 1997–98, the global financial crisis in 2008, and the euro crisis after 2009. The financial crises had a serious negative impact on economic growth, employment, and commodity prices in the crisis-affected countries. Accordingly, international financial institutions represented by the International Monetary Fund (IMF) and region-based multilateral intuitions have advanced preventive and rescue measures in the likely case of a future financial upheaval.

Although most economies in East Asia have achieved steady economic growth since the 1980s, financial turmoil has imposed a brake on such growth. In particular, the Asian financial crisis, which began in Thailand in July 2007, had region-wide contagious effects, making many economies in the region plunge into a serious depression. The cooperative framework among the members of the Association of Southeast Asian Nations (ASEAN) and China, Japan and South Korea (ASEAN+3) became the main locus to discuss collective measures designed to make regional economies more resistant to a financial attack. In 2000, member states launched the Chiang Mai Initiative (CMI), a network of bilateral swap agreements to provide liquidity support for a crisis-stricken member. The member states have striven to make the CMI a more institutionalised architecture with a collective decision-making mechanism, and expanded the scope of financial cooperation including the development of an Asian bond market as well as a credit guarantee and investment facility.

This chapter examines the initiation and development of financial and monetary cooperation in East Asia by focusing on the regional liquidity provision system and the regional surveillance system. It elucidates the policy preferences of China, Japan, South Korea, and ASEAN, and analyses their influences on the evolution of these two systems. This chapter also investigates the effect of financial crises on the trajectory of the building of financial institutions, and explores the meaningful involvement of and inputs from research institutes in the policy formation process for regional financial cooperation.

The launching of the CMI

The initiation of the CMI and regional surveillance system

The seeds of financial cooperation in East Asia were planted by a series of meetings of government financial authorities in the late 1990s. In September 1998, Japanese Finance Minister Kiichi Miyazawa proposed a meeting of Asian finance ministers and central bank governors, and six Asian countries not including China attended this meeting. Three months later, Chinese Vice-President Hu Jintao proposed a meeting of deputy finance ministers and central bank vice-governors of ASEAN members together with China, Japan, and South Korea. This proposal led to an ASEAN+3 finance ministers' meeting in Hanoi in March 1999. The third ASEAN+3 summit in November 1999 became a stepping stone to the development of regional financial cooperation. The leaders adopted the Joint Statement on East Asia Cooperation, in which they 'agreed to strengthen policy dialogue, coordination and collaboration on the financial, monetary and fiscal issues of common interest', with the recognition of need to enhance 'self-help and support mechanisms in East Asia through the ASEAN+3 Framework'.[1] At the meeting, China insisted on the significance of strengthening the ASEAN+3 financial process. The Chinese assertion was supported by other participants, leading to an agreement to institutionalise the ASEAN+3 finance ministers' meeting (Hamanaka 2008: 71).

At the second ASEAN+3 finance ministers' meeting in May 2000 in Chiang Mai, Thailand, ministers confirmed a set of objectives for regional financial cooperation such as policy dialogues, monitoring of capital flows, and the reform of international financial institutions. The most important outcome of the meeting was the CMI, which aimed to provide liquidity support to member countries that would face short-term balance of payment deficits. The CMI contained two pillars: to strengthen the ASEAN Swap Agreement of 1977 by raising the available amount from US$200 million to US$1 billion; and to develop a full series of bilateral swap agreements (BSAs) among 'ASEAN+3' involving China, Japan, and South Korea. By utilising the BSAs, crisis-hit countries would be able to borrow a predetermined amount of their counterparts' reserves for a period of 90 days (renewable for up to two years) to supplement their own reserves (Grimes 2006: 359).

In order to guarantee the CMI, ASEAN+3 members needed to establish a feasible surveillance mechanism. Such a mechanism was necessary both because it would help to establish and strengthen the domestic financial system as a supporting instrument and mechanism for regional financial arrangements and because it would contribute to identifying emerging issues and potential problems that would require countries to take collective action at the national, or jointly at the regional level (Kim and Yang 2011: 582–83). At the second ASEAN+3 finance ministers' meeting, the ASEAN+3 Economic Review and Policy Dialogue (ERPD) system was agreed. The ERPD consists of meetings at the minister level annually and at the deputy minister level twice a year, and is intended to facilitate information sharing, exchanges of views, and collaboration on financial, monetary, and fiscal issues of common interest. International organisations such as the Asian Development Bank (ADB) and IMF would provide economic reports in order to facilitate policy dialogues, information sharing, and exchanges of views (Kawai and Houser 2007: 8).

There are three critical features in the initiation of the CMI. First, the CMI was an incomplete collective aid delivery system. It was a collective system because a trouble-affected country would need to borrow money simultaneously from all other countries with which it maintained swap agreements. It was an incomplete system because participating countries could opt out of swaps from the start by negotiating swap contracts only with selected countries (Amyx 2008: 122). Second, the CMI carefully avoided the seeds of political conflict. It did not presuppose that any state supervised the overall framework, being considered just an assembly of BSAs. Such consideration was intended to prevent political rivalry among member states as well as political and economic tensions between member and non-member states (Nakatsuji 2009: 63). Third, the CMI had subtle relationships with the IMF. In the background of the CMI, there were widespread criticisms of the IMF's dealings with the economies hit by the Asian financial crisis in 1997–98. At the same time, the CMI aimed at supplementing the existing international financial arrangements represented by the IMF. Namely, 90 per cent of each bilateral swap line requires an IMF loan agreement as a precondition. Accordingly, only up to 10 per cent of the maximum amount drawn would be provided without linkages with the fund. This condition resulted from the fact that East Asian states did not have sufficient capabilities to undertake effective surveillance and monitoring of the members' macroeconomic and financial conditions.

The effect of the 1997 Asian financial crisis

A critical incident that had significant effects on financial cooperation in East Asia was the Asian financial crisis. The crisis questioned the role and presence of existing institutions in East Asia. While central bankers launched an Executives' Meeting of East Asia Pacific Central Banks in 1991, finance ministers began to hold a meeting through the APEC forum in 1994. These two facilities were important as symbols rather than as financial safety nets (Ciorciari 2011: 927). Five Southeast Asian countries had set up the ASEAN Swap Agreement in August 1977, but this arrangement involved tiny sums, not being accompanied by an independent surveillance mechanism. The dysfunction of the existing institutions in response to the crisis provided a background factor encouraging the states in East Asia to pursue a new institution under the ASEAN+3 framework. The crisis 'broke the institutional status quo by bringing the two East Asian sub-regions under the auspices of an embryonic economic and financial architecture', and opened windows of change for new regional institutions (Emmers and Ravenhill 2011: 135).

The Asian financial crisis had a significant effect on cohesion among East Asian countries in two ways. First, the crisis consolidated collective identity among East Asian states, making it apparent that the Southeast and Northeast Asian economies were interdependent and the regional economy as a whole was vulnerable to the vagaries of global finance. The crisis that occurred in Thailand in 1997 proliferated to its neighbouring countries and South Korea within that year. The contagion by which the crisis spread to countries throughout the region made East Asian leaders recognise that their countries have a common fate within the larger framework of East Asia. The economies of East Asia had common vulnerabilities resulting from high reliance on external markets – especially those in Europe and North America. The leaders developed a common understanding about the need to advance collective actions to reduce such vulnerabilities given the difficulty of withstanding the forces of global financial markets through individual efforts. The recognition of collective identity provided the foundation for promoting regional financial cooperation through tangible measures (Terada 2003).

Second, the crisis provoked the so-called 'politics of resentment' (Higgott 1998). The United States had maintained a strong political, security, and economic presence in East Asia. However, the US government, which had provided a massive US$20 billion to support Mexico in its 1995 financial turmoil, did not provide fund support for Thailand. Given this US attitude, the states in East Asia recognised that they had to pursue a regionally oriented support mechanism through their own collective initiatives. Moreover, the states that relied on the IMF rescue packages experienced worsening recessions largely due to misguided conditionality imposed by the fund with the US Treasury and the Federal Reserve exerting influence behind the scenes (Sussangkarn 2011: 206). The crisis made the states in East Asia come together to promote regional financial cooperation, independent of US influence.

The Asian financial crisis had a strong impact on the policy directions of two regional powers: Japan and China. Since Japan had forged close ties with the East Asian economies, with 41 per cent of its exports going to them in 1997, the Japanese economy suffered from downward pressure on its exports and economy as a whole. Accordingly, the Japanese government adopted measures to sustain the recovery of the crisis-hit economies represented by the New Miyazawa Initiative.[2] Importantly, the crisis provided the Japanese financial authorities with a critical stimulus to direct their concern to regional financial matters. The Ministry of Finance (MOF) strengthened internal organs that would deal with monetary and financial affairs in East

Asia after the crisis. In July 1998, the ministry set up the International Financial Market Office (the Japanese name can be translated literally as the Asian Currency Office) as the first division dealing specifically with Asian financial issues.[3] Other divisions also began to take up matters pertinent to East Asian countries and the ministry's awareness of issues and problems that the Asian economies faced rapidly increased (Sakakibara 1999: 46).

The Chinese financial market was under heavy government regulation and the Chinese economy had not yet forged close economic linkages with Southeast Asia. Accordingly, China did not experience significant negative effects from the Asian financial crisis. However, the crisis became a clue that Chinese policymakers took regional financial affairs seriously. They believed that the West in general and the United States in particular had taken advantage of the Asian financial crisis to advance particular economic agendas designed to serve self-interest, sharing with its Asian neighbours the sense of common victim *vis-à-vis* the western 'gang' (Sohn 2008: 320; Chey 2009: 462–63). Moreover, Chinese policy elites thought that the IMF-prescribed solutions to the crisis-hit economies dismissed the importance of the non-interference and independence principles that China and other Asian developing countries paid respect to (Sohn 2008: 320). An additional factor was relevant to Hong Kong, which had reverted to Chinese sovereignty on July 1, 1997. Given Hong Kong's heavy trade and financial interdependence with East Asia, its exposure to economic difficulties in the region sensitised the Chinese authorities to the broader volatility and potential danger of Asian monetary affairs. In particular, likely turmoil in Hong Kong would inevitably have political echo effects on mainland China, reducing the people's trust in the capabilities of top leaders (Calder and Ye 2010: 90–91).

There was one imperative factor that Chinese policymakers feared in relation to the effects of the Asian financial crisis. They experienced the fear of a financial crisis that could proliferate easily to neighbouring countries. In particular, the collapse of the Suharto regime in Indonesia due to the financial crisis stunned and worried the leaders of the Chinese Communist Party (CCP). To Chinese policy elites who had been concerned about political stability and CCP regime survival, the political transition in Indonesia portrayed the importance of financial and economic security to political security and even regime survival (Sohn 2008: 316). The CCP Central Committee convened a special session on financial security in May 1998, and organised a training course on finance for senior party and government officials in January 1999 (Sohn 2008: 317). Thus, Chinese policymakers were worried about the devastating effects that the financial crisis had on domestic society, and the possibility that such effects would provoke a political crisis.

Certainly, the Asian financial crisis constituted a critical juncture for producing new institutions and policy patterns towards financial stability in East Asia. During the financial crisis, the existing institutions could not provide effective counter-measures. The regional states observed the contagious nature of a financial crisis, perceived their collective identity as nations living in a region vulnerable to financial instability, and recognised the need for collective action to establish new institutional mechanisms to deal with a large-scale crisis. The crisis paved the way for the subsequent institutional path opened under the initiatives by ASEAN+3 members.

The parties' preferences and behaviour

Among four parties in East Asia, Japan played a significant role in pushing forward regional financial cooperation. During the Asian financial crisis, the Japanese MOF proposed the creation of the Asian Monetary Fund (AMF), which aimed at establishing a US$100 billion fund to offer various forms of assistance to the crisis-hit economies and a pool of reserve currency in case of a future financial crisis. However, the proposal was pushed aside by objections from the United States and IMF, which were apprehensive about the duplication of IMF operations, and lack of support from China, which was concerned about Japan's financial hegemony in East Asia. Afterwards, the ministry strove to create regional financial architectures carefully in a step-by-step manner.

Interestingly, it was unclear who took the lead in establishing the CMI. However, the Japanese MOF surely undertook informal negotiations behind the scenes in order to gain explicit support from the United States and other East Asian countries. Unlike with the AMF proposal, the US government did not oppose the launching of the CMI. This was partly because it recognised the need for regional facilities as measures to prevent the repetition of a financial crisis. At the same time, the Japanese MOF successfully persuaded the US financial officials about the necessity of the CMI. A senior MOF official recalls that it was tough to convince Washington that the initiative would be completely different from the AMF.[4]

Under the CMI the BSA networks deepened, centred on Japan. The progenitor of the CMI was the New Miyazawa Initiative, under which Japan signed BSAs with South Korea and Malaysia in January and July 1999, respectively. As of July 2002, Japan concluded BSAs with South Korea (US$7 billion), Thailand (US$3 billion), the Philippines (US$3 billion), Malaysia (US$3.5 billion), and China (US$3 billion). Japan was the key promoter of bilateral networks within a few years after the launching of the CMI.

Japan's commitment to regional financial cooperation derived from its desire to establish regional leadership in financial affairs. 'Tokyo has pushed one idea after another for new regional ventures, obviously hoping to consolidate whatever remains of Japan's position as a regional leader while there is still time' (Cohen 2010: 20). Japan had strength in the huge amount of foreign reserves it possessed, and with its connections to international financial institutions. While Japan had material power as the primary holder of foreign reserves for a long time until 2005, it had ideational power with nearly half a century of experience in participating in financial cooperation at the pinnacle of the international financial architecture (Grimes 2009: 108). Japan could take advantage of such assets and experience in guiding regional financial management.

At the same time, Japan's engagement in the CMI was complicated in relation to the internationalisation of the yen. After 1997, the Japanese MOF intensified its commitment to the internationalisation of the yen, exemplified by the statements by the finance minister at the APEC meeting in May 1998 and subsequently by Prime Minister Keizo Obuchi himself in January 1999 (Oba 2003: 160–63; Yoshimatsu 2003: 130–31; Rathus 2011: 118). The Japanese government believed that the internationalisation of the yen would stabilise currency relations in East Asia by reducing the risk of excessive dependence on the US dollar. This policy was also expected to produce substantial merits for the domestic economy by realising the stable growth of Japanese trade and investment and easing the fiscal burdens of public debt. However, international use of the yen did not expand, and East Asian countries continuously favoured the stabilisation of exchange rates with the dollar and the accumulation of foreign reserves to prepare for currency fluctuations. The CMI aimed to guarantee the East Asian countries' need for foreign reserves in the case of emergency. In relation to the internationalisation of the yen, the CMI did not necessarily reflect Japan's policy preferences (Hiwatari 2003).

In parallel to Japan, China played an important role in building regional financial architectures. As already explained, the first institutional framework among financial authorities in East Asia was established in response to a Chinese proposal. Moreover, the Chinese government began to provide training courses on regional economic and financial cooperation for ASEAN+3 finance and central bank officials in 2000 (Jiang 2010c: 612). Such positive engagements resulted from Chinese policymakers' willingness to proceed on financial cooperation, which was revealed in their formal statements. Chinese Premier Zhu Rongji claimed at the fourth ASEAN+3 summit in November 2000 that 'as for the next-step financial co-operation, China is open to all ideas.... China stands ready to work with other East Asian countries for the reform of the current international financial regime and the prevention and management of financial crisis'.[5] China continuously exhibited positive postures towards the development of regional financial architectures. Chinese Premier Wen Jiabao officially proposed converting the CMI's separate BSAs into a unified multilateral currency swap agreement at the ASEAN+3 summit in October 2003. This proposal aimed to request member states to contribute from their foreign reserves to a central fund (Dent 2005: 391–92; Nakatsuji 2009: 63).

China's positive engagement in regional financial cooperation derived from two factors. First, Chinese policymakers were motivated by a desire to raise their country's profile as a responsible player through discernible contributions to regional financial affairs. During the Asian financial crisis, China maintained the value of the RMB against the dollar, rather than devaluing it, and committed US$ 4.5 billion to the operational budget of the IMF to support financial packages to Thailand and Indonesia. These policies led to China's enhanced role and status in regional and international affairs (Bowles 2002). Beijing hoped to foster an image as a reliable and responsible country especially among Southeast Asian countries. Stable financial and monetary relationships were also important as China attempted to deepen trade relationship with Southeast Asian countries through the ASEAN-China Free Trade Area (ACFTA). The provision of stable monetary conditions was a prerequisite for the expansion of trade in goods and services.

Second, China became tolerant of accepting Japan's presence and role in regional financial affairs by attaching higher priority to reducing US influence in East Asia. China did not support Japan's proposal to establish the AMF largely because its officials worried that Japan would use a regional institution to leverage its immense reserves for political and economic gains at the expense of China (Ciorciari 2011: 928). However, China soon changed its stance. Chinese policymakers discovered that Japan's influence in East Asia increased as its New Miyazawa Initiative in 1998 was welcomed by Southeast Asian countries (Jiang 2011: 342). On the other hand, the Sino-US relationship worsened because of the bombing of the Chinese Embassy in Belgrade during the US-led North Atlantic Treaty Organisation (NATO) war in Kosovo in 1999, which raised Beijing's perception of Washington as the main security threat (Bowles 2002: 257). The development of regional financial cooperation by accepting Japan's initiative was regarded as not necessarily contradicting China's overall diplomatic interests.

Despite changes in its policy stance on regional financial cooperation, China was still careful about keeping an appropriate distance from both Japan and the United States. Beijing was passive about the idea that regional financial arrangements were independent from the IMF. Amyx (2005) stresses economic rationality and argues that China was afraid of risking its capital under the CMI because the initiative lacked an effective economic surveillance system, which would lead to a moral hazard risk for its borrowers. Equally important were nuanced relationships with both Washington and Tokyo. The indirect inclusion of the United States in East Asian financial arrangements through the IMF link was best for China, which feared that regional financial arrangements without the United States meant the dominance of Japan (Hamanaka 2008: 74; Grimes 2009: 104). Beijing hoped for a double-hedging condition in which it could prevent both financial domination by Tokyo and full involvement by Washington.

South Korea recovered quickly from the financial crisis due to successful reforms to improve corporate governance in financial institutions, and repaid its IMF loans in 2001.[6] However, harsh conditions attached to the IMF rescue packages created uneasy feelings towards the fund among government officials and the public. Accordingly, South Korea supported policy trends for regional financial cooperation created by Japan and China. The development of cooperative economic institutions in East Asia was desirable for South Korea, whose economy had gradually deepened interdependent relationships with other East Asian economies. In particular, it was desirable for Seoul to develop a region-based liquidity provision system, which would expand its leeway not to rely on the IMF in case of a financial emergency.

ASEAN members did not have robust and developed financial markets, apart from Singapore, and therefore ASEAN did not have sufficient capabilities to initiate a process of regional financial cooperation (Dieter 2008: 492). For most ASEAN members, the CMI implied a borrowing facility, allowing them to potentially draw on more foreign reserves than each alone possessed (Amyx 2008: 127). Accordingly, they had serious concerns about borrowing conditions under the CMI. Given their bitter experience of the conditions imposed by the IMF during the Asian financial crisis, they hoped to reduce their dependence on the IMF. Under pressure from the Malaysian government and other prospective borrowers, the +3 countries agreed that participants could borrow 10 per cent of CMI funds without an IMF programme for up to six months (Ciorciari 2011: 932). An additional merit that ASEAN members found in the CMI was relevant to China. The CMI provided the ASEAN members with insights into the development of possible changes in the Chinese financial system and foreign exchange regime (Amyx 2008: 127–28).

Research institutes and the beginning of financial cooperation

In the initial process of regional financial cooperation, several networks of research institutes were formed. The Japanese MOF proposed the establishment of the ASEAN+3 Research Group at an informal ASEAN+3 finance and central bank deputies' meeting in November 2002, and its establishment was agreed at the sixth ASEAN+3 finance ministers' meeting in August 2003. The group aimed to explore tangible measures to strengthen financial cooperation and promote financial stability in East Asia by soliciting academic input from researchers and research institutes in ASEAN+3 countries. The governments of China, Japan, and South Korea provided funds to finance research activities by institutes of their own countries or those of ASEAN members (Kawai and Houser 2007: 7).

ASEAN+3 finance ministers confirmed research agendas commissioned to the ASEAN+3 Research Group formally in their joint statements (see Table 4.1). In 2003/04, a research project entitled 'Towards a Regional Financial Architecture for East Asia' was commissioned to research institutes and its report was presented at the ASEAN+3 finance ministers' meeting in 2004. In this report, five think-tanks – the Institute for International Monetary Affairs (IIMA) of Japan, the Korea Institute for International Economic

Table 4.1 The research projects of the ASEAN+3 research group

Year	Research project
2003/2004	• Towards a regional financial architecture for East Asia • An exchange rate arrangement for East Asia
2004/2005	• Economic surveillance and policy dialogue in East Asia • Trade, investment, and financial integration in East Asia • Exploring ways to enhance the functions of the CMI in the medium term • The role of private sector development in regional economic growth and financial integration
2005/2006	• Liberalisation of cross-border capital flows and effectiveness of institutional arrangements against crisis in East Asia • Fostering the asset management industry for the development of capital markets in the region • Regional coordination of policy measures forward: financial market liberalisation and capital market development
2006/2007	• Towards greater financial stability in the Asian region: exploring steps to create regional monetary units • Financial conglomeration in the East Asian region: recent trends and implications for regional financial market development
2007/2008	• Towards greater financial stability in the Asian region: measures for possible use of regional monetary units for surveillance and transaction • Development of database on corporate credit information • Developing the capital market to widen and diversify SME financing
2008/2009	• Development of corporate credit information database and credit guarantee system • The trend of trade, foreign direct investment, and monetary flows in East Asia, and its policy implications • New financial products and their impact on the Asian financial markets
2009/2010	• Ways to promote foreign trade settlements denominated in local currencies in East Asia • Regulation and supervision for sound liquidity risk management for banks
2010/2011	• Possible use of regional monetary units • Lessons from Asia's experience with sudden capital flows • Fiscal and financial impact of the climate change and policy challenges in East Asia

Table 4.1 (Continued)

Year	Research project
2011/2012	• Dealing with commodity price volatility in East Asia • The roles and functions of the banking sector in the financial system of the ASEAN+3 Region • The role of regional financial safety nets in global architecture
2012/2013	• International discussions on the credit rating agencies • Enhancing infrastructure to strengthen the regional credit rating capacity in the ASEAN+3 Region
2013/2014	• Policy recommendations for the expansion of the securitisation market in the ASEAN+3 countries • SWOT analysis of the capital market infrastructures in the ASEAN+3 member countries and its implications

Source: Compiled by the author from data at ASEAN Secretariat (http://www.asean.org/communities/asean-economic-community/category/other-documents-7).

Policy (KIEP), the Chinese Academy of Social Sciences (CASS), the Thailand Development Research Institute (TDRI), and the Indonesian Danareksa Research Institute (DRI) – made concrete proposals on institutional designs for liquidity assistance and policy dialogue. The proposal contained valuable insights into the promotion of regional cooperation: arrangements under the CMI should be revised to strengthen their effectiveness, and surveillance and financial assistance should be coordinated under an ASEAN+3 institution (Shimura 2004: 4).[7] In 2004/05, the CASS, IIMA, and two additional economists conducted research on 'Exploring Ways to Enhance the Functions of the Chiang Mai Initiative in the Medium Term'. The recommendations based on the studies envisioned the CMI's development as a multilateral institution including the establishment of an Asian Monetary Organisation, which would oversee short-term capital flows, exchange rate equilibrium, capital account liberalisation, and monetary and financial policies in the region.[8] As explained later, agreements reached at the eighth ASEAN+3 finance ministers' meeting in May 2005 reflected initiatives in pursuing future directions exhibited in the recommendations.

Another crucial network of research institutes was formed under the initiative of the ADB Institute.[9] The ADB Institute established the Asian Policy Forum (APF) in December 1999 in order to strengthen intellectual capabilities to study the Asian economies and provide intellectual and analytical leadership in the Asian policy communities. The forum, composed of 17 research institutes all located in Asia, conducted research on economic and financial issues in Asia and the results were delivered to policymakers. For instance, the APF undertook a project on how to prevent another capital account crisis in 1999. The resulting policy recommendations were discussed at the ADB's annual meeting in 2000 and at the International Finance Seminar in Singapore. The final report, entitled 'Policy Recommendations for Preventing Another Capital Account Crisis', suggested policy prescriptions for crisis prevention (dealing with massive capital flows and minimising double mismatch) and crisis management (managing sudden reversals of capital flows and establishing regional financial arrangement) (ADB Institute 2000). The suggestions, produced by discussions among university scholars and think-tank researchers, provided signposts for creating stable domestic and regional financial order, and constituted the basis for high-level discussions in China, Indonesia, the Philippines, and so on.[10] The APF produced additional recommendations regarding 'designing new and balanced financial market structures in post-crisis Asia' and 'sequencing the next stage of domestic and external liberalisation for China'. Haas (1992) argues that post-crisis conditions of uncertainty raise the value of scientific expertise for policymakers who require professional insights and appropriate advice. The APF, taking advantage of such opportunities, issued a series of policy reports to prevent a recurrence of the financial crisis.

The research institutes played a role in assisting policymakers to initiate regional financial cooperation in East Asia. They provided professional knowledge and insights to formulate the design of regional institutions and directions of their activities. Since financial and monetary affairs were technically complex with high-level uncertainty, professional insights from a long-term perspective were indispensable for promoting regional financial cooperation. In authorising research activities by the ASEAN+3 Research Group, individual finance ministries of ASEAN+3 members commissioned important financial and monetary issues to specific research institutes. Importantly, research institutes and involved economists maintained institutionalised access to the policymaking process. Since some of the economists who were involved in the formulation of policy recommendations belonged to government-affiliated research institutes, they could secure privileged access to policymaking. The results of the research were explained at meetings of the CMI Task Force, which was composed of director-level government officials, and were sometimes presented at deputy ministers' meetings.[11] A critical point is that notwithstanding the established access to the policymaking process, recommendations by the ASEAN+3 Research Group had weakness in terms of cohesion. The research institutes that were involved in research under a specific theme exchanged views and opinions in an informal manner, but did not necessarily hold a formal gathering to discuss details of research aiming to produce a unified position on the topic.[12] Accordingly, recommendations were based on a combination of research outcomes by individual institutes, not presenting cohesive views and perspectives derived from such outcomes. The lack of 'one voice' might lead to the reduced influence of research institutes by undermining the legitimacy of scientific expertise in recommendations.

The APF had strength in presenting collective opinions of researchers on the basis of intensive policy deliberations. In preparing for the 2000 APF report, researchers' gatherings were organised six times from December 1999 until June 2000, and more than 30 researchers from 14 countries contributed to the formulation of the report (ADB Institute 2000). Such intensive engagements surely contributed to increasing common understanding of problems and solutions to them, which led to the production of integrated policy recommendations. Importantly, informal settings through research institutes could foster confidence-building among researchers. The informality in the track II networks helped to cultivate the ties of common interest, consensual knowledge and personal friendship (Sohn 2012: 600). The systematic research activities at the APF became possible with their integration into overall research operations and administrative coordination by the ADB Institute.

Slow progress in financial cooperation

The slow development of financial cooperation

The BSA network under the CMI developed rapidly. The total number of BSAs increased from eight in July 2002 to 16 by April 2005, and the cumulative value grew from US$17 billion to US$39.5 billion in the same period. All the agreements until 2005 were directed from the +3 countries to ASEAN members, and Indonesia, Malaysia, Thailand, and the Philippines networked with all their northern partners (Huotari 2012: 21). Despite such developments, the size of BSAs was still small and inadequate in relation to the amount required in the event of a crisis. Chalongphob Sussangkarn explicitly pointed out this inadequacy:

> Take the case of Thailand in 1997. With outstanding short-term debt of $43 billion and a current-account deficit running at about $1 billion per month, it was clear that the country was basically insolvent in terms of not having enough foreign-exchange reserves on hand to meet its forex obligations.... Given the current size of these agreements [BSAs under the CMI], Thailand could have drawn (during the crisis) $300 million from ASA (ASEAN Swap Arrangement) plus another $600 million from the 10 per cent of the bilateral swap facilities with the Plus Three countries available without the need to enter an IMF programme. These amounts are clearly insignificant compared to Thailand's problem in the middle of 1997.[13]

In addition, the CMI, a mechanism as an assembly of BSAs, had an inherent weakness in making speedy and effective responses in case of financial emergency.

In order to rectify the above shortcomings, finance ministers strove to strengthen a regional liquidity reserve through the CMI system. At the eighth ASEAN+3 finance ministers' meeting in May 2005, ministers exhibited a clear interest in the establishment of a collective decision-making mechanism of BSAs, or multilateralisation in which the relevant BSAs would be activated collectively and promptly in case of emergency. At the ninth meeting in May 2006, ministers requested the deputies to set up a new task force to further study various possible options for creating a more advanced framework for the regional liquidity support arrangement (CMI multilateralisation, CMIM). After 2007 finance ministers sought to consolidate their decisions to establish the CMIM. At the tenth meeting in May 2007, ministers reached an agreement that 'a self-managed reserve pooling arrangement governed by a single contractual agreement is an appropriate form of multilateralisation'.[14] At the following year's meeting, ministers 'agreed that CMI Multilateralisation will be underpinned by rigorous principles to govern its key aspects, including economic surveillance, borrowing accessibility, activation mechanism, decision making rules and lending covenants, while keeping to timely disbursement'.[15] They also reached an agreement that the total size of the CMIM would be at least US$80 billion.

Despite the rhetoric of commitment, actual progress towards the CMIM was slow. The multilateralisation of BSAs was first proposed by Chinese Premier Wen Jiabao in 2003. Even five years after this proposal, details of the multilateralisation were not determined. The slow development had much to do with the issue of contribution quotas under the CMIM. While ASEAN members quickly reached an agreement on individual quotas among themselves, the +3 countries took time to finalise coordination on individual quotas.

There were marked problems in the regional surveillance system. The ASEAN +3 members established the ERPD in 2000 as a regional surveillance mechanism. However, the ERPD provided member governments with broad discretion over the contents of individual reports, and the governments often submitted late or incomplete information and followed no common template, making it difficult to share and compare data (Kim 2008: 116; Ciorciari 2011: 945). Resources available to support the ERPD system were very limited, and officials involved in the system only carried out talks on a part-time basis alongside many other regular jobs. Furthermore, ministers' meetings mostly 'rubber stamped' what the officials prepared through the deputy meetings (Kawai 2010: 409–10; Sussangkarn 2010: 13).

Seeing these apparent shortcomings of the existing regional surveillance system, finance ministers sought to strengthen the system. At the eighth ASEAN+3 finance ministers' meeting in May 2005, ministers agreed to integrate the ERPD system into the CMI framework. This change was intended to allow for the quick detection of problems through enhanced capabilities to assess economic and financial conditions of the member states. At the ninth meeting in May 2006, ministers agreed to launch the Group of Experts and the Technical Working Group on Economic and Financial Monitoring to explore ways to further strengthen surveillance capacity in East Asia.

Despite the importance of the strengthened surveillance system, the progress of talks on concrete measures was slow. At the meetings in 2007 and 2008, finance ministers just restated the importance of strengthening cooperation on the regional surveillance system. The difficulty in regional surveillance derived from the fact that the strength of the ERPD would be a 'double-edged sword'. On the one hand, it would contribute to the strength of the CMI and independence from the IMF. Certainly, it was difficult to see how the CMI could operate without a dedicated institution to carry out economic surveillance, and the establishment of an independent regional surveillance system aimed to rectify this problem (Sussangkarn 2010: 9). This would then strengthen moves towards autonomy from the IMF because East Asian countries relied on the IMF for the monitoring surveillance of the member economies. On the other hand, the strength of the ERPD would run counter to basic norms long maintained in East Asia. The strength of the ERPD, which aimed to monitor compliance of policies adopted by individual states with agreed policy objectives, implied that regional governments would have to jettison a norm of non-interference in each other's internal affairs and surrender a portion of their economic and financial sovereignty to a multilateral institution. This was a step that most East Asian governments were reluctant to take (Nakatsuji 2009: 64).

The parties' complicated stances on the CMI development

Although ASEAN members and Northeast Asian countries were committed to the development of the CMI, their basic positions were diverse. China and Japan, the world's primary and secondary holders of foreign reserves, would be lenders in the event of a crisis, and four ASEAN members – Indonesia, Malaysia, Thailand, and the Philippines – would be potential borrowers. South Korea and Singapore stood as either lenders or borrowers in actual situations. Accordingly, China and Japan, and their collaboration as creditor nations were the most important factors advancing the CMI architecture.

Collaboration between China and Japan pushed forward the development of financial cooperation. In March 2002, the Bank of Japan and the People's Bank of China signed a yen–RMB swap arrangement equivalent to US$3 billion. Given that Japan and China were the world's two largest holders of foreign reserves, it was unlikely that the two states would activate the swap agreement. Accordingly, their agreement represented a political symbol that the two great powers had made firm commitments to financial cooperation in East Asia (Asami 2002: 3–4; Nakatsuji 2009: 63). China and Japan became the main contributors to studies of regional financial cooperation organised by the ASEAN+3 Research Group (Jiang 2010c: 612).

The Sino-Japanese collaboration was sustained by a broad range of common interests in regional financial cooperation. The IMF link aimed to evade outright opposition to the CMI from the United States and the IMF. At the same time, it reflected the common stance of Japan and China as creditor nations. Although ASEAN members who would stand in the borrowers' position requested a reduction of the IMF link, Japan and China rejected such requests. There were considerable political costs to reserve-rich countries in denying requests for money from crisis-stricken countries or attempting to attach their own conditions. However, the promise of money provision without the threat of conditions had the potential of creating a 'moral hazard' for recipient countries. The IMF link was a convenient method of avoiding both political costs and moral hazards for Japan and China.

China and Japan also had shared interests in taking advantage of the collective power of the East Asian grouping in handling international financial affairs. The two states hoped to see changes to IMF facilities, policy conditionality, and governance, especially with respect to the IMF granting them larger quotas and attached voting rights in the Executive Board and Board of Governors (Henning 2009: 3). They sought to use the East Asian grouping as political leverage to elevate their stance in the IMF. The joint statement of the finance ministers' meeting in 2005 contained a phrase which noted that 'we called for an urgent review of the quota of the Asian countries in the IMF to properly reflect the current realities and their relative positions in the world economy. This would strengthen the mutual understanding between Asia and the IFIs [International Financial Institutions].'[16]

Notwithstanding the existence of common interests that propelled regional financial cooperation, China and Japan were in serious confrontation over specific issues regarding regional financial architectures. A typical example was a controversy on the regional currency unit. Japan had a strong interest in this issue from the beginning of regional financial cooperation, and presented a joint report with France regarding the exchange rate system at the third Asia–Europe Meeting (ASEM) finance ministers' meeting in January 2001. The report suggested adopting a managed exchange rate regime, in which a currency moves within a band with its centre targeted on a basket of currencies that takes the dollar, euro, and yen as reference currencies (Nakatsuji 2009: 66). The Japanese Research Institute of Economy, Trade and Industry (RIETI) in collaboration with Hitotsubashi University also conducted joint research on the Asian Monetary Unit in 2005, made up from the ASEAN 10+3 currencies to monitor the deviation of movements of national currencies in relation to their common regional movement.[17] In 2006 a more formal initiative was presented by the ADB under the strong influence of the Japanese government. The ADB's Office for Regional Economic Integration proposed the relative weight of the currencies in the Asian Currency Unit (ACU) on the basis of three economic elements: the size of the economy defined by GDP, volume of intra-regional trade, and a capital control variable (international debt security by residence of transactions), which were simply averaged. Using this method, the yen was given a weighting of

36.9 per cent and the RMB 19.51 per cent (Rathus 2011: 119). China did not agree with the launching of the ACU. The Chinese government maintained heavy controls and regulations on the exchange rate and capital account, and consequently China's weighting was lower than those of some other states. Accordingly, the Chinese government argued that under the plan the ACU would be difficult to quantify and not useful for stabilising exchange rates (Jiang 2010c: 617).

An additional controversy was directly connected to development towards the CMIM. Japan, China, and to a lesser extent South Korea undertook fierce negotiations on individual contribution quotas in the proposed CMIM. The contribution quotas were crucial because they were linked to the voting weight that the countries would have in the new institution. Japan insisted that it should be the largest single contributor to the CMIM because it had the biggest economy in East Asia and its contribution to the CMI was the largest. Japan also considered that it could aid the development of regional financial cooperation due to its experience and expertise in international financial affairs. China claimed that its contribution should be at least equal to that of Japan because it held the world's largest foreign reserves, which reached US$2.4 trillion in 2009, and that the Chinese economy was on a clear trajectory to overtake the Japanese economy. South Korea desired to hold a share equal to China on the grounds that it had an advanced level of economic development and depth in its financial markets, and made large contributions under the CMI (Cho 2011: 11). South Korea was apprehensive that China and Japan would determine the direction and content of the CMIM through their own informal dialogues and formal negotiations. Accordingly, it hoped to retain considerable influence in the new institution.

Certainly, common interests between China and Japan propelled the development of the CMI. Under such conditions, the states in East Asia could identify absolute gains from collective action, and pursued a policy goal to develop the CMI into a multilateral framework. However, China, Japan, and South Korea cared more about relative gains from cooperation and struggled to secure a relatively advantageous position in the details of this new architecture. Such struggles became a significant hurdle to the creation of the CMIM.

The establishment of the CMIM and AMRO

Renewed moves towards financial cooperation after 2009

The year 2009 marked a watershed in the development of financial cooperation in East Asia. At the 12th ASEAN+3 finance ministers' meeting in May 2009, ministers 'reached agreement on all the main components of the CMIM, including the individual country's contribution, borrowing accessibility, and the surveillance mechanism'.[18] Japan and China would provide US$38.4 billion (32 per cent of total US$120 billion) each, and South Korea half of this amount (Table 4.2). The maximum amount of borrowing for each country follows its contribution multiplied by its respective borrowing multiplier, giving ASEAN members higher multipliers – 5 and 2.5 –, South Korea parity, and China and Japan half their quotas. The CMIM also enabled ASEAN members who were not previously connected by BSAs – Brunei, Cambodia, Laos, Myanmar, and Vietnam – to become full members of the CMI mechanism. The participation of these countries was significant in that it helped with the consolidation of East Asia as a unified region that accepted the same policy prescriptions in response to potential financial risks.

The CMIM Agreement was signed on December 28, 2009, and came into effect on March 24, 2010. The swap activation process would be coordinated by the two co-chairs of the ASEAN+3 Finance Ministers Process: one from ASEAN members and the other from the +3 members. This coordination method follows co-chair systems that were formally adopted at the tenth finance ministers' meeting in 2007. The agreement contained clauses regarding the decision-making mechanism. The weighted voting system was adopted on the basis of quota contributions. While fundamental issues such as the total size of the CMIM and contribution of each party would be determined by consensus at the ministerial level consisting of finance ministers, executive-level matters such as initial execution of drawing, renewal of drawing rights, and events of default would be determined by a two-thirds weighted majority vote at the deputy-level comprised of deputy-representatives from finance ministries and central banks. The adoption of the majority-based decision-making implied an outstanding achievement as it was the first case of joint decision-making overcoming the members' adherence to consensus-based decision-making. The agreement also contained a clause regarding conditions that a party which requests a drawing has to meet before the voting for a swap request can be initiated, such as completing a review of the economic and financial situation, and having no events of default.

The finance ministers endorsed the Operational Guidelines for Enhancing Effectiveness of the CMIM at the 14th meeting in May 2011. The IMF representative joined discussions at the CMIM taskforce on this matter, and the guidelines provided for operational procedures for activating the CMIM included those in relation to the existence of an IMF programme (Kurihara 2011: 18). The formulation of the guidelines implied practical preparation for a request for a currency swap under the CMIM.

There was marked development in the regional surveillance system. At the 13th ASEAN+3 finance ministers' meeting in May 2010, ministers reached an agreement on a regional surveillance unit called the ASEAN+3 Macroeconomic Research Office (AMRO), and the office was established in Singapore in April 2011.[19] The AMRO implements tasks to monitor and analyse regional economies, which contributes to the early detection of risks, swift implementation of policy measures, and effective decision-making of

Table 4.2 CMIM contributions, purchasing multiple, and voting-power distribution

Countries	Financial contribution (US$ billion) (%)		Purchasing multiple	Voting power			
				Basic votes	Votes based on contribution	Total (%)	
Plus three	96.00	80.00		4.80	96.00	100.8	71.59
China							
China	34.20	28.50	0.5	1.60	34.20	35.8	25.43
Hong Kong	4.2	3.50	2.5	0	4.20	4.2	2.98
Japan	38.4	32.00	0.5	1.60	38.40	40.0	28.41
South Korea	19.2	16.00	1	1.60	19.20	20.8	14.77
ASEAN	24.0	20.00		16.00	24.00	40.0	28.41
Indonesia	4.552	3.793	2.5	1.60	4.552	6.152	4.369
Thailand	4.552	3.793	2.5	1.60	4.552	6.152	4.369
Malaysia	4.552	3.793	2.5	1.60	4.552	6.152	4.369
Singapore	4.552	3.793	2.5	1.60	4.552	6.152	4.369
Philippines	4.552	3.793	2.5	1.60	4.552	6.152	4.369
Vietnam	1.0	0.833	5	1.60	1.00	2.60	1.847
Cambodia	0.12	0.100	5	1.60	0.12	1.72	1.222
Myanmar	0.06	0.050	5	1.60	0.06	1.66	1.179
Brunei	0.03	0.025	5	1.60	0.03	1.63	1.158
Laos	0.03	0.025	5	1.60	0.03	1.63	1.158
Total	120.00	100.00		20.80	120.00	140.80	100.00

Source: Created by the author with data from the AMRO home page.

the CMIM. The office began the surveillance mission in October 2011, and submitted a consolidated surveillance report with overall macroeconomic and financial assessments of member states and the region during the process of the ERPD.

Further progress on regional financial cooperation was seen at the 15th finance ministers' meeting in May 2012. Central bank governors joined the meeting for the first time, which facilitated better collaboration between financial and monetary authorities. The participants agreed to double the total size of the CMIM to US$240 billion, and increase the IMF de-linked portion from 20 per cent to 30 per cent in 2012 and further to 40 per cent in 2014 if conditions are suitable. They also decided to introduce a crisis-prevention facility called the CMIM Precautionary Line (CMIM-PL). As for the AMRO, ministers instructed the deputies to accelerate the preparation to institutionalise the AMRO as an international organisation, and authorised Singapore to work with the AMRO to come up with the first draft of the treaty.

The higher IMF de-linkage implied a further attempt to establish a self-help mechanism of liquidity support as well as the reduced possibility of the US commitment to financial affairs in East Asia. The strength of the AMRO has two contradictory effects. The higher IMF de-link portion surely requires the strengthened function of the AMRO. However, the strengthened function itself leads to the rising possibility of intervention in internal affairs of member states. This implies that ASEAN+3 members pursued the strength of the AMRO with due consideration to its side-effects.

The 2008 global financial crisis

The 2008 global financial crisis that originated with the subprime mortgage loan problems in the United States had a significant impact on the global and East Asian economies. Since most East Asian countries held relatively affluent foreign reserves, the recurrence of a region-wide financial crisis was avoided. However, despite policy dialogues and studies on the desirability of reducing dollar dependence, East Asia increased its exposure to the dollar in the ten years after the Asian financial crisis (Katada 2011: 282). Under these conditions, South Korea and Indonesia faced short-term liquidity problems with a risk that their central banks did not hold enough dollars to meet demand in the market.

The global financial crisis created two obstacles to financial cooperation in East Asia. First, policy options adopted by several East Asian governments in response to the crisis reduced the reliability of the CMI. During the crisis, South Korea did not rely on the CMI but entered into a swap agreement with the US Federal Reserve for US$30 billion. This option was adopted largely because the country could have access only to US$3.7 billion without the portion of an IMF programme out of a total US$18.5 billion under the CMI. Given the lingering, painful memory of the 'IMF crisis' in the public mind, it was politically too risky for the Korean government to seek IMF assistance again (Sohn 2012: 590). This was also the case for other countries. Indonesia hoped to have a similar swap agreement with the US Federal Reserve, but the US government did not grant this wish. Accordingly, Indonesia ended up with a swap agreement with China (Kawai 2010: 416; Sussangkarn 2011: 214). As Thai Finance Minister Korn Chatikavanij pointed out, given bitter memories during the Asian financial crisis, it would be equivalent to 'suicide' in terms of domestic politics to ask the IMF for assistance.[20]

Second, international power shifts during the global financial crisis reduced the relative importance of the 'region'. The global financial crisis provoked a shift in gravity from the G-7 to the G-20 through the holding of financial and summit meetings under the latter's framework. This shift in gravity incorporated a shifting focus in solving the problem of East Asia's economic vulnerability, from regional arrangements to national and global stages (Katada 2011). Hence, the relative importance of regional financial architectures represented by the CMI declined in the reforms towards new global financial governance structures with East Asia's increased representation.

At the same time, the global financial crisis had positive effects on financial cooperation in East Asia. The financial authorities of governments seriously considered the value of regional financial institutions in preventing a crisis and mitigating its negative impact on the economy. The three Northeast Asian countries consolidated their common stance on struggling against the crisis. In November 2008, finance ministers of China, Japan, and South Korea organised an informal meeting in Washington on the fringes of the G-20. The meeting, organised in the midst of grave challenges to the financial market and real economy, provided the ministers with chances to exchange views on the causes of the crisis and possible measures to address it. At the meeting, the ministers expressed their determination to expedite the process of the CMIM as the top priority and agreed to make further efforts to reach consensus on all the elements of the CMIM. The following month, leaders of the three countries held the first trilateral summit independent of ASEAN+3 in Japan. The summit, convened in the shadow of the deepest global financial crisis for at least three decades, was a landmark event. The three leaders issued a special statement on the international finance and economy, in which they 'confirmed the significance of measures that will reinforce growth and expand domestic demand and are determined to work closely and strengthen the trilateral cooperation to facilitate Asian countries' efforts in order to overcome the negative impact resulting from the current international financial crisis and achieve self-sustainable growth in Asia'.[21] ASEAN finance ministers also 'underscored the importance and urgency of launching the CMIM and agreed to work closely with our Plus Three counterparts to resolve the remaining issues in order to finalize the multilateralised initiative' at their finance ministers' meeting in April 2009.[22]

The ASEAN+3 finance ministers held a special meeting in February 2009 in order to respond to the global financial crisis. At the meeting, ministers adopted the Action Plan to Restore Economic and Financial Stability of the Asian Region, which included important agreements to expand the total size of the CMIM from US$80 billion to US$120 billion and to strengthen the regional surveillance mechanism into a robust and credible system that would facilitate prompt activation of the CMIM. The plan also implied the prospect that when the surveillance mechanism became fully effective in its functions, the ratio for de-linkage with the IMF would be increased to over 20 per cent. The action plan exhibited a clear road towards the CMIM by consolidating the basic elements required to realise it.

As indicated by the holding of a special meeting, finance ministers in East Asia recognised the enormous impact of the global financial crisis on their national and regional economies. They were increasingly aware of the need to push ahead with the CMIM largely because reliance on ad hoc BSAs would create political friction, such as in the case where a swap is refused, and the development of a liquidity support system in the form of a regional public good mechanism would be the most effective option economically and politically (Sussangkarn 2011: 214).

The global financial crisis articulated the shortcomings of the existing architectures. Korean non-usage of the CMI revealed the problem of IMF linkage and accordingly leaders searched for a lower linkage with the IMF. The insufficiency of a regional surveillance system underpinned the high linkage and thereby the leaders sought to strengthen regional surveillance capacity. The crisis provided the states in East Asia with an impetus to overcome differences in details of the CMIM, and paved the way to a new institutional architecture to secure regional financial stability. Moreover, the crisis contributed to expanding the scope of regional financial cooperation. The crisis accentuated the importance of a crisis-prevention system in parallel to a crisis-rescue one. In fact the IMF adopted new crisis-prevention facilities such as the Flexible Credit Line and Precautionary and Liquidity Line. The financial authorities of East Asian countries also recognised the need to establish a similar system, and agreed to adopt the CMIM-PL.

The coordination of the parties' interests

A critical factor in completing the CMIM was coordination of interests among China, Japan, and South Korea. The coordination on contribution quotas was skilful in terms of the voting ratio, which was decided as a combination of basic votes and contribution-based votes. The formula for the latter was determined with the ratio of 2: 2: 1 for China, Japan, and South Korea. The final vote for China, Japan, and South Korea was 28.41 per cent, 28.41 per cent (28.41 per cent for ASEAN as well), and 14.77 per cent, respectively.

As already explained, coordination on contribution quotas to the CMIM among the +3 countries was the most difficult barrier to launching the CMIM. Japan pushed for the highest weighting while China insisted on a weighting equal to Japan. A skilful compromise was that Japan and China contributed 32 per cent each but China's share included 3.5 per cent from Hong Kong, which was specially added to membership of the CMI. This allowed China to claim co-equality with Japan while allowing Japan to claim the largest individual contribution (Rathus 2011: 114). This compromise implied significant progress from debates on the ACU, when the lack of policy coordination disturbed the realisation of the ACU idea.

Japan considered that it had provided a much larger contribution to the IMF and World Bank and had led the development of the CMI by forging the largest number of BSAs. At the same time, Japanese government officials recognised the reality that Japan's economic power was declining *vis-à-vis* China, and the Chinese economy would soon overcome its own. Accordingly, it was desirable and indeed necessary to decide on contributions while Tokyo still retained relative advantage against Beijing in terms of the economic size. A senior official of Japanese MOF recalls that 'it might be possible to push through an assertion to get a slightly larger quota than China. But, when the Chinese economy becomes larger, China can throw the quotas in reverse.'[23]

China had confidence that it would become the world's second largest economy, soon superseding Japan. Accordingly, China was willing to play a more assertive role in regional financial affairs, and positioned its engagement in the CMIM within this overall policy objective. Such willingness was seen in its commitment to the internationalisation of the yuan. In September 2009, the Chinese government announced the issuance of 6 billion yuan worth of RMB-denominated treasury bonds in Hong Kong. The subsequent two issuances took place in November 2010 and August 2011 with treasury bonds worth 8 billion and 20 billion yuan, respectively.[24] Furthermore, the Chinese government signed currency swaps in RMB with countries within and beyond East Asia that had large trade payments to China.[25] The growing convertibility of the yuan with other currencies would surely strengthen China's position in the CMIM (Chan 2012: 204). At the same time, China made rational calculations regarding its relationship with Japan. The Chinese economy had exhibited rapid growth, but its domestic economic conditions still required a high level of financial regulations, which constrained the international use of the yuan. Accordingly, Chinese officials recognised a need to make some compromise with Japan in leading the development of regional financial architectures. The acquisition of a share substantially equal to that of Japan implied a big political success for China because this was the first time that Beijing was accorded equal weight to Tokyo in a multilateral body (Rathus 2011: 114).

Equally important for the Chinese strategy was that the country had specific motivations from a global perspective to promote regional financial cooperation. China had a desire to advance East Asian regionalism independent of US involvement. The main reason why the United States did not oppose the CMIM was the IMF link, which enabled Washington to exercise indirect veto power over the operation of the new institution. China hoped to reduce US influence by consolidating regional financial cooperation and by reducing the IMF link. Moreover, China intended to use a regional foreign reserve pool as leverage to win stronger bargaining power within the IMF. Despite its rapid growth in overall GDP, China did not get voting rights in the IMF equivalent to its economic power. The development of the CMIM into a regional foreign reserve pool would imply the declining presence of the IMF as lender of last resort. This pressure was expected to draw certain concession from the fund and grant China and other East Asian states a greater voice in the fund (Yuan and Murphy 2010: 4–5).[26]

The policy stance adopted by South Korea had much to do with its concern about the overshadowing of its presence by its two neighbouring great powers. Although South Korea's attempt to get a contribution quota equal to China did not succeed, a half quota was reasonably advantageous. Seoul's basic position under the CMIM was different from that of Beijing and Tokyo because it was not only a potential lender but also a potential borrower. South Korea could also obtain a relatively larger quota (16 per cent) than ASEAN (20 per cent) in terms of economic power because the former's shares of total GDP and foreign reserves in the ASEAN+3 (7 per cent and 6 per cent) were much smaller than the latter's (13 per cent and 14 per cent) (Ciorciari 2011: 940). Moreover, South Korea could hold the casting vote in real decision-making because two out of three parties (China, Japan, and ASEAN) (28.41 per cent each) would need support from South Korea (14.77 per cent) in order to get the two-thirds majority. The ratio was the smallest among the four parties but there were no substantial differences in implications for actual voting.

Compared with the three Northeast Asian states, the financial power of ASEAN members has been extremely weak, typically shown by their small amount of foreign reserves. Moreover, China, Japan, and South Korea, despite tensions over the details of financial architectures, have certainly advanced bilateral or trilateral institutions for policy dialogue to coordinate financial affairs.[27] Accordingly, the ASEAN members had strong preferences for reducing the possibility that the CMIM would be dominated by Northeast Asia. The ASEAN members, which feared the dominance by the +3 members of decision-making in any weighted share allocation system, searched for the possibility of a 'double majority' voting scheme in which both a majority of countries and a majority of votes would be required for decisions (Ciorciari 2011: 939–40). The ASEAN members showed interest in the CMIM as a mechanism to entangle China and Japan into a cooperative process to provide regional public goods, carefully hedging against a situation in which their collaboration would lead to the dominance of regional financial architectures. The enticement of the AMRO being given to Southeast Asia can be seen as a successful outcome of such a hedging strategy.

Research institutes and the development of financial cooperation

In the development of regional financial cooperation, the network of research institutes played an important role in identifying implications and directions of regional cooperation in evolving international settings. Such a role was typically played by the APF. The APF informed policy directions in response to the global financial crisis by issuing several recommendations. In March 2009 forum members proposed a wide range of policies covering monetary, fiscal, trade, and exchange rate fields, as well as international financial architectures. In relation to the CMI, they suggested making the CMI support more flexible by (i) delinking the CMI from IMF programmes; (ii) requiring no conditionality in a way comparable to the IMF's Short-Term Liquidity Facility; and (iii) supplementing the CMI by bilateral contributions from economies inside and outside the region (ADB Institute 2009). In October 2010 the APF submitted additional policy recommendations, which were signed by 35 think-tank representatives and university scholars. The recommendations contained important suggestions such as (i) enhancing the CMIM in terms of size of funding, development of surveillance capacity, and eventual elimination of IMF linkage; (ii) the establishment of a flexible precautionary (non-crisis) facility; (iii) the creation of a framework where ASEAN+3 finance ministers and central bank governors could work with each other; and (iv) the establishment of a fiscal funding mechanism to support fiscal stimulus measures (ADB Institute 2010).

The APF assisted the development of regional financial institutions in various ways. First, it stressed the need to adopt a coordinated approach in accordance with changes in global economic conditions. The recommendations strongly urged Asian leaders to develop 'a strong, unified, and clear Asian voice' with 'an increased opportunity to play a more important role for effecting change in the global economic and financial architecture' (ADB Institute 2010: 5). Second, the forum pointed out desirable policy directions going beyond policy considerations. The early establishment of a fully fledged AMF and the elimination of IMF linkage were desirable policy directions from professional and scientific standpoints although their realisation would take time due to limitations resulting from political considerations. Third, the APF's research activities contributed to the formation of transnational networks of professionals. Quite a few economists have been engaged in the formulation of the APF's policy recommendations for more than ten years since its foundation in 1999.

Another network of researchers regarding regional financial cooperation is provided by the Network of East Asian Think-tanks (NEAT).[28] The NEAT is a track II mechanism designed to provide intellectual support for and policy recommendations on regional cooperation in East Asia, and its establishment was one of 17 recommendations to promote regional cooperation suggested by the East Asia Vision Group (EAVG) in 2002 (Wong 2012: 91–92). China submitted the concept paper on the NEAT at the ASEAN+3 foreign ministers' meeting in June 2003, and the first NEAT conference was held in Beijing in September 2003. Since then an annual NEAT conference has been held in major cities in East Asia, and working groups to carry out research on specific policy areas have been organised with participation of research institutes or individual researchers.

'Financial cooperation' was one of six policy areas in which the NEAT originally organised working groups for policy talks and discussions among researchers in 2004. The 2010 working group report on East Asian financial cooperation in response to post-crisis challenges contained suggestions on regional financial cooperation such as the expansion of the function of the AMRO, the de-linkage of the CMIM loans from IMF conditionality, and the pursuit of the creation of an East Asian monetary fund. These points were included in the NEAT's policy recommendations that were delivered to the ASEAN+3 summit in 2010.

The activities of the Working Group on East Asian Financial Cooperation lasted from 2004 until 2010, issuing a working group report almost every year. Yet, recommendations in the reports did not necessarily have a substantial impact on the policymaking process for two reasons. The first was relevant to weakness in the working group itself. The activities of the group became routine tasks. After the formation of the working group in 2004, China alone assumed the role of country coordinator, preparing the drafts of working group reports. Other group members did not provide positive comments on the reports (CEAC 2010: 32). The second was related to weak links to the policymaking process. The recommendations were simply delivered to the ASEAN+3 summit, with no institutionalised formal linkages with the track I process such as explanation at the ASEAN+3 senior official meetings.

The network of researchers is able to play a crucial role in reducing uncertainty about the governments' intentions and likely behaviour. Informal settings formed through research networks are expected to provide government officials with a chance to deliver policy preferences to and get responses from other governments. Such a function is particularly important in politically sensitive relations such as those between China and Japan. The importance of research institutes in this respect was shown in policy talks on the role of the ASEAN+3 Research Group in relation to the introduction of a regional currency unit. One project commissioned to the ASEAN+3 Research Group in 2005/06 was 'Regional Coordination of Policy Measures Forward: Financial Market Liberalization and Capital Market Development'.

Importantly, the project covered the issues of exchange rate stability and the Asian Monetary Unit (AMU) in addition to financial and capital markets liberalisation (IIMA 2006). The IIMA became a leading institute in the implementation of the project, and research institutes from Singapore, Malaysia, and South Korea joined the project. However, no Chinese research institutes were invited to participate in this project, which naturally aroused China's suspicions about Japan's intention on the matter (Rathus 2011: 119). The ASEAN+3 Research Group continued the projects on regional monetary units in the following years, with the IIMA being a leading institute.[29] But Chinese research institutes were not involved in subsequent projects.

Conclusion

The empirical focus of this chapter is financial cooperation and the building up of monetary reserves in preparation for possible financial turmoil in East Asia. The East Asian countries launched the CMI in 2000 and developed it into a multilateralised mechanism ten years later. In parallel to this process, they established the surveillance and monitoring system called the ERPD and developed this system with the involvement of an independent and permanent surveillance unit.

The presence of China and Japan was particularly important in advancing regional financial institutions in East Asia. This was largely because the two states, which hold the primary and secondary foreign reserves in the world, are creditor nations which provide liquidity support for other Asian countries that have a risk of liquidity shortage. Accordingly, the formation of collaborative relationships between the two states had a vital impact on the evolution of financial cooperation. As is the case in other policy fields, the two states, which sought to maintain national interests and regional leadership, clashed over several issues such as the ACU and contribution quotas in the CMIM. While Japan sought to keep the initiative in advancing regional financial cooperation by taking advantage of its foreign reserves and experience in international financial affairs, China sought to check Japan's attempts to lead regional financial affairs and to acquire influence in the financial sector equivalent to its growing economic capabilities in the region.

South Korea and ASEAN members supported the development of regional financial cooperation. Since Seoul and some ASEAN members suffered serious damage from IMF conditionality during the Asian financial crisis, they welcomed the formation of an alternative mechanism to guarantee liquidity provision. At the same time, they were anxious about the dominance of regional financial affairs by China and Japan, and made efforts to maintain their presence in the building process of financial architectures.

There are two additional factors that underpinned the development of regional financial cooperation. The first was the financial crises that caused devastating damage to the regional economies. During the Asian financial crisis, the existing institutions including the ASEAN Swap Agreement provided virtually no effective measures, and the dysfunction of the existing institutions urged policymakers in East Asia to consolidate their desires to launch the CMI. The CMIM process was completed due to the financial authorities' clear recognition of the need to advance feasible collective mechanisms to respond effectively to a global financial crisis in 2008. The two financial crises surely constituted critical junctures that changed the perception of reality among policymakers and elevated regional institutions to a new level at which a policy option to reverse direction became difficult or impossible.

The second was the meaningful involvement of research institutes. The research institutes provided policymakers with professional knowledge and expertise that helped them to address problems in financial management and policies of member countries, as well as recommendations on feasible ways to rectify the problems and develop collective mechanisms to tackle common challenges in regional financial and monetary affairs. Policymakers commissioned specific themes to research institutes, and researchers maintained close connection with government officials. Accordingly, their views were delivered to the policymaking process relatively easily, and were reflected in actual initiatives. At the same time, research institutes sometimes failed to create one voice, which is a critical factor in raising the legitimacy of scientific expertise.

A distinctive feature of institution-building in the financial case was that China and Japan reached compromise on critical issues, which finally led to the successful launching of the CMIM in 2010. The Japanese government, which admitted an inevitable transition in economic power between Japan and China, accepted realistic compromise in order to retain its power and interests from a long-term perspective. The Chinese government sustained the development of regional financial institutions in order to create a stable regional financial order that underpins domestic economic stability. It also accepted compromise with Japan due to recognition that the domestic financial market still requires considerable regulations. The prudent calculations on domestic and regional matters coupled with common interests in maintaining a stable financial order produced political acquiescence between the two states and paved the way for the development of regional financial institutions.

5
Food Security Cooperation through Emergency Rice Reserve

One of the most salient features of East Asia is diversity. The region is diverse in terms of its degree of economic development, political systems, resource endowments, and cultural traditions including religions. However, East Asia has an important commonality in diet: rice is the main staple food, being an integral part of the culture and the people's life style. Accordingly, East Asia has maintained a special status in rice production and rice trade in the world. Some two-thirds of world rice production originates in East Asia, and nearly half of global rice exports come from this region.

Another salient feature of East Asia is vulnerability to natural calamity. The region is vulnerable to various kinds of natural disasters such as flood, storm, drought, volcano eruption, and seismic activity. Accordingly, East Asia has an imperative need to maintain mechanisms for emergency food relief to a region hit by a disaster. Rice, which is suitable for relatively long-term storage, is the main foodstuff used for such emergency circumstances. The countries in the disaster-prone region can find common interests in maintaining food security by establishing a rice storage mechanism in preparation for emergency relief.

In the early 2000s, a concrete initiative to enhance food security in East Asia was launched. The ASEAN Plus Three (ASEAN+3) members agreed to investigate the establishment of a rice reserve system for emergency circumstances. The members accumulated expertise to operationalise the rice reserve system through a pilot project, and finally reached an agreement on the ASEAN+3 Emergency Rice Reserve (APTERR) in 2011. Progress towards the agreement was far from steady, though, largely because the member governments had different preferences for and expectations about food security and the rice reserve system.

This chapter examines the process of institution-building for regional food security in general and a rice reserve system in particular. It traces the development process towards the APTERR by shedding light on political interactions among China, Japan, South Korea, and ASEAN as well as motivations underpinning their commitment to a rice reserve system. This chapter also investigates how specific international events drove the development of regional food security externally and how policy networks formed by non-state actors influenced its development internally.

The introduction of the EAERR

Proposal for the EAERR

In the new millennium, an important initiative to enhance food security through rice reserve was launched in East Asia. At the first meeting of ASEAN+3 ministers on agriculture and forestry (AMAF+3) in October 2001, ministers agreed to begin studying specific cooperation to alleviate poverty in rural areas and strengthen food security in East Asia, and agreed to commission Thailand to coordinate a study of a rice reserve system.[1] Two months later, a study team on the rice reserve system began to conduct the review on rice reserve among the ASEAN+3 countries. The results of the study were discussed at the Technical Meeting on Rice Reserve (TMRR), a gathering of directors general of relevant government agencies, which were held three times between April and October 2002. One of the recommendations put forward by the TMRR was to undertake a three-year pilot project designed to investigate the feasibility of a rice reserve system in East Asia, prior to the establishment of the East Asia Emergency Rice Reserve (EAERR). The proposal on the pilot project was approved at the third AMAF+3 meeting in October 2003, and the project began in April 2004. The project aimed to establish stock release guidelines to provide a mechanism for utilising emergency rice reserve, stock release under poverty alleviation programmes, and food aid for disaster-hit regions (ASEAN 2009a).

The overall supervisory body of the EAERR was the Project Steering Committee that reported to the AMAF+3 meeting, and daily management was conducted by the Management Team of the EAERR (MT-EAERR). In 2004, the EAERR Secretariat was set up within the Thai Ministry of Agriculture and Cooperatives (MOAC) in order to manage the pilot project and coordinate social development activities. Although the secretariat was a small body, its establishment had critical significance as it ensured steady progress in implementing ministers' decisions through the institutional system.

In addition to the EAERR project, agricultural ministers approved ASEAN's proposal for the establishment of the ASEAN Food Security Information System (AFSIS) project at the second AMAF+3 meeting in October 2002.[2] The AFSIS project, started in January 2003, consisted of two main pillars: human resource development and information network system development. The project aimed to facilitate food security planning, implementation, monitoring, and evaluation for ASEAN+3 countries through the systematic collection, analysis, and dissemination of food security data and information (ASEAN 2009b). The information available through the AFSIS was crucial in determining possible strengths and weaknesses of the countries in the region in terms of achieving food security (Danõ 2006: 43). Accordingly, the AFSIS played a role as a technical body for the EAERR since the AFSIS data were used for judging whether the EAERR's programmes would be implemented for a particular country with specific conditions.

The EAERR implied a cross-supply arrangement for rice from food-surplus to food-deficit countries during normal conditions and in times of emergency. The EAERR planned to hold a rice reserve of 1,750,000 tonnes with two methods. The first was earmarked rice reserve, under which member countries voluntarily designate a certain quantity of rice for meeting emergency requirements. The second method was stockpiled (physical) rice reserve, under which member countries donate a certain quantity of rice as an emergency stock to provide preparedness for an emergency.

The release of rice under the two reserve methods was based on the three-tier programmes (Table 5.1). The tier 1 programme was the release of the earmarked reserve rice through commercial transactions. This reserve was

Table 5.1 Release of reserved rice under the EAERR

	Reserve type	**Character**	**Mechanism**
Tier 1	Earmarked	Commercial rice trade through a forward contract between members	A member informs the MT-EAERR of amount, date, delivery time, etc., and the MT-EAERR makes assessment and shipping arrangement.
Tier 2	Earmarked	Long-term loan or grant agreement between members	A member in emergency notifies degree of emergency, necessary amount, etc., and the MT-EAERR makes assessment and negotiation arrangement.
Tier 3	Stockpiled (under reserve)	First food aid on request or automatic trigger system	A member in emergency informs the MT-EAERR of degree of emergency, necessary amount, etc., and the MT-EAERR makes an assessment and arranges shipping and distribution.
PAME	Stockpiled (after reserve)	The release of rice after stockpiled rice is not used for a certain period	A member submits a plan to the MT-EAERR, and the MT-EAERR gives approval.

Source: Created by the author with data from the APTERR home page, JICA documents, and others.

part of the national rice reserve of each member, which would assume the costs for purchasing, storing, and maintaining rice. The MT-EAERR would evaluate the degree of emergency and provide a supply–demand matching service between a deficit member country and a country with a rice surplus. The tier 2 programme was the release of the earmarked reserve rice as emergency food assistance. The terms of release would be governed by a loan or grant agreement, after an appeal from a member country or an international organisation such as the Food and Agriculture Organisation (FAO) and the World Food Programme (WFP). The tier 3 programme was the release of stockpiled rice reserved as first aid in an emergency. The release would be initiated by a request from a member country or an international organisation, and the MT-EAERR would evaluate the request (Toyoda 2009: 236–37; Briones 2011: 14). In addition to these three programmes, a rice release on the poverty alleviation and malnourishment eradication (PAME) programme was prepared. When stockpiled rice reserve was not used in the designated period (12 months), it would be released for humanitarian purposes by accepting a plan from a member government.

The Asian financial crisis and its impact on food security

In Southeast Asia there existed a rice reserve mechanism dedicated to emergency circumstances. In October 1979, ASEAN foreign ministers signed the Agreement on the ASEAN Food Security Reserve in New York. Under the agreement, ASEAN members created the ASEAN Emergency Rice Reserve (AERR) as an earmarked rice reserve in which they promised to provide a part of national rice stock for the purpose of meeting emergency requirements.[3] The members also set up the ASEAN Food Security Reserve Board (AFSRB) in order to supervise and coordinate the implementation of cooperation on food security.

Despite its idealistic objectives, the AERR had never been utilised in an emergency in more than 30 years due to several inherent flaws. The rice reserve under the AERR increased from the initial 50,000 tonnes to 87,000 tonnes as ASEAN accepted five new members. However, the reserve volume, which equalled only 0.4 days' consumption quantity of ASEAN countries, was extremely small in response to a real food emergency (MAFF no year). The AERR also lacked an effective information system, indispensable for bringing the release of reserved rice into effect (Oba 2004: 27). Moreover, the AFSRB was unable to operationalise the AERR as a functional body due to the lack of funds for administration at the secretariat. The board remained as an information clearing-house with no mandate to operationalise and implement rice reserve.

In addition to the above functional limitations, political factors discouraged the member governments from putting the AERR mechanism into operation. The release of reserved rice would be coordinated on a bilateral basis: a member country applying for a release would first make a direct request to a rice-surplus member regarding prices, terms and conditions of payment, and so on (Briones 2011: 12). This condition virtually prevented the member governments from putting the AERR mechanism into practice. Any politically shrewd government suffering from a food shortage would not admit to its neighbours that it was experiencing an emergency situation, which might aggravate domestic unrest and put the country in a weak political position in the region. The bilateral nature of negotiations for terms in tapping the rice reserve under a supposedly multilateral scheme might put a country in need at the mercy of a more powerful rice-surplus neighbour (Danõ 2006: 40). Thus, a state's adherence to maintaining political and society stability internally and political autonomy externally made it extremely difficult to utilise the ASEAN institution designed to respond to an urgent condition of food shortage.

The AERR's inefficiency in addressing food emergencies became apparent during the 1997–98 Asian financial crisis. Economic and social turmoil caused by the financial crisis hit people's daily lives through the rise of prices of major foodstuffs and confusion of food delivery in Southeast Asia. The crisis raised political leaders' concern with the importance of maintaining a stable food supply for the people in a critical condition. More specifically, Indonesia was confronted with serious food problems in 1997–98. The El Nino-induced drought and forest fires in Eastern Indonesia caused a decline in food production. Rice production dropped by 3.7 per cent in 1997 and again by 8.8 per cent in 1998, the biggest single-year fall over 20 years. The reduction in food production led to soaring food prices. The retail rice prices in 27 major cities increased from 1,021 rupiah per kilogram in May 1997 to 1,290 in January 1998 to 3,009 in September 1998 (Tabor et al. 1999: 3). Under such serious conditions of food shortage, Indonesia was forced to increase imports of major foodstuffs. Imports of rice increased dramatically from 0.41 million tonnes in 1997 to 5.77 million tonnes in 1998 (Sidik 2004: 6). Despite such critical conditions, the Indonesian government did not seek to procure rice from its neighbouring countries through the AERR. 'Rather than tapping the ASEAN rice reserve to address the serious rice crisis it was facing, the Indonesian government opted for International Monetary Fund-World Bank (IMF-WB) loans to import food from other countries' (Danõ 2006: 40).

Through experience during the Asian financial crisis, ASEAN policymakers recognised the flaws of the AERR – the existing regional institution for food security – and began to embark on an alternative institutional path to improve the food security system. At the 20th AMAF meeting in September 1998, agricultural ministers endorsed the Strategic Plan of Action on ASEAN Cooperation in Food, Agriculture and Forestry (1999–2004), which pursued the strength of food security including the reviews of the agreement on the ASEAN Food Security Reserve and the AERR system.[4] Moreover, ASEAN members encouraged China, Japan, and South Korea to share the recognition to enhance regional food security. The Joint Statement on East Asia Cooperation, issued at the third ASEAN+3 summit in November 1999, raised agricultural cooperation as one area in the economic and social fields for East Asian cooperation.[5] The ASEAN members' interest in food security provided the foundation for subsequent cooperation on the establishment of the regional rice reserve system.

Bitter experience gained during the Asian financial crisis was reflected in strengthened rice reserve mechanisms under the EAERR. In addition to earmarked reserve, the EAERR prepared for a mechanism to maintain physical reserve, which enabled a country in emergency to access rice swiftly and easily. Moreover, the EAERR established collective mechanisms to realise emergency rice relief. The terms of procurement and pricing were addressed at the regional level by the MT-EAERR (Danõ and Peria 2006: 10).

Japan's political initiatives with Thai support

ASEAN policymakers deepened their recognition of the need for strengthening emergency rice reserve in Southeast Asia, which provided an impetus for food security cooperation in East Asia. A specific country in East Asia played a pivotal role in changing such recognition into a practical process to launch a concrete project. A formal agreement to set up a rice reserve system in East Asia was reached at the AMAF+3 meeting in October 2001, but prior consultation was undertaken with Japan's involvement. When Yoichi Tani, the Japanese Agricultural Minister, made a formal visit to Manila in August 2000, his counterpart Edgardo Angara, the Philippine Secretary of Agriculture, proposed the holding of an agricultural ministers' meeting of ASEAN members as well as Japan, China, and South Korea. Tani and Angara agreed to promote cooperation on the holding of this ASEAN+3 gathering.

After ASEAN+3 agricultural ministers agreed on a study of a regional rice reserve system in October 2001, the Japanese government offered practical support through the Japan International Cooperation Agency (JICA). JICA commenced a survey on project research in January 2002 and conducted the Development Study on an East Asia/ASEAN Rice Reserve System from May to November 2002. The discussions at the TMRR were undertaken in accordance with the progress of this study (Pacific Consultant International 2002: 1–4). JICA also provided Thailand with personnel and with technical assistance in holding the TMRR. The mechanisms for the EAERR reflected recommendations in the final report of the survey. Japan's intensive support continued after the pilot project began in April 2004. The Japanese Ministry of Agriculture, Forestry and Fisheries (MAFF) provided financial assistance for the pilot project and the holding of the EAERR Project Steering Committee, the main decision-making body after the start of the pilot project.

Japan also committed to the development of the AFSIS project. Although Thailand had formal responsibility for coordinating the project, the Japanese

MAFF provided financial support for it. The AFSIS project was conducted in close collaboration with other Japan-funded projects such as an FAO regional project, 'Strengthening Regional Data Exchange System on Food and Agricultural Statistics in Asia and Pacific Countries', and a JICA project, 'Agricultural Statistics and Economic Analysis Development'. JICA assisted human resource development by organising the Seminar for the Directors General of Agricultural Statistics and Information in ASEAN in January 2003.

Japan's commitment to regional rice reserve derived from two motivations. First, the commitment reflected its willingness to play a leadership role in advancing agricultural cooperation and food security in East Asia. During the 1998 food crisis in Indonesia, the Japanese government provided 700,000 tonnes of rice for the country. In 2000–01, the government also provided 500,000 tonnes of rice for North Korea through the WFP. Such experiences broadened Japan's interest in considering the provision of rice as part of critical support for emergency conditions in developing countries. The country took the view that it could enhance its international profile as a generous neighbour by initiating an institution to provide food aid for developing countries in emergency.

The second and practical motivation concerned WTO agricultural negotiations. Japan stood in a defensive position at the WTO agricultural negotiations that began in January 2000, as it faced strong demands for market liberalisation from agricultural exporting countries. In response to such demands, the Japanese government submitted a proposal entitled 'Negotiating Proposal by Japan on WTO Agricultural Negotiations' in December 2000. The five pillars of the proposal were: (i) consideration of the multifunctionality of agriculture; (ii) ensuring food security that is the basis of society in each country; (iii) redressing the imbalance between rules and disciplines applied to agricultural exporting countries and those applied to importing countries; (iv) consideration for developing countries; and (v) consideration for the concerns of consumers and the civil society.[6] The securing of food security in parallel to the multifunctionality of agriculture was Japan's counter-argument against WTO members who advocated free trade in agriculture, and the basis for gaining support from developing countries for Japan's stance (Oba 2004: 29). In the proposal, Japan linked food security concerns to consideration for developing countries, proposing an examination to establish a framework for international food stockholding as a means to address food security concerns in developing countries. Then, a study group of the international food stockholding concept was established in April 2001 as an advisory body to the head of the Food Agency. The group was tasked with developing a new framework for international food stockholding that the Japanese government had proposed at WTO agricultural negotiations. The group's final report contained a section entitled 'International Stockholding Concept and Its Practice in Asia', proposing that it is appropriate to cooperate with initiatives in advancing regional food security and rice reserve in East Asia as the first step towards realising the international food reserve concept.[7] Thus, Japan's commitment to the rice reserve system in East Asia derived from an intention of strengthening its advocacy of food security and food stockholding at WTO agricultural negotiations. It sought to expand advocates among East Asian countries for food security by sustaining a concrete food stockholding project in the region.

There was a specific Southeast Asian country that pushed forward the revision of the existing rice reserve system in ASEAN: Thailand. At a senior officials' meeting of the AMAF+3 in April 2001, the Thai government presented a report that addressed the state and problems of rice in East Asia and the necessity of rice reserve in East Asia. In response to the report, it was decided to hold a workshop and report the results of the workshop to an AMAF+3 meeting. Three months later, the ASEAN Workshop on Food Security Cooperation was organised under the sponsorship of the Thai MOAC and Chulalongkorn University. The participants recommended that a feasibility study should be undertaken on the creation of a new rice reserve system in East Asia so as to improve and reinforce the AERR (Oba 2004: 31–33).

After the beginning of the cooperative projects, Thailand continuously sustained them by assuming the secretariat role. When agricultural ministers decided to begin a study of a rice reserve system in East Asia at the AMAF+3 meeting in October 2001, Thailand was appointed as the coordinating country of the study. After the start of the EAERR pilot project, the MOAC assumed its secretariat. Moreover, the ASEAN Food Security Information and Training (AFSIT) Centre was established under the ministry as the secretariat of the AFSIS project. The centre coordinated various programmes such as a training course on statistical survey technique (December 2003), a workshop on the construction of the information network system (February 2004), and a workshop on improvement of the quality of agricultural statistics (April 2005).

Thailand, as the world's top rice-exporting country, had a special interest in rice affairs. In fact, when ASEAN members agreed to establish the AFSRB in 1979, the Thai Ministry of Commerce assumed the board's secretariat (Briones 2011: 12). The Thai government had a strong desire to become the leading country in managing rice-related affairs in Southeast Asia by assuming secretariat functions.[8] Moreover, Thailand had a practical interest in promoting rice reserve in East Asia. The country regarded the EAERR project as a prospective market for its rice exports especially in the midst of cut-throat competition in the international rice market (Danõ 2006: 37). The provision of stockpiled rice during a food shortage might have negative effects on exports for Thailand. However, Thailand could get substantial benefits from the project. The tier 1 programme, which formulates commercial based transactions, was expected to create a reliable system in which Thailand could export its rice to neighbouring countries facing a food shortage.

Thus, the initiation of regional cooperation in food security through the EAERR project was sustained by Japan and Thailand. The two countries played a supplementary role in advancing the project: while Japan set up financial resources to advance the project, Thailand mainly provided material resources to offer offices for the secretariat. The two countries had specific interests that they could advance through the development of the regional rice reserve system.

The prolonged EAERR project

The difficulty in institutionalising the EAERR

After the EAERR pilot project began in April 2004, several cooperative activities were implemented. Nearly 3,000 tonnes of stockpiled rice were distributed under the project to disaster victims and poor households in Cambodia, Indonesia, Laos, Myanmar, and the Philippines (APTERR no year: 3).[9] As already explained, the EAERR project envisioned the PAME programme in which stockpiled rice would be used for poverty alleviation after a certain storage period had passed. In December 2004, the EAERR concluded an agreement with the Lao government on the cooperation project on PAME, which pursued the development of rice production areas by the refurbishment of irrigation canals and improvement in water reservoirs as well as the enhancement of household food security through the provision of nutritious food and clean water.

Notwithstanding practical activities for rice provision, the EAEER remained an undeveloped body as an institution. The EAERR was originally projected to increase the total quantity of earmarked rice reserve to 1,750,000 tonnes. However, it continued to hold just 337,000 tonnes with Japan's contribution of 250,000 tonnes in addition to ASEAN's 87,000 tonnes, failing to draw contributions from China and South Korea. The average number of staff at the EAERR Secretariat since its establishment was six including a coordinator from JICA. The posts for two managers handling trade issues and IT issues were often unoccupied.[10]

While the AERR is a formal agreement signed by member governments, the EAERR began as a mere management project for cooperation on food emergencies. Accordingly, it was necessary to enhance the EAERR's institutional foundation. At the fifth AMAF+3 meeting in September 2005, ministers 'agreed to emphasize the importance of converting the EAERR into a permanent scheme on a voluntary basis'.[11] However, the ministers decided to postpone the decision on the future form of the EAERR three times at the following years' meetings, and the pilot project was postponed. Eventually, the pilot project was extended to February 2010, three years longer than originally planned. Thus, it took a long time to elevate the status of the EAERR to a fully fledged institution that would have the authority and capabilities to establish the sound foundation for food security in East Asia.

Political interactions among the four parties

Stalemated talks on the future form of the EAERR derived from different expectations and commitments by ASEAN+3 members. Japan, the main initiator of the EAERR, had a strong desire to convert the EAERR into a permanent institution to manage a regional rice reserve system, and this desire derived from two motivations. The first concerned the protection of domestic agricultural interests. The Japanese MAFF aimed to take advantage of the EAERR as a means to mitigate the negative impact of international obligations on domestic agriculture. The Japanese government accepted the minimum access volume (MAV) as a part of the Agreement on Agriculture of the GATT Uruguay Round in 1993. The MAV was formulated in the form of 'national trade' in which the government purchased the whole volume of imported rice in order that the price of domestically produced rice would not be adversely affected by an increase of imported rice. The government used imported rice for processing and foreign aid in addition to principal foodstuff. The quantity of imported rice under the MAV increased from 426,000 tonnes in 1995 to 767,000 tonnes in 2000, and maintained this level afterwards (MAFF 2009: 7). The establishment of the EAERR as a permanent institution would enable Japan to absorb imported rice coming in through the MAV and physically keep the imported stock in other locations within Southeast Asia (Danõ 2006: 37–38). This was beneficial for the MAFF, enabling it to avoid a situation where the price of domestic rice would be affected by imported rice and to reduce the financial burden of spending on rice stocks under the MAV. [12]

Second, Japan hoped to reduce the financial burden of sustaining the EAERR. The Japanese government assumed the entire operational costs of the EAERR pilot project.[13] Given that the rice reserve system was a cooperative scheme to give benefits to all participating members, it was difficult for the MAFF to persuade the financial authorities that Japan alone should assume the entire cost. Accordingly, the ministry hoped to establish a burden-sharing mechanism in which other members would also make contributions towards maintaining the regional rice reserve system.[14]

The Japanese government made a proposal to change the EAERR into a permanent body at each meeting of the AMAF+3. However, it was unable to get an accord from other countries on the shift to a permanent institution. Japan's engagement in sustaining the EAERR project could be superficially regarded as the provision of regional public goods. However, other ASEAN+3 members had a suspicion about Japan's hidden self-interest in the EAERR project: to comply with international trade obligations under the WTO to open up its domestic rice market while at the same time protecting the interests of domestic rice producers against the upsurge of imported cheaper rice (Danõ 2006: 37).

China's position on regional agricultural cooperation was complicated. China exhibited willingness to promote agricultural cooperation with ASEAN members particularly in relation to trade initiatives. At the ASEAN-China summit in 2001, China proposed promoting cooperation on five priority areas: agriculture, information and communications technology (ICT), human resource development, Mekong River Basin development, and two-way investment. The proposal, which contained practical programmes in non-controversial areas, became a cue to invite positive postures from ASEAN towards the ASEAN-China Free Trade Area (ACFTA) (Onishi 2007: 112). In November 2002, ASEAN and China signed the Memorandum of Understanding (MOU) on Medium and Long-Term Plan of Agricultural Cooperation. In this memorandum, China promised to carry out training courses in various fields such as hybrid rice, cultivation skills, fertilizer and water management, and so on. The two parties signed the extension of the MOU on Agricultural Cooperation (2007–11) in January 2007, and various activities regarding personnel training, technical exchange, demonstration programme, and trade promotion programmes were implemented.

The agricultural sector was important in the ACFTA as China proposed the early harvest programme (EHP), which committed to reducing tariffs for agricultural products in advance. Market liberalisation through the EHP was expected to have a negative impact on the agricultural sector in China, and caused serious concerns among producers in the sector. In fact, the Ministry of Agriculture and the local government of the Guangxi Province submitted internal reports to the Ministry of Commerce regarding the negative effects of the EHP (Ravenhill and Jiang 2009: 40). In response to such concerns, the central government sought to create and expand opportunities for local producers through closer economic ties with Southeast Asia. The Chinese government successfully made the Guangxi Province a member of the Greater Mekong Sub-region (GMS) Economic Cooperation Programme in 2005, although the province was not, geographically speaking, part of the Mekong River Basin. The relationship with ASEAN in the agricultural sector was crucial for China in terms of trade strategy and the development of the southern provinces.

Despite China's positive engagements in agricultural cooperation with ASEAN members, it did not exhibit a keen interest in the EAERR project. This was typically shown in its involvement in the EAERR Project Steering Committee. The fourth committee meeting in March 2005 was important because the Guidelines for Release of EAERR Stock and the implementation plan for the second year of the pilot project were approved at the meeting. At the meeting, the member countries were also expected to report contributions to earmarked reserve for the EAERR.[15] The delegates from China (and South Korea) did not attend this important meeting, and the proposed contributions to the earmarked reserve were Japan's 250,000 tonnes and ASEAN's 87,000 tonnes.

China's low interest in the EAERR derived from two factors. First, Beijing had a weak international aspiration in rice-related affairs. China has been the world's primary country in terms of rice production and rice consumption, and the government has maintained a policy of domestic production and domestic consumption. Accordingly, Beijing had limited concern with providing rice for external uses such as export and foreign aid. The second was relevant to domestic administrative jurisdiction. The Ministry of Agriculture was in charge of domestic agricultural development and rural economic development. While the ministry dealt with the production field of the agricultural sector, it did not have authority to manage trade and foreign aid issues (Toyoda 2009: 239). Accordingly, the ministry could not make decisions, without the explicit approval of senior political leaders, on the provision of rice for the EAERR, which incorporated elements of economic diplomacy in trade and foreign aid.

South Korea was another country that did not exhibit sufficient interest in the EAERR project. The Korean government did not host the EAERR Project Steering Committee, and sent a low-ranking assistant director to the committee meetings.[16] South Korea's passive postures towards the EAERR had much to do with the complexity of rice-related issues. In South Korea rice production declined gradually from 6.05 million tonnes in 1988. However, the self-sufficiency rate remained nearly 100 per cent, largely because changes in people's diet led to the decline in rice consumption. Accordingly, Seoul could afford to provide domestic rice for external commitments, and rice provision was undertaken for strategic objectives. The Korean government exported rice to North Korea as food aid between 2002 and 2007 with a quantity of 105,000 tonnes at minimum and 400,000 tonnes at maximum (Kuramochi 2012: 220). A more critical element in rice-related issues was the obligation of rice imports under the MAV. The Korean government accepted the MAV in order to avoid tariffication of rice imports. In 2004 the government made efforts to continue its MAV for ten years from 2005, and its agricultural ministry was preoccupied with this issue. The Korean government, which had its own important agendas on the rice issue, did not find the rationale to make substantial commitments to the Japan-initiated EAERR project. Seoul regarded the EAERR as a project initiated by Tokyo for advancing its own interests, rather than sharing the perception that it was a region-based cooperative institution to enhance food security in a collective manner.

As far as ASEAN members were concerned, different positions in terms of rice production and rice trade hampered the formation of a cohesive front on the EAERR. Although Southeast Asia as a region has been the primary rice-producing area, the position of each country was different. Thailand and Vietnam, the world's largest rice producers and exporters, paid close attention to the issue of how the provision of rice under the EAERR project would influence their rice exports. The less developed Mekong countries – Cambodia, Laos, and Myanmar – have been among the top recipients of rice food aid from the WFP. The Philippines, Malaysia, and Indonesia were among the world's biggest rice-deficit and importing countries. Indonesia and the Philippines were recipients of rice food aid from the WFP, especially the calamity-affected provinces in the former and the war-torn Muslim South in the latter (Danõ and Peria 2006: 18). The countries that received rice food aid showed an interest in maintaining such a position, seeking to avoid costs associated with rice reserve under the EAERR.

When a member of the EAERR was faced with a food shortage, it could expect the provision of rice through this scheme. At the same time, the EAERR procedure required financial burdens for the food-shortage country. The EAERR presented a model where food aid for emergency would be readily accessible with physical stocks kept in actual locations, but costs of handling and distribution would be borne by the country in need. The countries that would need emergency assistance in providing rice supplies for their people would most likely be the ones without sufficient financial resources to provide for their own needs (Danõ 2006: 39). This implied that most countries requiring food support still hoped to extend their begging bowls to UN agencies and receive free rice food aid for their populations (Danõ and Peria 2006: 18). These countries did not find sufficient rationale to agree on the institutionalisation of the EAERR.

The road to the APTERR

The agreement on the APTERR

After 2009, East Asian countries began to reconfirm the importance of cooperation on food security and rice reserve. At the ninth AMAF+3 meeting in November 2009, ministers 'expressed their commitment to develop a comprehensive strategy on sustainable and integrated food and bio-fuels production and consumption that will promote better allocation of resources for the production of both food and bio-fuels'. They then 'agreed to work towards the transformation of EAERR into a permanent mechanism under the ASEAN Plus Three Emergency Rice Reserve (APTERR) and early realization of APTERR'.[17] At the following AMAF+3 meeting in October 2010, ministers agreed to formalise the APTERR as a permanent institution for meeting emergency requirements and achieving humanitarian purposes. The ministers originally planned to sign an agreement on emergency rice reserve on this occasion. However, Singapore requested the postponement of the signature, due to its concern about ASEAN centrality. It had been agreed that the chair for the APTERR Council would be rotated in alphabetical order among ASEAN+3 members, which implied that China, Japan, or South Korea would assume the chair independently in the future. Singapore was apprehensive that such a system would undermine ASEAN's central position to manage regional cooperation in East Asia.[18]

At the 11th AMAF+3 meeting in October 2011, ministers signed an MOU that confirmed the advancement of cooperation in food, agriculture, and forestry sectors in East Asia. By signing the MOU, ministers welcomed the development of the ASEAN +3 Cooperation Strategy, which consists of six strategic areas: food security, biomass energy development, sustainable forest management, climate change mitigation and adaptation, animal health and disease control, and cross-cutting issues. The ministers then signed the agreement on the APTERR, and the agreement came into force in July 2012.

Under the ten-article agreement, members agreed to strengthen food security in East Asia by establishing a rice reserve system to meet emergency requirements and achieve humanitarian purposes, while avoiding a distortion in international rice markets. The APTERR Council was positioned as the main decision-making body to assume the responsibility of the APTERR's operation. The council is co-chaired by an ASEAN member and a member from the '+3' countries, and its decision is made on the basis of consensus. The daily management of APTERR business is undertaken by the secretariat, and a small secretariat with a staff of less than ten was established within the Thai MOAC.

The APTERR Agreement is a simple accord. The members' obligations under the agreement are to earmark a certain quality of rice, to provide information on policies and programmes for rice reserve as well as on food security and other aspects of food supply and demand situations, and to make contributions to the APTERR Fund and the operational cost. The agreement does not contain even basic terms and conditions for rice releases, just stipulating that 'the release of rice reserved in the APTERR and replenishment of the earmarked rice shall be implemented in accordance with the rules and procedures to be set forth by the Council' (Article 4.3).

The agreement accompanied attachments that indicated rice and financial contributions to sustain the APTERR operation. The member countries are required to provide a total of 787,000 tonnes of earmarked rice. While ASEAN members provide 87,000 tonnes, the rest is offered by China, Japan, and South Korea – 300,000 tonnes, 250,000 tonnes, and 150,000 tonnes, respectively (Table 5.2). The ministers also agreed on an endowment fund to cover costs for running and maintaining emergency rice reserve: China, Japan, and South Korea disburse US$1 million respectively; seven ASEAN members contribute US$107,500 respectively; and Cambodia, Laos and Myanmar contribute US$83,000 each. Furthermore, the members agreed to provide US$300,000 to finance the operational costs of the office running the rice programme over the first five years, and ASEAN, China, Japan, and South Korea disburse US$75,000 respectively.

The programmes for releasing rice reserved in the APTERR followed the three-tier mechanism under the EAERR. Under the tier 1 programme,

Table 5.2 Members' contributions to the APTERR

Country	Earmarked rice quantity (tonnes)	Contribution to endowment fund (US$)	Contribution to operational costs (US$)
Brunei	3,000	107,500	8,000
Cambodia	3,000	83,000	6,000
Indonesia	12,000	107,500	8,000
Laos	3,000	83,000	6,000
Malaysia	6,000	107,500	8,000
Myanmar	14,000	83,000	6,000
Philippines	12,000	107,500	8,000
Singapore	5,000	107,500	8,000
Thailand	15,000	107,500	8,000
Vietnam	14,000	107,500	8,000
China	300,000	1,000,000	75,000
Japan	250,000	1,000,000	75,000
South Korea	150,000	1,000,000	75,000

Source: Created by the author with data from the 'APTERR agreement'.

earmarked stock is released to meet emergency demand by employing pre-arranged commercial contracts between supplying and recipient countries. The tier 2 programme is the release of earmarked stock to meet emergency demand, based on a long-term loan agreement or a grant between supplying and recipient countries. The tier 3 programme is the release of stockpiled rice to meet acute emergencies and other humanitarian responses to food insecurity, based on a request or an automatic trigger system.

The establishment of the APTERR implied crucial progress in cooperation on food security. First, the APTERR became an independent institution that was established with a formal agreement. Unlike the EAERR, the APTERR has legal authority to manage regional rice reserve with an agreement signed by ministers or vice-ministers. The APTERR is also equipped with the financial basis to sustain its operation and activities. Second, the APTERR envisioned policy coordination on rice policies among member countries. The preamble of the agreement contains the phrase 'the need to coordinate national rice stock policies, which take into account the policies of other ASEAN Plus Three Countries'. Third, the APTERR has the potential to become the comprehensive institution to manage overall food security in East Asia by expanding the scope of targeted products and issues. At the joint press statement of the 11th AMAF+3 meeting in October 2011, ministers referred to 'the possibility of expanding coverage of the APTERR other than rice in times of emergency and in supporting countries in a vulnerable position as a result of food price volatility and a surge in food demand'.[19] The APTERR was deemed to be a stepping stone to deal with more general price volatility in staple foods other than rice.

Political interactions towards the agreement

The process to adopt the APTERR accompanied complicated politics over food security and food trade. Politics over rice trade among ASEAN members indicated difficulty in forming regional solidarity. The rice-exporting countries in the region tended to opt for pursuing economic benefits by meeting the global food demand or restricting food exports rather than raising food security by ensuring supplies for rice-importing countries in the region. In Malaysia, for instance, the price of Thai rice tripled in the last few months of 2007, which was partly caused by the reluctance of rice-producing counties in the region to provide rice for Malaysia (Chandra and Lontoh 2010: 14). Moreover, rice-exporting countries in Southeast Asia sought the possibility of a rice export cartel. In April 2008, the Thai government launched an idea to establish the Organisation of Rice Exporting Countries (OREC), comprising Thailand, Vietnam, Cambodia, Myanmar, and Laos. The OREC, modelled on the Organisation of the Petroleum Exporting Countries (OPEC), aimed to control world rice prices at a level that would increase farmers' incomes and to exchange information about food stability. This concept was based on discussions between Thailand and Vietnam to harmonise the control of export volume to increase the price of rice since the two countries had undertaken intensive export competition, which led to the stagnation of international rice prices (Suzuki 2008: 45). Practically, the OREC would have difficulty in managing exports of rice by a numerous number of producers. Politically, the idea was denounced by rice-importing countries such as the Philippines and the Asian Development Bank. Accordingly, Thailand abandoned the idea rather quickly.

As the above moves indicate, diverse stances on the rice trade hampered the formation of a unified front on rice affairs among ASEAN members. The enhancement of food security by ensuring adequate access to food at all times for all ASEAN peoples is one of the major pillars of the ASEAN Community that ASEAN members intend to create by 2015 (ASEAN 2010: 73). However, in handling rice-related affairs practically, the members tended to give priority to individual interests rather than regional collective interests. At the same time, as explained later, the global food crisis became a catalyst in urging ASEAN leaders to advance collective measures to enhance regional cooperation on food security and rice reserve.

A driving force for regional cooperation on rice reserve was provided by China, which changed its posture towards cooperation on food security after 2009, showing willingness to offer material resources to sustain the EAERR. In April 2009, the Chinese government revealed a plan to contribute 300,000 tonnes of earmarked rice to the EAERR. This decision came from Premier Wen Jiabao's initiative (Toyoda 2009: 239). At the ASEAN+3 summit in October 2010 Premier Wen declared that China would work together with other regional countries to promote the establishment of a feasible regional rice reserve system, proposing a US$1 million donation for this aim.[20] This donation was a significant step towards resolving the financial problems that accompanied the APTERR management. China also sought to make ideational contributions to enhancing food security in East Asia. Its government proposed holding the ASEAN+3 Roundtable on Food Security Cooperation Strategy, and its first meeting was held in Beijing in September 2009. After the second round table was held in Tokyo in May 2010, the third round table took place in Nanning, Guangxi Province, in November 2011. The round table was critical in sharing the importance of avoiding food insecurity and exploring channels and mechanisms for strengthening strategic cooperation on food security.

China's new commitment to regional food security derived from at least three factors. First, they were parts of China's intensified international cooperation in the agricultural field. China originally had a 'right to speak' on matters relating to international food security because of its own miraculous achievement in feeding a huge population, and food security became a critical arena for its international cooperation (Morton 2012: 31). In 2008, the Chinese government decided to deepen agricultural cooperation by doubling the number of experts and technical personnel sent overseas and offering training programmes to 3,000 people from developing countries. In the same year, Beijing also announced a contribution of US$30 million to the FAO to support developing countries in improving their agricultural productivity to achieve the Millennium Development Goals (FAO 2011: 7). China's commitment to rice reserve in East Asia could be regarded as a part of such cooperative policies. Second, China's initiative in food security was a pillar of its strategic regional diplomacy. The country did not expect that it would receive rice from other countries when a domestic natural disaster occurs because it has adhered to a norm of self-sufficiency in food.[21] Accordingly, China's commitment derived from its interest in external relations. China's pledge to provide earmarked rice was originally announced as a series of economic initiatives towards ASEAN, which included the establishment of the China–ASEAN Investment Cooperation Fund and the provision of US$15 billion credits to less developed ASEAN members (Sutter and Huang 2009). Thus, food security was a desirable area where China could show its willingness to deepen political linkages with ASEAN members. Third, favourable conditions in domestic grain production provided the Chinese government with leeway to make contributions to rice reserve. Grain output had been increasing for five years in a row since 2004, reaching a record high of over 500 million tonnes in 2008.[22] After 2005 rice production became larger than rice consumption and rice stock gradually expanded. In 2007, for instance, storage capacity of grains mostly comprised of rice and wheat reached between 150 and 200 million tonnes, or roughly 30–40 per cent of total grain production for that year (501.5 million tonnes) (Morton 2012: 20–21). This situation allowed the Chinese government to take advantage of commitments to the EAERR as a means to promote ASEAN+3 cooperation.

China's new diplomacy influenced South Korea's policy approach. In October 2009, the Korean Ministry for Food, Agriculture, Forestry and Fisheries decided to commit to the EAERR, pledging to provide 150,000 tonnes of earmarked rice.[23] After China announced substantial contributions to the EAERR, South Korea feared that it would be left out in moves towards regional cooperation on food security, an increasingly important policy field.

The global food crisis in 2007–08

In 2007 and 2008, there were significant global events and trends that provoked high and volatile food prices. They extended from draughts and floods due to climate change, growing food demand in the newly emerging economies, and rising energy prices and consequent shifts towards biofuel production. The prices of major foodstuffs exhibited a sharp rise. By March 2008, average wheat prices rose by 130 per cent above their level a year earlier, soy prices were 87 per cent higher, and maize prices climbed 31 per cent (Holt-Giménez and Peabody 2008: 1). In the case of rice, export restraints in rice-exporting counties contributed to a further hike in price in the thinly traded international rice market. The export prices (FOB) for all kinds of rice in major exporting countries in Southeast Asia began to increase from November 2007 and reached their peak in May 2008. For instance, the average of FOB prices for Thailand milled rice 5 per cent rose by three times in a year from US$320 per tonne in May 2007 to US$973 in May 2008 (AFSIS 2008: 7).

The above events and movements on the international scene brought about a sharp rise in domestic prices of major foodstuffs in Southeast Asian countries. In Cambodia, between March and July 2007 and March and July 2008, the prices of major foodstuffs rose sharply: 100 per cent for rice, 50–70 per cent for meat, and 20–30 per cent for fish and vegetables. Given that the poorest 40 per cent of the population had spent 70 per cent of their incomes on food, such hikes in food were disastrous (CDRI 2008: 9). Indonesia, which gradually strengthened reliance on imported food, was faced with a rise in the price of basic foodstuffs by as much as 60 per cent in 2008 (Arnst 2009: 9). The hike in food prices caused social unrest in several Southeast Asian countries. In Indonesia, hundreds of meat sellers took to the streets in Jakarta to complain about the rising prices of beef, and more than 10,000 people protested against surging prices for tofu and tempeh.[24] In April 2008, the Philippine government deployed troops to guard government-subsidised food distribution centres in Manila, and politicians in opposition parties called on the government to declare a state of emergency over food prices.[25]

The food crisis in 2007–08 raised political leaders' sense of urgency about food emergencies. At the 14th summit in March 2009, ASEAN leaders issued the Statement on Food Security in the ASEAN Region, which adopted the ASEAN Integrated Food Security (AIFS) Framework and the Strategic Plan of Action on Food Security in the ASEAN Region (SPA-FS) (2009–13). The framework provides four components of cooperation: food security arrangements and emergency short-term relief; sustainable food trade development; integrated food security information system; and agricultural innovation. The strategic plan explicitly stated a commitment to 'support the establishment of a long-term mechanism for ASEAN Plus Three emergency rice reserve'.[26] At the 12th ASEAN+3 Summit in October 2009, ASEAN+3 leaders adopted a special statement on food security and bio-energy development, which clearly stated an intention to 'support the continuation of the East Asia Emergency Rice Reserve (EAERR) pilot project and explore the possibility of establishing an ASEAN Plus Three Emergency Rice Reserve (APTERR) based on the experience of the EAERR'.[27] These frameworks and statements indicated political leaders' deep concern about widespread food emergencies and their political and social impact, and the recognition of the APTERR as a feasible mechanism to mitigate food emergencies.

The food crisis raised the value of a regional rice reserve system as a mechanism to mitigate food insecurity. The Japanese government gradually curtailed its commitments to the EAERR, no longer sending a coordinator to its secretariat. However, it re-evaluated the EAERR as a valuable project to respond to food emergencies, and restored a budget to dispatch a coordinator in 2008.[28] The food crisis urged some ASEAN members to change their policy stances on regional cooperation on rice reserve. Before the food crisis occurred, there was an internal divide over a method to make an interim assessment on the EAERR project. While Indonesia and the Philippines supported a positive method in that such an assessment should be made in accordance with progress of the project, others favoured a prudent method in that the assessment should be made after the completion of the whole project. The food crisis and the resultant hike in food prices changed the situation, and Thailand, Malaysia, and Brunei converted their stances to support the positive method (Toyoda 2009: 239). Importantly, the food crisis contributed to broadening the possible function of rice reserve to stabilise the prices of staple foods. Surin Pitsuwan, Secretary General of ASEAN, made this point, stating that 'obviously, to prevent spiralling food prices, we need a concerted effort to further strengthen the scope of regional cooperation in food security, including stabilization of prices'.[29]

The 2007–08 food crisis became a critical juncture when policymakers in East Asia changed their perception of food security. Before the crisis, the policymakers were generally cautious about developing the EAERR project into a fully fledged institution. However, volatility in food prices and surges in food demand made them recognise the risk that food emergencies would provoke social unrest and political instability. Accordingly, they began to pursue a new policy pattern to take advantage of the APTERR as an institution to smooth out the erratic fluctuation of rice prices in addition to supporting food emergency relief.

Research institutes and cooperation on food security

This section investigates the likely influence of networks formed by researchers and research institutes on the initiation and development of food security cooperation in East Asia. Unlike in other policy fields, there were no long-standing networks linking agriculture-related researchers or research institutes covering the whole of East Asia. The networks were formed in the sub-regions – Northeast Asia and Southeast Asia.

China, Japan, and South Korea began cooperation on agriculture-related research by launching the Forum for Agricultural Policy Research in North East Asia in October 2003.[30] The forum, established by the Chinese Academy of Agricultural Sciences, the Policy Research Institute under the MAFF of Japan, and the Korea Rural Economic Institute, has conducted the exchange of information about agriculture and rural communities in each country. The forum has also organised an international symposium where researchers from the three countries have discussed critical agriculture-related issues. It has created transnational networks of research institutes through the exchange of information and journals, the holding of international meetings and seminars, as well as the advance of joint studies.

The impact of the forum on food security in East Asia has been limited because major agendas at the forum have been common agricultural issues and policy coordination in Northeast Asia, not extending to cooperative affairs in the broader East Asia. Moreover, this track II policy network has been functioned without policy networks at the track I level. It was in 2012 that agricultural ministers of the three governments began a regular meeting.[31] Given that the three institutes have strong institutional, financial, and personnel connections to government agencies, their research collaboration provided one foundation for the initiation of formal ministerial linkages. However, it is premature to deduce meaningful impacts of research activities or research outcomes on concrete policy agendas and directions at the government level.

In Southeast Asia, ASEAN forged collaboration with one agricultural research institute in discussing various rice issues. The International Rice Research Institute (IRRI), the world's leading rice-related institute, has conducted activities for improving the well-being of rice farmers and consumers as well as for ensuring environmental sustainability. The IRRI, based in the Philippines and with offices in other ten Asian countries, is one of 15 centres funded through the Consultative Group on International Agricultural Research. At the 30th AMAF meeting in 2008, ministers gave support to the ASEAN Rice Action Plan prepared and submitted by the IRRI. The seven-point plan contained items such as 'bring about an agronomic revolution to reduce existing yield gaps', 'accelerate the delivery of new postharvest technologies', and 'accelerate the introduction and adoption of higher-yielding rice varieties'.[32] At the 33rd AMAF meeting in October 2011, ministers further supported the Global Rice Science Partnership, led by the IRRI, as an expansion of the ASEAN Rice Action Plan. As shown in growing linkages with the IRRI, ASEAN certainly strengthened linkages with research institutes as food security emerged as a critical policy agenda. The institutes' scientific expertise and practical knowledge were indispensable for formulating feasible agricultural policies and food security strategies. However, the scientific expertise and knowledge were used to discuss common agricultural issues in Southeast Asia, not extending to the wider East Asia.

An exceptional network involving agriculture-related researchers in both Northeast Asia and Southeast Asia was formed under the Network of East Asian Think-tanks (NEAT). The NEAT Working Group on East Asian Food Security functioned in 2009–10 with participation of some 20 experts from ASEAN+3 members. Japan assumed the role of country coordinator of the group and an international meeting was held twice, in July 2009 and July 2010. The group presented the 'NEAT Working Group on East Asian Food Security: Final Report' at the NEAT annual conferences in 2009 and 2010. The 2009 report suggested exploring the possibility of an East Asian common agricultural policy, stressing the need for setting up a consultative organisation in ASEAN+3 countries including a permanent secretariat to advance common food security policies in East Asia.[33] The 2010 report paid attention to aspects of food safety in food security in East Asia. It suggested taking the step-by-step approach towards the establishment of common regional standards and/or regulations in order to improve national food safety.[34] The essence of the reports, which were included in policy recommendations on East Asian cooperation, was delivered to ASEAN+3 summit meetings. Accordingly, the reports could become one reference for the leaders in making decisions on regional food security affairs.[35]

However, the working group did not have enough capabilities to form transnational policy networks. It operated for only two years, organising an international meeting just twice. This short-term operation made it impossible to provide a venue for promoting social learning through objective interpretation of facts regarding politically sensitive food security affairs. The reports certainly identified major challenges and future policy agendas regarding food security in East Asia. But the reports, of some 2,000 words, did not provide concrete action plans to tackle these challenges and agendas.

Researchers and think-tanks have been involved in policy discussions on agricultural cooperation including food security in East Asia, and provided some professional expertise. However, such commitments were fragmented in terms of the scope of regional area and interest. Unlike regional cooperation in finance and the environment examined in other chapters, policymakers did not establish an internal body to discuss rice emergencies from a scientific standpoint. Accordingly, substantial policy networks involving non-state actors have not developed in the discussions of rice reserve in East Asia. The development of regional cooperation on food security has proceeded under the intergovernmental initiative alone.

The weak presence of policy networks involving non-state actors had two crucial effects on cooperation on food security in East Asia. First, it constituted one cause of a failure to create well functioning, reliable institutions for managing regional food security affairs. The institutions themselves were proposed and established with state actors' political initiatives. However, their functions were far from effective, largely due to the lack of operational systems and guiding rules to implement concrete practical programmes. The intensive debates through policy networks should have provided ideas and knowledge to overcome such deficiencies. In particular, the involvement of non-state actors would have been crucial in gaining expertise in the storage of reserve and the logistics of delivery and distribution (Briones 2011: 18). Secondly, the lack of policy networks led to a failure to deepen the recognition of the importance of food security. In the process of food security cooperation, Japan as the initiator of the EAERR encouraged ASEAN members to re-examine the performance of their food security initiatives. However, they were slow in fully recognising that food insecurity would lead to a serious challenge that would undermine domestic social and political stability. Frank dialogues through policy networks formed with the involvement of non-state actors might have contributed to changing such recognition.

Conclusion

In this chapter, I examined how East Asian countries have engaged in the formation of regional institutions for food security. While ASEAN members established the AERR in 1979, it had not been utilised for more than 30 years largely because of its small quantity of rice reserve and political sensitivities involved in its operation. In order to enhance food security and tackle poverty problems in rural areas, the countries in East Asia sought the establishment of a more fully fledged regional institution for rice reserve. Through discussions at the AMAF+3 meetings, the EAERR was introduced as a pilot project for reserving rice for emergencies. The EAERR pilot project was implemented from April 2004 for six years, and in 2012 the APTERR was launched on the basis of EAERR experience. Japan, China, South Korea, and ASEAN members provided earmarked rice reserve, the endowment fund, and operational costs for the APTERR. Although it took a long time to set up the new regional institution for rice reserve and the APTERR is still at a preliminary stage with a small secretariat, countries in East Asia have established collective mechanisms to respond to common challenges in food security.

A salient feature in the development of the rice reserve system was Japan's initiative. Japan provided the blueprint for the EAERR, financial support for managing the EAERR Secretariat and meetings, and emergency rice for crisis-stricken countries. Despite its seemingly altruistic character, the EAERR initiative was closely linked to Japan's national interests. The Japanese government proposed the EAERR as a means to gain support from developing countries for its assertions at WTO agricultural negotiations. Moreover, the provision of physically reserved rice helped to absorb imported rice under WTO obligations and thereby protect the domestic rice market. Other regional countries were suspicious about Japan's intentions, which led to their passive postures towards the strength of the Japan-initiated EAERR project. ASEAN members failed to establish a cohesive stance on regional rice reserve largely because of diverse positions on rice trade. While Thailand and Vietnam, two major rice-exporting countries, hoped to expand rice exports through the EAERR, rice-importing countries in the Mekong region and the Philippines desired to receive rice food aid, seeking to avoid assuming costs for rice storage. A major actor that propelled the process towards the APTERR was China, which proposed offering the largest quantity of earmarked rice and organised an international round table on food security. The new commitments derived largely from its willingness to deepen international cooperation in the agricultural field and strengthen political and economic linkages with ASEAN.

A critical background factor that drove the initiative on rice reserve was a food crisis. The food shortage during the Asian financial crisis encouraged ASEAN members to recognise essential shortcomings of the existing AERR and seek a more reliable institution for emergency rice reserve. A similar food shortage in 2007–08 also urged East Asian countries to reconsider the existing food supply system, and finalised a political decision to transit the EAERR to the APTERR. Thus, these two periods became a historical breakpoint of institutional change by highlighting the limitations of the exiting institutional structures. They became critical junctures to raise the institutional path to a new level at which the parties concerned deliberated on a new structure for cooperation.

The APTERR, a regional institution for rice reserve, was established with political will, but the process of establishing it took considerable time and its structure is unlikely to undertake effective operations, at least in the short term. This is partly because research institutes were irrelevant to the development of regional food security affairs. There existed several research networks engaging in agricultural issues, but they did not highlight regional rice reserve issues. Although the NEAT research networks showed interest in food security issues, policy reports produced from this network did not have substantial influence on policy debates among government officials. The establishment of a feasible rice reserve system requires scientific analyses and professional knowledge regarding storage and distribution methods, linkages to international trade, and so on. The weak or non-existent input of such expertise from research institutes led to the weak institutionalisation of regional rice reserve in East Asia.

6

Energy Security Cooperation under ASEAN+3

In the new millennium, East Asia as a group has consolidated its status as a main driver of economic growth in the world. Steady economic growth has led to increasing demand for energy because of input expansion in the industrial sector and consumption growth in the household and transport sectors. The rising demand for energy inevitably fuels steep competition among the countries for securing stable energy resources represented by oil and natural gas. A relevant issue is that major East Asian countries have been heavily dependent on oil imported from the Middle East. High dependence on oil from the volatile Middle East means that political instability in the region has a direct impact on energy supply, and that any accident in certain sealanes such as the Malacca Strait will have significant effects on oil supply to East Asian countries. Moreover, improvement in energy efficiency is a critical issue for managing greenhouse gas emissions and climate change, and energy efficiency remains relatively low in most East Asian countries.

Given the above multifaceted challenges, hedging against the likely risk of energy insecurity by establishing a stable energy supply system is an urgent issue for governments in East Asia. Some of the challenges are common concerns for the countries in the region, and the creation of regional institutions to react to common concerns should become a feasible policy option. In the 1990s, however, existing regional frameworks – the Association of Southeast Asian Nations (ASEAN) and Asia-Pacific Economic Cooperation (APEC) – did not necessarily provide effective initiatives in responding to evolving conditions in energy affairs in East Asia. In the new millennium, East Asian countries began to deliberate on the possibility of collective actions to pursue stable energy supplies and enhanced energy security under the new frameworks of ASEAN Plus Three (ASEAN+3) and the East Asia Summit (EAS).

This chapter examines the development of ASEAN+3 institutions to sustain energy security in East Asia. It examines political interactions among China, Japan, South Korea, and ASEAN and strategic motivations pertinent to such interactions. This chapter also explores the manner of development of the ASEAN+3 institutions and the impact that specific external incidents had on this development, and elucidates possible contributions by energy experts and energy research institutes to the building of regional institutions.

The creation of the EPGG

The launching of the EPGG and policy forums

In the early 2000s, formal dialogues to advance energy cooperation in East Asia began under the ASEAN+3 framework. In July 2002, the first ASEAN+3 Senior Officials Meeting on Energy (SOME+3) was held in Bali, Indonesia. One year later, the second SOME+3 meeting was organised in Langkawi, Malaysia. At the meeting, senior officials agreed that the SOME+3 Energy Policy Governing Group (EPGG) would be established to provide overall policy directions and programme management for cooperation, and that common issues and concerns in energy security, natural gas development, oil market studies, oil stockpiling, and renewable energy would be discussed. Based on the agreement, the first SOME+3 EPGG meeting was held in Bangkok the following month. Through discussions at the two meetings, the basic framework for ASEAN+3 energy cooperation was consolidated.

In order to undertake concrete cooperative activities, forums were set up under the SOME+3 EPGG in five policy areas: energy security, oil market, oil stockpiling, natural gas, and new and renewable energy and energy efficiency and conservation (NRE and EE&C) (Figure 6.1). The Energy Security Forum focuses on the development of emergency energy security communication. The Oil Market Forum discusses various issues in the oil market and oil industry in Asia in general and the Asia Premium issue in particular. The Oil Stockpiling Forum deliberates on the possible development of stockpiling programmes in member countries. The Natural Gas Forum examines investment in the exploration and production of natural gas as well as the development of gas transport infrastructure. The NRE and EE&C Forum seeks the improvement of energy efficiency and renewable energy. The SOME+3 EPGG designated the ASEAN Centre for Energy (ACE) as coordinator for ASEAN and the Japanese Ministry of Economy, Trade and Industry (METI) as coordinator for the +3 countries (Tanabe 2011: 100). The name 'forum' was adopted in order to stress the voluntary and non-binding nature of this cooperative framework (Tanabe 2004: 231). The first Oil Market Forum and Oil Stockpiling Forum took place in Bangkok in November 2003, and the first Energy Security Forum was organised in Cebu, the Philippines, in February 2004. The first Natural Gas Forum and the NRE and EE&C Forum also took place within 2004.

In June 2004, the first ASEAN+3 Ministers on Energy Meeting (AMEM+3) was held in Manila. At the meeting, the ministers confirmed common goals of greater energy security and energy sustainability in East Asia, which would become the largest energy consumption region in the world. They then referred to three general principles: an equal and mutual relationship,

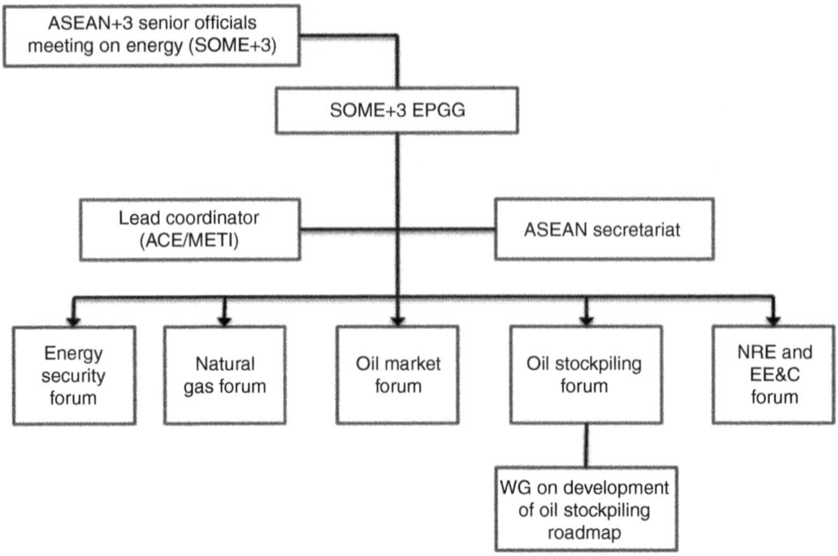

Figure 6.1 The structure of ASEAN+3 energy cooperation
Source: Created by the author with internal documents from the Japanese METI.

taking diversity among countries into account; diversity in sources of primary energy supply; and the importance of the market mechanism.[1] The ministers decided to meet on a regular basis to discuss cooperation on common policy goals and work on further relevant studies and activities at senior official level. The ministerial meeting was institutionalised, and a meeting took place annually thereafter.

Among five policy areas for cooperation, one that had the potential to produce a concrete project was oil stockpiling. The development of oil-stockpiling facilities is important for increasing insurance against short-term supply shortages and reducing competition among oil-consuming countries. Moreover, the holding of oil stockpiles is crucial for oil-consuming countries to gain freedom from price controls by oil-producing countries and deal with fluctuations in world oil prices. Oil stockpiling had significant implications for East Asian countries largely because they were heavily dependent on oil imported from the volatile Middle East. If exports of crude oil had been suspended due to a civil war or a terrorist attack, the East Asian countries would have suffered from the disruption of oil supply. The development of oil reserve facilities could reduce the risk accompanying such emergency situations.

The development of oil-stockpiling facilities is generally regarded as a critical pillar of a state's national strategy for energy security. However, it is not easy in reality to find an appropriate site for an oil tank base because the site requires solid ground to endure the weight of oil and a port with sufficient depth for a large-scale tanker (Goto 2004: 167). Moreover, the huge initial costs of constructing the facilities become crucial financial burdens, especially for developing countries. Accordingly, it is feasible to consider oil reserve collectively and develop stockpiling facilities in a region. The shared oil stockpiling among countries in a given region can generate a larger storage capacity and produce greater benefits than oil stockpiling by a single country. Thus, shared oil reserve through regional cooperation can increase the resiliency of oil stockpiling and produce greater benefits to the countries concerned.

At the beginning of the new millennium, the degree of development in oil stockpiling was diverse among East Asian countries. Japan and South Korea, members of the International Energy Agency (IEA), established the national and private oil-stockpiling systems as the agency's membership obligation.[2] The Chinese government decided to establish the national oil-stockpiling system in the tenth five-year plan (2001–05), approved at the National People's Congress in 2001. In 2003, the Energy Bureau was created under the National Development and Reform Commission (NDRC), and the National Oil Stockpiling Office was set up by the bureau in order to formulate the strategic oil reserve policy. After intensive consultations with the IEA and oil companies, the bureau formulated a plan to establish national oil-stockpiling bases with a total storage capacity of 14 million tons in Dalian in Liaoning Province, Huangdao in Shandong Province, and Daishan and Zhenhai in Zhejiang Province (Ehara 2005: 43). With the construction of the oil-stockpiling facilities, the National Oil Reserve Centre (NORC) was created in 2007 to undertake the management and operation of oil stockpiling.

The oil stockpiling was crucial for Southeast Asian countries. While Indonesia, a major oil exporting country in Southeast Asia, gradually fell to the status of an oil importer, other oil-consuming countries like Thailand, the Philippines, and Vietnam increased their oil demand. However, oil stockpiling was underdeveloped in the region. No ASEAN members had a plan to establish a national oil-stockpiling system, and oil stockpiling by the private sector was undertaken by only four countries – Thailand, Indonesia, Singapore, and Brunei (Koyama 2001: 69). A unique attempt to rectify this by ASEAN was a collective arrangement for oil supply. In 1986, ASEAN members signed the ASEAN Petroleum Security Agreement (APSA), which provided for oil-sharing systems in terms of both shortage and oversupply.[3] The APSA aimed to offer preferential oil supplies to an oil-importing country whose oil procurement becomes less than 80 per cent of normal consumption requirements, and to offer preferential oil purchase to assist an oil exporting country to increase its exports to at least 80 per cent of the normal level (Ravenhill 2013: 51–52). Soon after the adoption of the APSA, it became apparent that the agreement did not work effectively. When oil provision was suspended during the Gulf War in 1990–91, Malaysia proposed offering oil to the Philippines under the APSA. The Philippine government declined the proposal in view of prices and kind of oil, and procured Saudi oil from the international market (Ehara 2005: 45). This incident revealed the limitation of the APSA. Later, ASEAN members organised a task force under the ASEAN Council on Petroleum (ASCOPE) in 2002 to revise the APSA (Koyama 2002: 32).

The start of ASEAN+3's energy cooperation became a valuable opportunity to encourage several ASEAN members to formulate a plan to develop the oil-stockpiling system. The Philippines and Thailand had strong interests in advancing regional stockpiling systems. The Philippine government hoped to be a centre of stockpiling in Southeast Asia by taking advantage of a former US military base at Subic Bay, which had large fuel storage facilities. The Thai government planned to construct an oil storage site for Asian countries as part of the Land Bridge Project (Shin and Savage 2011: 2822).[4] The Philippines, Thailand, and Vietnam conducted a feasibility study to introduce the oil-stockpiling system, and presented a plan for its development at the meetings of the Oil Stockpiling Forum.

The Osaka IEF meeting as a critical juncture

After the late 1990s, significant movements surrounding energy issues occurred in several dimensions. The first movement was growing fluctuations in the international oil market after 1998. The crude oil price declined from US$17.4 per barrel in early 1998 to US$10.7 in December 1998, and rose to US$37.2 in September 2000. The fluctuations had a significant influence on energy-related policies in Southeast Asia. While the Philippine government suspended import tariffs on petroleum products (3 per cent) from November 2000 to January 2001, the Thai government requested the Petroleum Authority of Thailand (PTT) to refrain from increasing oil prices (Koyama 2002: 25). These measures aimed to prevent social unrest resulting from a rise in the prices of petroleum products. The second was relevant to geopolitical concerns. The 9/11 terrorist attacks in 2001 had a broad range of impacts on the world economy and international politics. The terrorist attacks led to an economic recession in the United States, which had a significant negative impact on the countries that relied on the US market through the decline of their exports. The terrorist attacks also provoked concerns about energy security in the Middle East. In particular, the US government exhibited its determination to conduct military attacks on Iraq, which became reality in March 2003. Such disorder in the Middle East was a great anxiety for the countries that relied on the region for their oil supply. The oil-importing countries were forced to enhance responsiveness to growing energy risks through the creation of an emergency network for energy security, the strength of oil reserve, and so on.

The new developments encouraged policymakers in East Asia to consider energy security seriously. In China, the new developments contributed to shifting a primary perception of energy policy from 'economic' to 'strategic'. In the wake of the 9/11 terrorist attacks and the subsequent retaliatory military actions by the United States, Chinese leaders learned the 'high politics' aspect of and rising strategic concern with energy security policy (Choo 2006: 96). The new developments also encouraged the Japanese government to formulate a new strategy for energy security. In 2001, METI set up a working group on energy security under the Advisory Committee for Natural Resources and Energy in order to analyse evolving energy affairs in the world and deliberate on possible measures to maintain energy security in response to them. The working group's report regarded price volatility in the international oil market and geopolitical risks in the Middle East such as the regression in the peace process, the introduction and development of mass-destruction weapons, and religious conflicts as serious risks. Given these growing risks, the report proposed region-based measures to enhance energy security such as the sharing of information and perceptions about energy security, the securing of stable oil supply, the development and use of alternative energy resources, and cooperation in the diffusion of energy conservation and new energy (METI 2001).

With crucial backgrounds surrounding international energy affairs, an event that had a direct impact on the initiation of ASEAN+3 energy cooperation took place. In September 2002, the Japanese government hosted the eighth International Energy Forum (IEF) in Osaka, where energy ministers and delegations gathered from 65 countries and ten relevant organisations.[5] The main agendas of the meeting, which was held for the first time in East Asia, were 'World Energy Situation and Outlook', 'Facilitating Investment in the Energy Sector', 'Interaction among Energy Security', 'Environmental Issues and Economic Growth' and 'The Way Forward of the IEF in Addressing International Energy Issues'. The participants reconfirmed the importance of fostering collaborative relationships between oil-producing and oil-consuming nations to stabilise the oil market, and shared the awareness of a rapid increase in energy demand in developing countries, especially in Asia.

On the fringes of the forum, the Japanese government hosted an informal energy ministers' meeting of China, Japan, South Korea, and ASEAN countries. The participants expressed their opinions regarding the importance of sea-lane security and coal. With respect to oil stockpiling, representatives from the Philippines and Thailand brought up the oil-stockpiling projects envisioned by their countries (Tanabe 2004: 227). Moreover, in addition to a willingness to develop oil-stockpiling systems at the country level, an idea to coordinate the timing for providing reserved oil at emergency circumstances was presented (Horii 2006: 452). Towards the end of the meeting, Takeo Hiranuma, Japanese Minister of Economy, Trade and Industry, proposed a five-point initiative (Hiranuma Initiative) to undertake concrete actions for energy cooperation in East Asia: (i) the establishment of an emergency network; (ii) the promotion of oil stockpiling; (iii) the launching of joint studies of the Asian oil market; (iv) natural gas development; and (v) the improvement of energy conservation and renewable energy. Within one year after the launching of the Hiranuma Initiative, ASEAN+3 members reached an agreement to set up forums to materialise cooperation on the five suggested policy fields.

The informal ministerial meeting had critical implications for initiating ASEAN+3 energy cooperation. The meeting became the first chance of institutional linkages among energy ministers from ASEAN+3 members, and offered a venue where the ministers exchanged views on and concerns with energy-related affairs. Besides, since the meeting was held on the fringes of the IEF, the ministers were able to confirm a unified stance as energy consumers. More concretely, the Hiranuma Initiative provided clear guidelines for bringing forward ASEAN+3 energy cooperation. The initiative identified five areas of cooperation and consultative forums were formed exactly in these areas. The new self-reinforcing path for regional cooperation began as the forums organised an annual meeting and the SOME+3 EPGG coordinated the forums' activities.

In sum, growing uncertainty in geopolitics in the Middle East coupled with volatile oil prices made policymakers in East Asia nervous about oil market conditions, and encouraged them to consider seriously concrete measures to prepare for emergency situations. In such a milieu, the IEF meeting in Osaka became a catalyst in developing a regional institution to tackle challenges in energy security. It became an opportunity to begin an energy ministers' meeting under the ASEAN+3 framework, and provided the foundation to commence a new cooperative trajectory under the SOME+3 EPGG. Afterwards, concrete forums were organised to deepen policy dialogues on specific issues for energy security.

The major parties' stance on regional energy cooperation

ASEAN+3 energy cooperation began with Japan's initiative in organising an informal energy ministers' meeting. Before this initiative, Japan established institutional linkages for energy cooperation with ASEAN. The SOME-METI Consultation started in 2000, targeting cooperation on energy security planning, EE&C, and NRE. At the second SOME-METI Consultation meeting in July 2001, six ASEAN members gave presentations on their energy-related policies.[6] Afterwards, Japan and ASEAN co-organised a series of workshops and seminars: an ASEAN+3 /IEA joint workshop in Tokyo in December 2002; a Japan-ASEAN Clean Development Mechanism (CDM) seminar in Jakarta in January 2003; and an ASEAN+3 petroleum security workshop in Kuala Lumpur in June 2003.[7] Thus, institutional linkages between Japan and ASEAN provided the foundation for cooperation in the ASEAN+3 framework.

After the formal start of ASEAN+3 energy cooperation in 2003, METI played the key role in advancing cooperation. METI has an energy-specific agency, the Agency for Natural Resources and Energy. The agency took advantage of its affiliated organisations such as the Japan Oil, Gas and Metals National Corporation (JOGMEC), the Institute of Energy Economics, Japan (IEEJ), and the Japan Coal Energy Centre (JCOAL) in order to provide support for the holding of relevant meetings and intellectual inputs for sustaining concrete activities. Furthermore, METI made substantial commitments to advancing specific policy issues. For instance, the ministry took the lead in diffusing the importance of oil stockpiling to East Asian countries. During the second SOME+3 meeting in July 2003, Japan floated a proposal for oil stockpiling as an emergency response mechanism, with an offer of soft loans and technical know-how for the construction of stockpiling facilities.[8] Japan then proposed assisting feasibility studies of oil stockpiling for ASEAN members at the first meeting of the Oil Stockpiling Forum in November 2003. METI offered support for formulating a master plan for the development of oil stockpiling for Thailand and the Philippines in 2004–05, and the result of the formulation was presented at the fourth SOME+3 meeting in July 2005. METI also assisted in the formulation of a master plan for Vietnam by showing prospects for energy demand and instructing Japan's experience in design, operation, and support for the system.

Japan hoped to achieve two objectives in initiating ASEAN+3 energy cooperation. First, regional energy cooperation was expected to contribute to Japan's energy security. Large demand for energy and high import dependence has made energy security one of the priorities of any government of Japan (Vivoda 2012: 135).[9] Growing energy demand in one country has a significant impact on the energy security of other energy-consuming countries like Japan by reducing the export capacity of energy-producing countries. Japan regarded Asia's growing share in the world's energy demand as a critical factor that influenced its energy affairs, imports of crude oil from the Middle East in particular (METI 2001). Such a perception encouraged the Japanese government to initiate bilateral or multilateral cooperation with East Asian countries to develop measures for enhancing energy security under the banner of 'Asian energy partnership' (Tanabe 2004). In this context, a particularly important issue was how to integrate China into a collaborative framework. The idea that a trilateral framework of China, Japan, and South Korea would be more feasible was presented at prior discussions to launch an Asian energy partnership. However, there was a possibility that head-to-head confrontation might occur in the trilateral framework. Since cooperation under the ASEAN+3 framework had already started with the holding of the SOME+3 meeting in July 2002, it would be easier and less risky to embrace China, whose response was uncertain in a broader framework involving Southeast Asia (Tanabe 2004: 227).

The second objective was to show leadership in providing regional public goods. Japan formulated various policies to secure sufficient oil stock, reduce energy reliance on oil, and create a highly energy-efficient economy in its industrial development process after the experience of the two oil shocks in the 1970s. Moreover, Japan's unique identity enabled it to push forward formal and informal arrangements for managing energy issues and energy cooperation in East Asia (Jain and Mito 2014). While Japan could take advantage of its long experience in international institutions such as the Organisation for Economic Cooperation and Development (OECD), IEF, and the Group of Seven/Group of Eight (G-7/G-8) to diffuse formal rules and internationally accepted norms, it was accustomed to an Asian style of informal, soft institutions. In particular, METI regarded the pursuit of energy efficiency as an effective way to promote regional cooperation both because Japan had accumulated various technologies and policies as a world leader in creating an energy-efficient economy and because energy efficiency remained low in Asian countries.[10]

How did China respond to an initiative in promoting energy cooperation in East Asia? China did not exhibit keen interest in ASEAN+3 energy cooperation. This is confirmed by the fact that the Chinese government sometimes did not send a head of energy administration – vice-chairman of the NDRC – to ASEAN+3 meetings. While the Chinese Embassy's Councillor in Cambodia, on behalf of the government, attended the second AMEM+3 meeting in July 2005, the Director General of the Energy Bureau only joined a meeting two years later. Moreover, China's presence was generally weak and selective in the forums. While Japan, South Korea, and Malaysia each became a lead country of the two forums, China assumed this role only in one forum: the Natural Gas Forum. The Chinese government held the inaugural meeting of the forum in Shanghai in March 2004 and the fifth meeting in Beijing in October 2008. In the Natural Gas Forum, the Natural Gas Business Dialogue was organised in parallel to the forum meeting so as to explore how to facilitate commercial activities of wider use and development of natural gas, and the Chinese government hosted the business dialogue in October 2008.

China's passive commitment to ASEAN+3 energy cooperation derived from two factors. The first concerned its preference for bilateralism rather than multilateralism in external energy affairs. For a long time, China was able to maintain energy independence largely because of abundant natural resources including oil and coal. This situation left China without experience in energy cooperation and with neither real need nor pragmatic desire to engage in formal or informal cooperative arrangements (Jain and Mito 2014). The maintenance of energy independence was also necessary because advanced nations had set up multilateral frameworks in energy through the OECD, IEF, and G-7/G-8, and developed international norms and principles to manage their energy policies and relations. China was not a member of such multilateral frameworks, and had a suspicion that the international oil market was manipulated by large oil companies from advanced nations (Horiuchi 2007: 292). After China was forced to rely on energy resources from overseas sources, it tended to pursue bilateral arrangements to cultivate and secure deals with external energy suppliers. China advanced bilateral commitments in East Asia in the form of long-term crude oil/ liquid natural gas (LNG) supply contracts and equity investments in oil and gas fields abroad under the 'going-out' strategy (Lai 2009).[11] A crucial peculiarity in China's external energy cooperation lay in its narrow and selective scope, and most partners for energy cooperation were current energy producers or those with energy production potential (Choo 2006: 97).

The second factor is relevant to domestic administrative configuration under the Chinese Communist Party (CCP) regime. For a long time, China's energy bureaucracy was extremely complicated and fragmented with several government agencies to administer the energy sector, which were not subordinate to each other but held overlapping areas of jurisdiction. The administrative reform in March 2003 that replaced the State Development Planning Commission with the NDRC led to the creation of the Energy Bureau under this new commission with the mandate to formulate energy policy, draw up plans for sector reform and undertake routine oversight of the country's energy sector. Given electricity shortages that began in 2002 and growing concerns about the security of oil supply on the eve of the Iraq War, there was a strong anticipation that the CCP leadership would create a high-level agency to manage the energy sector. However, the anticipation was not realised due to opposition from the NDRC and energy companies (Downs 2006: 18). The newly established bureau, with insufficient manpower – a staff of 30 – and limited political clout was unable to perform its mandate adequately, and its officials were preoccupied with the project approval process and had neither time nor resources to ensure that policies drove projects (Downs 2006; Andrews-Speed 2012: 146). In contrast, three national oil companies (NOCs) – China Petrochemical Corporation (Sinopec), China National Petroleum Corporation (CNPC), and China National Offshore Oil Corporation (CNOOC) – were wealthy entities that retained autonomous power to pursue their own interests. These NOCs retained full and vice-ministerial ranking and membership of key executives in the Central Committee of the CCP, as well as direct connections to senior political leaders (Downs 2008: 42). The NOC executives were inclined 'to use government policies to justify decisions they would like to make for commercial reasons' (Jakobson 2008: 123). The powerful NOCs constrained the Energy Bureau's political legitimacy as a central agency to supervise energy affairs, and their corporate interests restricted the bureau's autonomy to formulate and implement external energy policy.

The weak government bureaucracy and strong energy companies explain China's distinctive commitment to ASEAN+3 energy cooperation. Since Chinese NOCs hoped to advance natural gas projects in East Asia, China became a lead country in the Natural Gas Forum, in which linkages with business actors were pursued intensively. The meetings of the forum and the business dialogues were valuable opportunities to exchange information about the natural gas development plan in East Asia and present the Chinese NOCs' business models and plans. In fact, mangers of Sinopec, CNPC, and CNOOC explained their corporate strategies in the natural gas field at the fourth Natural Gas Business Dialogue in October 2008. Thus, the Chinese government took advantage of ASEAN+3 cooperation to acquire pragmatic benefits that were directly linked to the oil companies' business strategies.

As being seen in other policy areas, South Korea's primary geographical target for regional cooperation is Northeast Asia, and the energy sector was no exception. In June 2001, the Korean government organised an international symposium on energy cooperation in Northeast Asia in Seoul, and proposed starting a senior officials' committee that would hold informal dialogues on energy cooperation. This proposal developed into the launching of the Intergovernmental Collaborative Mechanism on Energy Cooperation in North-East Asia, which was formally established in November 2005 (Christoffersen 2009: 191–97). The expected members of this gathering were South Korea, North Korea, China, Japan, Mongolia, and Russia. This mechanism did not develop smoothly as a multilateral framework, largely because of indifference from China and Japan. While China did not find much interest in the narrow scope of cooperation in a mechanism with inter-Korean collaboration as the core, Japan would not participate in a multilateral framework that included North Korea (Fallon 2006: 190–91). Japan remained as an observer and China participated in most of the activities informally. Under these conditions, South Korea was involved in ASEAN+3 energy cooperation, which had the broader geographical scope of East Asia.

ASEAN had a long history of internal energy cooperation, organising the AMEM meeting from 1980. Such a long history of cooperation enabled ASEAN to develop specialised bodies such as the ACE, the ASCOPE, the Forum of Heads of ASEAN Power Utilities/Authorities (HAPUA), and the ASEAN Forum on Coal (AFOC), as well as concrete strategies and actions for energy cooperation. The accumulation of long-term energy cooperation made it possible to appoint the ACE as a coordinator of ASEAN+3 energy cooperation and manage its overall development. A critical challenge for ASEAN in promoting regional energy cooperation was how to secure sufficient financial and technological resources to flesh out cooperative programmes. Accordingly, Japan's initiative in ASEAN+3 energy cooperation was welcomed by ASEAN members. Malaysian Energy Minister Leo Moggie, who assumed the chair of the 21st AMEM meeting in July 2003, stated that the global energy environment was becoming much more challenging and less predictable, and therefore Southeast Asia needed to cooperate with the three countries to attract investment, funding and expertise to exploit untapped energy resources including oil, gas, and hydro-power.[12]

As for the oil-stockpiling issue, Japan earnestly encouraged ASEAN members to consider the issue seriously and provided financial support for a feasibility study for several countries. However, the members were reluctant to raise this issue as a common agenda for ASEAN cooperation, not referring to the issue at the AMEM meetings. There were significant divisions on the issue between oil-consuming countries and oil-producing countries. While oil-consuming countries such as the Philippines and Thailand positively examined the development of oil stockpiling, oil-producing countries such as Indonesia and Malaysia asserted that the oil buried in the ground implied oil stockpiling to be offered to oil-consuming countries in the region, and its exploitation and provision should be given priority (Ehara 2005: 45). As fundamental problems, ASEAN members were apprehensive that the establishment and maintenance of oil stockpiling facilities would impose enormous financial burdens and the facilities might become a possible target of terrorist attacks (Shin and Savage 2011: 2823).

The involvement of research institutes

As already explained, ASEAN+3 energy cooperation was based on bilateral cooperation between Japan and ASEAN. Japan's engagement in energy cooperation with ASEAN was sustained by professional inputs from a research institute: the IEEJ. The IEEJ was established in 1966 as an institute to contribute to the sound development of Japan's energy supply/consuming industries and the improvement of people's lives by providing energy-related data and information and undertaking an analysis of energy problems. The institute has some 180 staff with several internal research units such as the Oil Information Centre and the Asia Pacific Energy Research Centre. The IEEJ is a general incorporated foundation, but has close connections with METI. While the institute has implemented numerous research projects commissioned by METI annually, its chairman post has been restored for the ministry's retired senior bureaucrats.

The IEEJ was deeply involved in research on energy affairs in East Asia. In 2000, the institute conducted comprehensive research on energy markets and energy security policies in ASEAN countries. The research comprised overall analyses of energy demand and supply in ASEAN and country reports on ten ASEAN members. The final report of the research highlighted several issues and trends: the growing importance of energy security in ASEAN in a prospect that oil exporting nations would become oil importers in the future; the formation of broader pipeline networks of natural gas; the growing importance of coal and the need to reduce air pollution accompanying the use of coal; the potential of water power and NRE; the securing of stable oil imports by way of strengthened economic relationships with oil-producing nations; and the development of oil-stockpiling systems. Based on the comprehensive analyses, the report proposed that the Japanese government examine cooperation with ASEAN countries by taking into account Japan's comparative advantage and the most crucial needs for ASEAN. In particular, the report referred to cooperation on the development of oil-stockpiling systems and capacity-building for the formation of energy security policies (Koyama 2001). In the following year, the IEEJ conducted additional research on the international oil market and energy security in ASEAN. This research confirmed ASEAN's challenges in response to energy security such as limitations to huge investment, the existence of diverse and important policy agendas for ASEAN, and consideration for environmental protection. It stressed the need for fostering a common perception that an energy security issue is a vital problem to be tackled by the entire region, not by individual (oil-importing) countries (Koyama 2002). From this standpoint, it emphasised that Japan would need to promote linkages with ASEAN, China, and South Korea in order to implement efficient policies for strengthening energy security.

The IEEJ's research had critical implications for promoting regional energy cooperation. On the basis of professional knowledge and expertise, the institute identified challenges for ASEAN countries resulting from uncertainties in the global economy and international politics in general and the international oil market in particular. Its research indicated desirable policy goals to enhance energy security in ASEAN countries and Japan's guiding role in achieving them. The research reports had a direct impact on the Japanese government's policies for stressing the development of oil-stockpiling systems and a policy direction to establish institutional linkages in East Asia involving China and Southeast Asia. The IEEJ's special position of maintaining close linkages with METI enabled it to gain access to the policymaking process and reflect the outcomes of research on practical policies.

The IEEJ's research activities had the potential to promote social learning for regional energy cooperation involving policymakers in other countries, especially those in Southeast Asia. However, the institute's research was undertaken with a narrow scope of objective and publicity. Its research was commissioned by METI, and proposals were directed towards instructing the Japanese government on desirable areas and means for regional cooperation. Accordingly, the IEEJ's research did not have a direct impact on interests and concerns among policymakers in other countries.

The complicated development of ASEAN+3 energy cooperation

Stagnated progress in energy cooperation

After the start of ASEAN+3 energy cooperation in 2003, a major development in cooperation was the inclusion of three new policy areas as the target of cooperation. The two areas – civilian nuclear energy and CDM – were confirmed as new issues at the fourth and fifth AMEM+3 meetings in 2007 and 2008. The cooperation on civilian nuclear energy was relevant to rules, regulations, technologies, and guidelines on the safe use of nuclear power. The CDM cooperation aimed to assist in the reduction of greenhouse gas emissions and the promotion of sustainable development. The ministers had discussed coal-related issues in terms of energy security from the first ministerial meeting, and coal was formally integrated as a target of the Energy Security Forum. The members explored cooperation on clean coal technologies, and coal trade and regulation, as well as environmental concern in coal use. At the seventh AMEM+3 meeting in July 2010, ministers formally reformulated the forums, consisting of: (i) the Natural Gas and Oil Market Forum; (ii) the Energy Security Forum, which includes oil stockpiling, coal, and civilian nuclear energy; and (iii) the NRE and EE&C Forum including CDM. The reformulation was a response to ASEAN's concern about the holding of too many meetings for energy cooperation.[13] In fact, forum-related meetings were organised nine times within one year, 2008.

ASEAN+3 energy cooperation functioned as a valuable platform to establish information sharing mechanisms. The sharing of information through an oil price database for ASEAN+3 countries was established. The participating countries also exchanged information through presentations on individual energy conditions and policies, which contributed to deepening understanding about concrete policy objectives and measures to enhance energy security and learning from precedent examples and best practices adopted by other countries. Moreover, regional cooperation led to capacity-building through the combination of training, site visits, and small group discussions. While the exchange of information was an important initial step in fostering confidence-building among participants, capacity-building programmes organised by advanced members provided practical benefits for developing members. However, a crucial limitation in the ASEAN+3 energy cooperation was that the exchange of information did not lead to an advanced form of cooperation to develop some kind of policy coordination for managing regional energy affairs.

In some policy areas, member governments agreed to engage in a concrete joint project. However, it took a long time for the project to yield fruit, which was seen in the form of oil stockpiling. Through policy talks at the Oil Stockpiling Forum, common understanding was fostered among member governments on the need to reinforce energy security in response to the rise in future oil demand and import dependency of East Asia as a whole, as well as on the vital role played by oil stockpiling in meeting such a need. Moreover, consensus was reached on the pursuit of the possibility of establishing an oil-stockpiling programme by making use of the experience gained by Japan and South Korea (Koyama and Koide 2004: 2). Despite such understanding and consensus, it took a long time to convert them into concrete policy actions.

It was at the sixth Oil Stockpiling Forum meeting in January 2008 that the ACE formally proposed commencing the Oil Stockpiling Roadmap (OSRM) programme. The formulation of the OSRM was approved at the fifth AMEM+3 meeting in August 2008. The Philippine Department of Energy was appointed as the lead coordinator for ASEAN. The lead coordinator was not determined for the +3 members, and government agencies of the three countries were appointed with equal status. It was also confirmed as an important matter that the OSRM would be developed on the basis of four principles: (i) a voluntary and non-binding nature; (ii) mutual benefits; (iii) mutual respect and respect for bilateral and regional cooperation; and (iv) a step-by-step approach with a long-term perspective. The third principle implies respect for each country's national stockpiling policy and regional oil-stockpiling cooperation (Nakai 2009). The principles clearly derived from the ASEAN Way, which stressed voluntarism, informality, gradualism, and non-intervention in domestic affairs, and reflected China and ASEAN members' preferences for avoiding likely intervention in their domestic oil-stockpiling policies.

In order to advance the formulation of the OSRM, the Working Group on the Development of the OSRM was set up and its first meeting took place in November 2008. The working group organised five rounds of meetings until June 2010 in order to exchange knowledge and experience on roadmaps and discuss the procedure and template for the OSRM. The final report on the OSRM was submitted to the seventh AMEM+3 meeting in July 2010. The report presented country-based plans for commercial, processing, and national oil stocks in the period of 2010–25. The report put ASEAN members into two categories: category A for countries that are able to draw concrete targets and will state their targets on a voluntary basis; and category B for countries that are unable to state concrete targets but may state their intention to set up an oil-stockpiling system and/or an expected target with a rough timeframe.[14] The countries that selected category B, such as Malaysia and Brunei, had a weak understanding of the need for establishing the oil-stockpiling programme. In particular, Malaysia did not subscribe to the idea of a national oil stockpile since production could be easily increased to meet its oil demand (Nicolas 2009: 26).

Although the OSRM had a critical value as the first attempt to integrate oil-stockpiling plans of ASEAN+3 members into the common format, it did not become a substantial roadmap due to its critical flaws as a collective project. While China and Malaysia did not submit a report on situations and future plans of oil stockpiling, even the countries that submitted a report did not provide full information about the future plans. Such divergent commitments derived primarily from differences in economic conditions and the needs of the OSRM of each country, and voluntarism – no formal obligation – allowed the members to report on the roadmap according to their own convenience.[15] At the subsequent AMEM+3 meetings energy ministers repeated recommendations on continuing studies and development of the OSRM, collecting annual information on the progress of each country's oil-stockpiling activities, and organising workshops to promote the implementation of each ASEAN member's OSRM.

A major feature in ASEAN+3 energy cooperation was the expansion of targeted policy areas without the deepening of cooperative activities in the existing policy areas. At the annual AMEM+3 meetings, ministers stressed the importance of further cooperation and integration in response to evolving energy climates. However, member governments were unsuccessful in shifting from the exchange of information to the coordination of national plans and/or the adoption of non-binding principles of behaviour for enhancing energy security (Ravenhill 2013: 44–46). They also failed to produce substantial outcomes in a joint project which was based on voluntarism and gradualism.

A relevant development regarding energy cooperation in East Asia was the launching of the EAS energy cooperation. In December 2005, the first EAS meeting was held in Kuala Lumpur, and leaders of ASEAN+3 members, Australia, New Zealand, and India confirmed basic principles to seek the creation of a community in the region. Importantly, the energy sector became one of the main pillars of EAS cooperation. At the second EAS meeting in January 2007, leaders signed the Cebu Declaration on East Asian Energy Security, which spelled out measures to set individual goals and formulate action plans voluntarily for improving energy efficiency, and to work together towards freer trade on biofuels and a standard on biofuels used in engines and motor vehicles.[16] Like the ASEAN+3 framework, an energy ministers' meeting was organised under the EAS framework, and its first meeting was held in Singapore in August 2007. Afterwards, EAS energy ministers confirmed progress in three work streams: EE&C, biofuels for transport and other purposes, and energy market integration.

The launching of the EAS energy cooperation had a crucial merit in integrating three additional countries into the multilateral framework to promote concrete energy cooperation. Given that East Asian countries are dependent on oil and gas imports from the Middle East as well as Australian gas and coal, the participation of India and Australia was valuable in securing safety of marine transportation routes that pass through their territorial waters (Ishida 2012: 9). Furthermore, the inclusion of India, whose energy demand attracted more international attention, was important because the country did not belong to any of the regional energy frameworks (Christoffersen 2009: 188). At the same time, the EAS framework produced the 'nested institutional structure' in relation to the ASEAN+3 framework and the possibility of duplicating energy initiatives in East Asia. Similar activities were undertaken under the two frameworks, which led to the inefficient use of limited resources. For instance, energy efficiency and conservation is one of the three pillars of the EAS cooperation, and this issue has been dealt with by the NRE and EE&C Forum under the ASEAN+3 cooperation. Moreover, the launching of the EAS led to the declining position of the ASEAN+3 as a comprehensive framework for energy cooperation in East Asia. A loose consensus gradually developed that the EAS functioned as a venue to establish the overall direction of energy cooperation in East Asia, while ASEAN+3 provided a venue for the sharing of basic information and statistics as well as capability-building.[17]

The four parties' preferences for regional energy cooperation

Japan has continuously provided substantial support for ASEAN+3 energy cooperation. As the sole lead country for the Energy Security Forum and Oil Stockpiling Forum, Japan has organised the forums' meetings. METI sustained the activities of the ACE, a coordinator of ASEAN+3 cooperation, by commissioning some tasks of energy cooperation through the IEEJ. For instance, in 2007 METI commissioned the project for ASEAN+3 energy cooperation to the IEEJ with a budget of 50.8 million yen (US$0.43 million), 2.1 million yen of which was recommissioned to the ACE.

Japan has maintained a keen interest in regional energy cooperation. The energy demand in East Asia had steadily increased with its economic growth, and geopolitical risks in the Middle East and North Africa became worse with prolonged economic sanctions on Iran and a series of democratic revolutions. Given these conditions, cooperation under the East Asian framework remained as a critical pillar for maintaining Japan's energy security. After the Fukushima nuclear power plant accident in March 2011, the overall policy for the development and use of nuclear energy became extremely ambiguous. This element also increased Japan's incentive to promote regional energy cooperation in East Asia.

While Japan remained as the pivotal player in ASEAN+3 cooperation, its relative interests in energy cooperation shifted to those under the EAS.[18] In September 2011 EAS energy ministers agreed on new research to be undertaken by the Economic Research Institute for ASEAN and East Asia (ERIA).[19] Japan allocated 1.5 billion yen (US$18.8 million) to sustain the ERIA's new research, and the institute set up the Energy Unit in April 2012 in order to undertake research in five areas: (i) energy outlooks for the medium to long term; (ii) the strategic use of coal through clean coal technologies; (iii) optimum electric power infrastructure; (iv) nuclear power safety management; and (v) smart urban traffic for promoting energy efficiency in the transport sector. These research areas had much to do with Japan's new orientation in economic diplomacy. The Japanese government gradually put emphasis on the deployment of integrated infrastructure systems as a means to assist the advance of Japanese companies into the dynamic Asian economies (Yoshimatsu 2012a). The electric power infrastructure, nuclear power safety management, and the smart urban traffic were relevant to the deployment of integrated infrastructure systems. Given the maturity of domestic energy demand, the Japanese government and companies intended to find new business opportunities in the growing Asian market, and the EAS was used as a platform to attain such a mercantilist objective.

China exhibited complicated postures towards regional energy cooperation. After 2006, China promoted bilateral cooperation with Japan in the energy sector. In May 2006, the first Japan–China Energy Conservation Forum was held in Tokyo. The three-day forum, involving some 500 participants from Japan and 300 from China, provided high-level speeches and theme-specific discussions. The forum became an annual event where the governments and companies of both countries sought to expand business chances in the increasingly important energy-saving field. When Chinese Premier Wen Jiabao made a formal visit to Tokyo in April 2007, the first Japan-China energy ministers' policy dialogue was organised. The working-level policy dialogues had been organised since 1996, but there were no ministerial-level linkages.[20] Accordingly, the dialogue was an important step in advancing energy cooperation and managing energy-related affairs. Furthermore, in June 2008, both governments reached a political agreement on cooperation in the East China Sea, which contained joint development in the northern part of the East China Sea and the participation of Japanese legal persons in the development of the Chunxiao (Japanese name: *Shirakaba*) oil and gas field.

Notwithstanding improvement in its bilateral relationship with Japan, China maintained a passive posture towards ASEAN+3 energy cooperation. Chinese delegates' attitudes at individual forum meetings were generally cautious and passive. For instance, a plan for future meetings was presented at the first meeting of the Working Group on the Development of the OSRM in November 2008. The plan was important in advancing cooperation on oil stockpiling in a speedy manner. The Chinese delegate suggested that the proposed timeframe of the future meetings is pressurised and the topics should be decided later as the economic situation changes rapidly.[21] Afterwards, the Chinese government lost interest in the working group's activity, and its delegate skipped the meeting three times.[22]

China's passive posture towards energy cooperation became more salient after 2009. The Chinese government did not send its delegate to the eighth SOME+3 EPGG in March 2009 or the 11th in July 2012. While China assumed a role as a lead country for the Natural Gas Forum, it did not send a delegate to the seventh forum meeting in November 2010. After the reformulation of the forums, China remained a lead country for the Natural Gas and Oil Market Forum. However, it did not play the expected role as a lead country. The first and second forum meetings were held in Bali, Indonesia and Inchon, South Korea, respectively, and China did not dispatch a delegate to the first forum meeting. The three-forum framework aimed partly to make the role of the +3 countries more clear, and China, Japan, and South Korea were expected to assume responsibility for leading each of the three forums. While Japan and South Korea met this expectation by assuming the chair of the forum meetings, China's commitments were far from fulfilling such an expectation.

China's weak interest in ASEAN+3 energy cooperation was a little abnormal from the standpoint of its overall regional diplomacy. This is because the Chinese authorities had a strong aspiration for the development of ASEAN+3 among various regional frameworks. For instance, Chinese Premier Wen Jiabao stressed the cohesive force created under the ASEAN+3 framework with its 50 dialogue mechanisms and 100 cooperation projects and put forward a five-point proposal on strengthening and deepening cooperation in this framework at the 11th ASEAN+3 summit in November 2007.[23] As chapters 4 and 5 indicated, China constructively engaged in the development of financial and food security cooperation under ASEAN+3, which contributed to the successful development of cooperative institutions. However, China's positive commitments to ASEAN+3 cooperation were not seen in energy security.

There are three factors that impeded China's positive engagement in the development of ASEAN+3 energy cooperation. The first is the growing strategic importance of the energy sector. China's continuous economic growth increased the consumption of fossil fuels, and deepened dependence on overseas sources for energy resources and raw materials. While the combined consumption of oil, natural gas, and coal increased from 974 million tonnes of oil equivalent (MTOE) in 2001 to 1,719 MTOE in 2006 to 2,419 MTOE in 2011, imports of crude oil increased from 60.3 million tons in 2001 to 145.2 million tons in 2006 to 252.6 million tons in 2011.[24] China intensified its strategy for the procurement and development of energy sources, raw materials, and natural resources in Africa, the Middle East, and the Americas (Cáceres and Ear 2012). The energy cooperation in East Asia was a small portion of such a global energy strategy. More specifically, a new approach, pursued in the process of ASEAN+3 energy cooperation, contradicted China's energy strategy. In the past, the concealment of information was important for energy security because the disclosure of information about domestic energy conditions and energy policies was regarded as leading to reduced energy security. In promoting ASEAN+3 energy cooperation, Japan pursued 'an open approach' to enhancing energy security by sharing information about energy affairs openly and pursuing collective action. From this baseline, it encouraged other members to set up and publish an individual oil-stockpiling plan.[25] However, China was passive about revealing information about the development of national oil-stockpiling facilities, which was regarded as a strategic and sensitive matter. Given the growing need for securing energy resources in the world, China did not find sufficient returns from ASEAN+3 cooperation in exchange for risks to encourage it to reveal information about its energy strategy.

Secondly, China's commitment to energy cooperation was influenced by domestic administrative reform. As a consequence of an administrative reform in August 2008, the National Energy Administration (NEA) was newly established, replacing the NDRC's Energy Bureau. The establishment of the

NEA aimed to strengthen energy development strategy and policy coordination by absorbing other energy offices from the NDRC, the Office of National Leading Group, and the nuclear power administration of the Commission of Science, Technology, and Industry for National Defence (COSTIND) (Downs 2008: 43). The NEA also assumed the daily running of the National Energy Commission (NEC), which was established in January 2010 as the highest decision-making body for energy policy. The NEC, headed by Premier Wen Jiabao, supervised overall energy security and development affairs through the setting of strategic direction and policy coordination. The administrative reform certainly broadened the NEA's mandate from the management of energy industries, to the planning and implementation of energy policies, to international commitments of energy affairs. However, the NEA remained a vice-ministerial body without political legitimacy to coordinate diverse interests among more powerful actors, and its manpower was still inadequate for the broadened mandate. While energy policy was regarded as an increasingly important policy field, its administration was still fragmented and porous with the key energy bureau having limited authority and capabilities. Such domestic administrative conditions constrained the NEA's commitment to ASEAN+3 energy cooperation.

The third factor was relevant to the relationship with Japan. Tokyo maintained a high profile in the development of ASEAN+3 energy cooperation by coordinating the forums' operations and providing financial and intellectual resources, and this factor discouraged Beijing from exhibiting a positive posture towards the cooperation. China's commitment to regional energy affairs became more reactive as its diplomatic relations with Japan deteriorated in the second half of 2010. In September 2010, the Japanese Coastguard arrested the crew of a Chinese fishing boat on suspicion of operating in Japanese territorial waters and obstructing the public duties of coastguard personnel by deliberately hitting patrol vessels. The incident occurred in the Senkaku/Diaoyu Islands that have been a source of conflict between Japan and China over the sovereign right to the islands and surrounding waters. The Chinese government reacted to the Japanese actions decisively, summoning the Japanese ambassador five times in a week after the incident and deciding to suspend ministerial-level exchanges with Tokyo and restrictions on exports of rare-earth elements. Importantly, the Chinese government also announced the postponement of talks with Japan over a treaty concerning joint gas field development in the East China Sea.[26] The dispute over the Senkaku/Diaoyu Islands is relevant to the sovereign right, but the development of energy resources cast a long shadow over the dispute. Growing tension with Japan over the territorial dispute undoubtedly reduced China's willingness to make positive engagements in regional energy cooperation.

Unlike China, South Korea has made positive commitments to ASEAN+3 energy cooperation. South Korea as a lead country assumed the chair of the Oil Market Forum as well as the NRE and EE&C Forum, and became a sponsor for other forums' meetings. The country has positively introduced its experience and expertise in oil stockpiling and the development of NRE. More significantly, South Korea took the lead in making civilian nuclear energy and CDM new targets for ASEAN+3 energy cooperation. The Korean government formally proposed the Nuclear Human Resource Development Programme at the fifth AMEM+3 meeting in August 2008. The programme was a three-year plan (2009–11) for senior policymakers and working-level officials to transfer experience, information and knowledge regarding nuclear power development. The Korean government also proposed cooperation on CDM projects in energy in order to help ASEAN members elevate greenhouse gas reduction plans and promote sustainable development. The three-year plan (2009–11) comprised capacity-building for experts, collaborative feasibility study of priority areas of CDM projects, and workshops on CDM promotion.

South Korea's engagements in energy cooperation were unique compared with those in other policy fields. Unlike in the cases of trade and the environment, the country gave support to Japan-initiated regional initiatives and did not adhere to primarily promoting cooperation in Northeast Asia. South Korea's commitments undoubtedly sprang from its benign intention to assist ASEAN countries to develop policies for civilian nuclear energy and CDM as well as human resources in these policy areas. At the same time, the country expected that policy dialogues would lead to business opportunities in these two fields. South Korea was eager to expand overseas inroads of its commercial nuclear reactors. After the first nuclear power plant was commissioned at Kori in 1978, 20 reactor units were built at four sites – Kori, Wolsong, Ulchin, and Yonggwang – (Kim et al. 2011: 6889). As of 2007, the country was ranked sixth in the world in terms of atomic energy generation with 20 reactor units, which generated roughly 40 per cent of the country's electricity output.[27] South Korea, which could design and manufacture its own reactors, did not export a single unit, being limited to some components and consultation. Accordingly, Seoul sought to take full advantage of opportunities created under the ASEAN+3 framework to expand its opportunity to export nuclear reactors and related components to Southeast Asia. Such a hope was reasonable because Southeast Asian countries increased their interest in pursuing nuclear energy programmes.[28] ASEAN also included 'civilian nuclear energy' as the seventh pillar of cooperation in the newly formulated APAEC, 2010–15.[29] As for the CDM, South Korea did not belong to the Annex I parties of the Kyoto Protocol who were obligated to reduce greenhouse gas emissions. However, the country would certainly be forced to assume greater responsibility in the post-Kyoto Protocol since it was the ninth-largest emitter of carbon dioxide in the world in 2004–08. Accordingly, the government decided to set up a domestic market for emissions trading at the second meeting of the National Energy Committee in August 2007 (Kokusai Keizai Koryu Zaidan 2011: 42). The pursuit of the opportunity to expand the CDM business in Southeast Asia was important for promoting the new CDM policy. Given the above conditions, South Korea tried to strengthen policy dialogues with ASEAN members, aiming to reap long-term mercantilist rewards in the energy field.

An additional factor that sustained South Korea's constructive commitments had much to do with its relationship with Japan. As can be seen in the area of trade and environmental cooperation, South Korea stood in rivalry relations with Japan, which discouraged it from exhibiting positive postures towards Japan-initiated regional institutions. However, this was not the case in the energy sector, as was exemplified by Seoul's cooperative posture towards Japan's energy initiatives. When the Japanese METI organised the first LNG Producer–Consumer Conference in Tokyo in September 2012, Hong Seok-woo, Korean Minister of Knowledge Economy, contributed to its success as one of five ministers who joined the conference. Hong's participation was extraordinary because the Japanese–Korean diplomatic relationship was at a critical moment after Korean President Lee Myung-bak's unprecedented visit to the Dokdo/Takeshima Islands in August 2012.

South Korea's cooperative relationship with Japan in the energy sector derived from substantial common interests. Indeed, the two countries stood in rivalry relations in international nuclear power business. For instance, consortiums involving the two countries fought over gaining a contract to build civilian nuclear power plants in the United Arab Emirates in 2009. At the same time, both countries shared similar vulnerabilities in terms of scarce domestic energy resources and high dependence on oil imported from the Middle East, as well as similar energy structures such as primary energy supply and electricity generation (Bustelo 2008). These similarities allowed the two governments to identify shared interests in major agendas for energy policy. South Korea and Japan have also shared a common position in international energy institutions such as the IEA and IEF as the two oil-consuming countries in East Asia. These elements facilitated Seoul and Tokyo to find consensus on the agendas and methods of regional cooperation.

As in other policy areas, ASEAN has striven to maintain its central position in the development of regional energy cooperation. When the EAS energy ministers' meeting was launched, an idea to integrate the AMEM+3 into this broader framework was proposed. ASEAN objected to this idea, fearing that its presence would decline in the EAS framework with a larger membership including India.[30] While Japan and South Korea have provided financial and technological contributions for ASEAN+3 energy cooperation, ASEAN has maintained a grip on its 'conference diplomacy' by organising relevant meetings in Southeast Asia. Among 11 annual meetings of the SOME+3 EPGG in 2003–12, all meetings except for the ninth in Tokyo in 2010 were held in cities among ASEAN members.

ASEAN has sought to entangle the +3 countries in its own energy strategy. Coal has been a core area of ASEAN's energy cooperation, being made one of the seven cooperative areas in the APAEC. ASEAN has urged Northeast Asia's positive engagements in the transfer of clean coal technologies and assistance in environmental planning and assessment of coal projects. For this objective, ASEAN has continuously encouraged the +3 members to participate in the meetings of the AFOC, an institutional body to formulate and advance ASEAN's coal-related strategies. ASEAN also aimed to link energy cooperation in East Asia to the ASEAN Connectivity programme.[31] The physical connectivity, one of three pillars of the programme, envisioned the formation of a regional energy security framework through the ASEAN Power Grid, the Trans-ASEAN Gas Pipeline Project, and so on (ASEAN 2011). The joint statement of the eighth AMEM+3 meeting in September 2011 contained the phrase that 'enhancing intra-ASEAN connectivity will bring the region closer to its goal of achieving greater energy security'.

The four parties engaged in ASEAN+3 energy cooperation with due attention to maintaining individual self-interest. ASEAN members sought to integrate ASEAN+3 cooperation into its own energy strategy, aiming to draw financial and technological support from the +3 countries. While the nesting institutional framework weakened Japan's engagement in ASEAN+3 cooperation, it still found crucial value in practical cooperation for its own energy security and a leadership role. For South Korea, the ASEAN+3 framework was a useful platform to exhibit its cooperative postures and pursue mercantilist benefits. Despite divergent motivations, the three parties shared an interest in promoting ASEAN+3 energy cooperation. The crucial factor that disturbed the deepening of energy cooperation was China's passive posture. China, which pursued a global energy strategy, did not find sufficient value in promoting ASEAN+3 energy cooperation, in which Japan played a key role.

The 2008 energy crisis and its influence

The price of crude oil showed an upward trend after 2004, largely because of the outlook for growing demand in the newly emerging economies. After the revelation of the subprime loan problem in the United States in the second half of 2007, funds shifted from the sluggish stock market to the crude oil market. As a consequence, the crude oil price went above US$80 per barrel in September 2007, US$100 in January 2008, and reached a historical peak of US$147 in July 2008. Afterwards, crude oil prices began to drop, since the demand for oil declined as the real economy slowed down due to the deepening of the global financial crisis. The price dropped to US$60 in October 2008 and reached US$39 in February 2009.

The sharp rise in oil prices had significant effects on the economy and society in East Asia. In particular, the high oil price imposed significant burdens on the national budgets for major Southeast Asian countries where domestic energy prices were set below market rates, and the governments provided massive energy subsidies for fuel and electricity (Mendoza 2012: 59–70).

In Malaysia, for instance, the total amount of government subsidies to oil products increased from 4.79 billion ringgit (US$1.31 billion) in 2006 to 12.2 billion ringgit (US$3.55 billion) in 2007 (METI 2009: 33). In 2008 government policies to increase fuel prices invited large-scale demonstrations in Malaysia and Indonesia. In the same year, labourers and labour unions went out on strike, demanding that the governments adopt effective measures to respond to large hikes in fuel prices in Vietnam and South Korea. The price mechanism did not work in the energy sector in many developing countries in East Asia where energy prices were under strong government regulation. However, the rise in oil prices placed enormous financial burdens on governments and provoked serious unrest in societies. These effects should have encouraged the governments to promote EE&C as well as the development of NRE.

The oil price hike in 2008 was recognised as an alarming matter for policymakers in East Asia. The joint statement at the fifth AMEM+3 meeting in August 2008 referred to 'serious concerns about the unprecedented current high oil prices which pose a downward risk to global economy and are against the interest of both consuming and producing countries'.[32] Naturally, the high oil price became a critical agenda item at the Oil Market Forum. At its sixth meeting in November 2008, Paul Stevens of Chatham House, one of the most renounced specialists on the international oil market, gave a presentation on the current volatility and future prospects of oil prices, and major oil-producing ASEAN members introduced the current states and future prospects of oil and gas production. On the basis of these presentations, participants discussed the development of institutional and investment environments designed to strengthen supply capabilities of oil and gas in the ASEAN+3 region.

After 2009, energy ministers remained concerned about the highly volatile oil price, but their anxiety about the high oil price itself decreased, stressing the need to promote greater stability in the international oil market through greater market transparency. Indeed, the rise of oil prices was a long trend from 2004, but a sharp rise occurred in a rather short time-span between autumn 2007 and summer 2008. Accordingly, there was not sufficient time for policymakers to recognise the genuine need for deepening regional attempts for energy cooperation as a means to complement national efforts. Moreover, the drop in crude oil prices had a negative influence on investment in new energy, energy conservation, and nuclear energy. During the price-hike period, the governments and companies had strong incentives to develop alternative energy sources and energy saving. In the renewable energy sector, for instance, new investment increased by 4.2 times from US$35 billion in 2004 to US$148 billion in 2007. However it began to decline in 2008: investment in the second half of the year was down 17 per cent on the first half, and down 23 per cent on the second half of the previous year (Fritz-Morgenthal et al. 2009: 8). Furthermore, emissions trading prices declined due to economic slowdown, which reduced economic incentives to explore new energy, energy conservation, and nuclear energy.

In brief, the oil price hike in the first half of 2008 created an urgent moment, but ended in a short time. Consequently, it did not become a catalyst in elevating the level of regional cooperation in East Asia and creating a new institutional trajectory for deepening energy cooperation. The global financial crisis, which brought about a sharp drop in crude oil prices, had reverse effects on regional energy cooperation. The crisis undermined policymakers' willingness to promote energy cooperation in general and reduced incentives to develop alternative energy sources in particular.

The involvement of research institutes

As already explained, the IEEJ was the key research institute that was involved in the initiation of ASEAN+3 energy cooperation. After the start of regional energy cooperation, the IEEJ sustained its development by providing intellectual input on the basis of intensive research activities. The institute prepared a presentation for the ASEAN+3 Energy Outlook describing the current state and outlook of the oil market in Asia and the world. The IEEJ also conducted capacity-building programmes in energy statistics and civilian nuclear energy. After the Fukushima nuclear power plant accident in March 2011, the IEEJ reported on knowledge and lessons from the accident and Japan's nuclear power policy.[33] Another research institute that has engaged in ASEAN+3 energy cooperation is the Korea Energy Economics Institute (KEEI). The KEEI has delivered outcomes of its research activities to the ASEAN+3 meetings. For instance, the institute introduced the current status and future prospects of the Asian gas market at the Natural Gas Forum and the SOME+3 EPGG.

The professional knowledge and expertise of the IEEJ and KEEI have contributed to showing the current status, development, and challenges of major policy areas in the energy sector. Their research outcomes helped policymakers to deepen their perception of challenges that the region is facing and provide guidance to overcome such challenges. At the same time, their research activities had inherent limitations. A critical feature in the institutes' engagement was that they had committed to ASEAN+3 cooperation primarily as administrative arms of the governments. For instance, the researchers of the KEEI, in parallel with officials of the Korean Ministry of Knowledge Economy, joined the forums' meetings and made presentation on the Korean energy strategies. The institutes implemented cooperative policies and presented energy strategies according to the governments' guidance in order to increase their interests. The institutes to a large extent became internal players with limited ability to present objective, third-party interpretations of energy affairs from the outside as autonomous non-state actors.

A critical role played by research institutes in promoting regional cooperation is the formation of transboundary networks among research institutes or individual researchers in multiple countries. The IEEJ and KEEI have not played this role sufficiently and have developed collaborative projects only with Chinese organisations. For instance, the 'Northeast Asia Petroleum Forum' has been held in rotation in China, Japan and South Korea since 2003 under the auspices of the IEEJ, KEEI, and the Petroleum Economics Commission of the Chinese Petroleum Society (Kanekiyo and Kobayashi 2013: 78). In April 2007, the IEEJ and the Energy Research Institute of the NDRC exchanged a memorandum of understanding regarding joint research on energy conservation policy. The two institutes undertook three-year research on the Energy Conservation Law and relevant legal systems as well as a bench-mark analysis of high energy consumption industries in China (Yoshimatsu 2012b). Despite such attempts to promote trilateral or bilateral cooperation, research linkages did not develop into systematic transboundary networks in the broader East Asian framework. In Southeast Asia, there are several energy-related research institutes such as the Foundation of Indonesian Institute for Energy Economics and the Institute of Energy in Vietnam. However, direct linkages with these institutes for energy cooperation in East Asia have not developed.

Another initiative from experts in regional energy affairs was provided by the NEAT. The NEAT Working Group on Energy Security Cooperation in East Asia was organised in 2004 and undertook research operations in 2005–07. At the first meeting in May 2005, the working group members deliberated on the energy outlook, energy maritime security cooperation, the harmonisation of oil diplomacy, and so on. The second working group, meeting in June 2006, focused on energy efficiency and energy conservation, followed by a third meeting in April 2007 where participants discussed energy diversification in terms of the energy mix and sources of energy supply. The reports of the working group meetings were presented at the annual NEAT conferences, and became a part of the NEAT recommendations for ASEAN+3 leaders. The recommendations contained the facilitation of the sharing of information, technology, and know-how on the use of both fossil and non-fossil fuels, the exploration of renewable sources of energy, and removal impediments to cross-border investments for energy diversification projects.

The activities of the working group were undertaken relatively effectively largely because they were well coordinated by the East Asian Institute of the National University of Singapore, the country coordinator for NEAT Singapore. Several research papers presented at the working group's meetings in 2005 and 2006 were published in an academic monograph with the title 'Asian Energy Security: The Maritime Dimension' (Lai ed. 2009). Moreover, the working group's recommendations were delivered to the policymaking process and had an influence on regional cooperation.

Many of the recommendations were incorporated into the Second Joint Statement on East Asian Cooperation in November 2007, and particularly into the attached Work Plan, which proposed 11 concrete actions to pursue energy security, sustainable development, and economic growth (Lye 2013: 121–24). The recommendations undoubtedly contributed to indicating desirable directions of regional energy cooperation to political leaders.

At the same time, the working group's activities have at least two limitations that result from weak institutional linkages between the track I and track II processes. First, the activities of the working group (track II) were not closely linked to ongoing practical operations undertaken under the SOME+3 EPGG, the main body of ASEAN+3 energy cooperation (track I). Accordingly, the working group's recommendations did not necessarily reflect the priorities of intergovernmental energy cooperation and practical challenges faced by policymakers in advancing concrete cooperative projects. Second, linkages between track I and track II tend to be one-way, not two-way communications. It would be extremely useful for the track I bodies to provide feedback to the working group's recommendations and continue mutual dialogues for developing better policies (Lye 2013: 123–24). In reality, however, the working group's operation ended after the submission of the recommendations, not forging substantial linkages for continuous communications.

Conclusion

In 2003, the SOME+3 EPGG was formed as a mechanism for promoting regional energy cooperation, and began dialogues on cooperation in the fields of oil stockpiling, natural gas development, NRE, and so on. While senior officials' meetings and field-specific forum meetings have been organised quite a few times, collective institutions with policy coordination going beyond information exchange and capacity-building programmes have not been produced from such meetings. The OSRM in oil stockpiling was an exception, but not all members committed to it.

The ASEAN+3 energy cooperation has developed through complicated interactions among China, Japan, South Korea, and ASEAN. Japan took the lead in fostering the cooperative move with motivations to enhance its own energy security and exhibit leadership in providing regional public goods. South Korea has been actively involved in the development of cooperation by providing capacity-building programmes in civilian nuclear energy and CDM. The development of NRE and oil stockpiling requires advanced technologies, experience, and know-how. While ASEAN had common interests in obtaining such expertise from the +3 members with the maintenance of its central position in the ASEAN+3 cooperation, its members could not form a common front on the development of the oil-stockpiling programme.

China has maintained a passive posture, which was displayed in its occasional absence from meetings and unwillingness to reveal information about its energy policies. Not only did China identify the energy policy as a vital strategic issue to be pursued through bilateral, not multilateral, engagements but it was also reluctant to sustain Japan's prominence in advancing regional energy collaboration.

Contrasting engagements in regional energy cooperation between Japan and China derived partly from domestic political conditions. The Japanese METI was able to establish integrated systems for promoting regional cooperation by taking advantage of systematic linkages with its affiliated organisations such as the IEEJ and JOGMEC. In contrast, the Chinese energy administration has remained fragmented and functionally weak even after administrative reforms in 2003 and 2008. The function of the Energy Bureau has been constrained by other government agencies and energy companies, and CCP leaders were unsuccessful in producing an integrated administrative system for energy policy.

The fluctuation in international oil prices after the late 1990s and a likely US attack on Iraq provoked great concerns about energy security among policymakers in East Asia. In such a move, the IEF Osaka meeting in 2002 became a valuable opportunity to put energy ministers from ASEAN+3 members together and identify concrete fields for energy cooperation. This event became a critical catalyst in creating a new path on regional energy cooperation under the ASEAN+3 framework. The international oil prices entered into an upward trend in 2004, reaching a peak in July 2008. However, the prices dropped sharply afterwards. Such volatility in oil prices alarmed policymakers in East Asia on energy security for a short period, but did not function as an incentive to elevate the building of energy institutions to a new level. The institutional inertia remained almost unchanged.

Research institutes certainly mattered in regional energy cooperation. The IEEJ, Japan's representative research institute in the energy sector, provided the foundation for ASEAN+3 energy cooperation by offering scientific data and professional insights to underscore the importance of collective action to enhance energy security. After the start of regional energy cooperation, the KEEI in parallel to the IEEJ were involved in the cooperative process. However, their roles involved undertaking administrative tasks commissioned by the governments, not elevating regional cooperation to a higher level by way of input of intellectual resources. Moreover, their commitments did not lead to the formation of transboundary networks involving research institutes in other countries.

7

Environmental Cooperation: The Monitoring of Transboundary Air Pollution

In East Asia steady economic growth has contributed to the overall development of the society and the improvement of people's lives. However, rapid industrialisation has been accompanied by various environmental problems from water pollution to greenhouse gas emissions. The excess atmospheric deposition of acidic substances is one such environmental problem. Emissions of air pollutants such as sulphur dioxide (SO_2) and nitrogen oxides (NOx) have increased due to the growing consumption of fossil fuels for electric power utilities, industrial activities and transport, and caused various adverse effects on the environment such as damage to forests and agricultural crops, as well as human health problems. Importantly, atmospheric deposition is transboundary in nature, flowing from one country to its neighbouring countries. This makes the resolution of atmospheric pollution problems complicated, requiring scientific knowledge to elucidate mechanisms for pollution migration and political bargaining among governments trying to agree on collective action.

In the early 1990s moves to protect regional environments and achieve sustainable development gained momentum in both Northeast Asia and Southeast Asia. The multilateral institutions to deal with transboundary atmospheric issues were established in such a move. Particularly important in this respect was the launching of the Acid Deposition Monitoring Network in East Asia (EANET). The network, which was formed following a model from Europe, began its regular-phase activities in 2001 with institutional bodies including a secretariat and a network centre. EANET has conducted the monitoring of acid deposition in 13 participating countries by employing standardised methods.[1] The members attempted to strengthen the financial basis and expand the operational scope, and such an attempt was carried out in political interactions among participating countries.

This chapter traces the development of EANET from policy talks before its formal launching to the adoption of an instrument to consolidate its foundation. It analyses political interactions among member countries and motivations underpinning their policy behaviour. This chapter also explores the likely influence that international and regional moves on air pollution had on the development of EANET, and the contributions made to its development by involving scientists' knowledge and expertise.

The formation of EANET

The process towards the formation of EANET

As East Asia as a region achieved rapid industrialisation, an increasing risk regarding the excess atmospheric deposition of acidic substances was recognised among scientists, government officials, and researchers. In order to take concrete actions to meet such a risk, the first expert meeting took place in October 1993 in Japan to discuss transboundary air pollution problems, and three subsequent expert meetings were organised between 1995 and 1997. The meetings were organised by scientists and government officials from ten countries in East Asia – Japan, China, South Korea, Mongolia, Russia, Indonesia, Malaysia, the Philippines, Thailand, and Singapore (later changed to Vietnam) – together with representatives from relevant international organisations such as the United Nations Environmental Programme (UNEP), the European Monitoring and Evaluation Programme (EMEP), and the US National Acid Precipitation Assessment Programme. The participants discussed the state of acid deposition, effects on ecosystems, and future steps towards regional cooperation, and reached an agreement on the necessity of establishing a regional monitoring network with standardised monitoring methods and analytical techniques. At the fourth expert meeting in 1997, the participants finalised three technical manuals, one set of guidelines for monitoring acid deposition, and the 'Design of the Acid Deposition Monitoring Network in East Asia (EANET)', which addressed activities and institutional arrangements of the network (Takahashi 2002: 235).

On the basis of shared recognition formed through the four expert meetings, the first intergovernmental (IG) meeting of EANET was organised in March 1998 in Japan. The participating government officials discussed the Tentative Design of EANET and agreed to start the preparatory phase activities of EANET from the following month to 2000.[2] During this phase, each participating country prepared for the implementation of acid deposition monitoring in its local areas in order to assess the state of acid deposition and its ecological impact (Wangwongwatana 2001: 155).

At the second IG meeting in October 2000, participants issued the Joint Announcement on the Implementation of EANET and the Tentative Design of EANET. The announcement contained three objectives of EANET: to create a common understanding of the state of acid deposition problems in East Asia; to provide useful inputs for decision-making at the local, national, and regional levels; and to contribute to cooperation on issues pertinent to acid deposition among the participating countries. It also evaluated the preparatory phase as having ended successfully, and decided to begin the regular-phase activities of EANET from 2001. The two pillars of the activities were to implement the monitoring of wet and dry depositions and their impacts on soil, vegetation, and inland aquatic environments by using common methodologies, and to promote quality assurance and quality control (QA/QC) activities for gaining high quality monitoring data.

At the third IG meeting in November 2001, participants adopted the Rules of Procedure for EANET, which addressed rules for admission and withdrawal, sessions of the IG meeting, and relevant bodies. Moreover, the first meeting of the Scientific Advisory Committee (SAC) was organised in the same month. By that time, the network's institutional framework was established with four main bodies: the IG meeting as the decision-making body, the SAC, the secretariat, and the network centre that provides member governments with scientific and technical support (Figure 7.1). The UNEP Regional Resource Centre for Asia and the Pacific (UNEP RRC.AP) in Bangkok, Thailand was chosen as the secretariat. The Acid Deposition and Oxidant Research Centre (ADORC, currently the Asia Centre for Air Pollution Research, ACAP) located in Niigata, Japan, was designated as the network centre.[3] Furthermore, three subsidiary bodies were established under the SAC: the Task Force on Monitoring for Dry Deposition, the Task Force

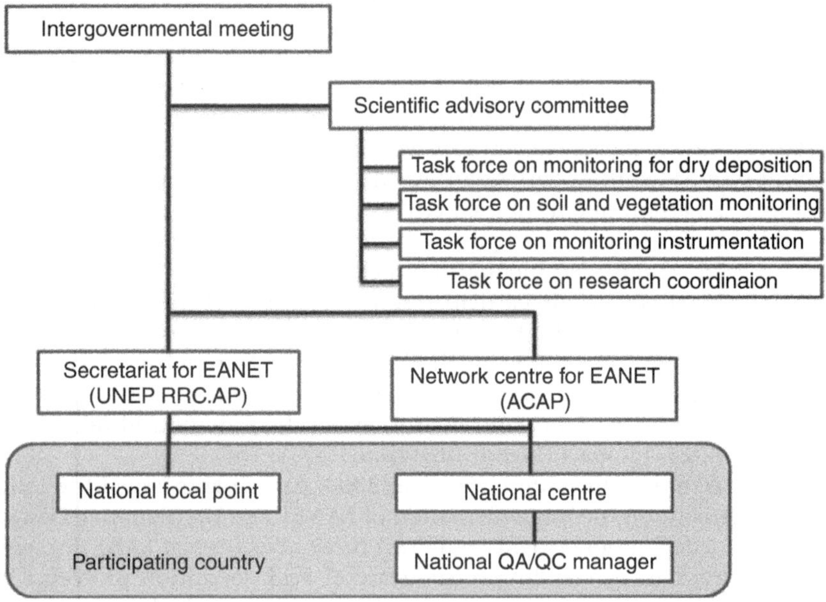

Figure 7.1 Organisational structure of EANET
Source: Created by the author with data from the EANET home page.

on Soil and Vegetation Monitoring, and the Network of Soil and Vegetation Specialists. It was also agreed that national QA/QC managers from participating countries should meet to discuss important technical issues related to the network and exchange information about their monitoring activities.

EANET has several distinctive features in its composition and operations. First, it developed as a comprehensive East Asia-based institution to deal with environmental issues in the region. Indeed, there were several multilateral institutions to tackle transboundary air pollution problems in Northeast Asia, and ASEAN pushed forward environmental cooperation by organising the ASEAN Ministerial Meeting on Environment (AMME). However, there were few environment-related institutions that covered the whole of East Asia.[4] EANET is substantially the sole institution that covers almost all countries in East Asia (except for Singapore, Brunei, and North Korea) and undertakes concrete joint activities to tackle acid deposition problems.

Second, EANET adopted a form of soft institution. A major concern about EANET participation for developing countries was that EANET might become a strict regime and impose legal obligations on members. In order to remove such concerns, EANET adopted a form of soft institution that stressed the consultation process, consensus-based decision-making, and agreements without legal obligations. Moreover, EANET formally adopted the step-by-step approach in pursuing its development (Akimoto 2000: 46; Wangwongwatana 2001). In reality, EANET developed from the unofficial expert-meeting phase in 1993–97, when experts from participating countries discussed technical matters regarding monitoring, to the IG meeting phase after 1998, when government representatives discussed concrete activities and management. The IG meeting phase shifted from the preparatory phase in 1998–2000 to the regular phase after 2001. The soft institution and gradualism derived from the Asian style of institution-building, which is typically seen in the 'ASEAN Way'.

The 1992 UNCED and its influence

The launching of EANET had much to do with international moves towards the protection of the global environment. In June 1992, the United Nations Conference on Environment and Development (UNCED) was held in Rio de Janeiro.[5] The conference adopted an action plan called Agenda 21, which recommended, in the chapter on protection of the atmosphere, that the European experience of controlling long-range transboundary air pollution needed to be shared with other regions of the world.[6] In Europe, the EMEP was launched in 1977 in order to gather data on acid deposition, and the Convention on Long-range Transboundary Air Pollution (LRTAP) was signed two years later among nations in Europe and North America. The LRTAP was regarded as one of the most successful regimes for regional environmental cooperation.

The UNCED stirred moves to advance environmental protection in Northeast Asia. In Japan, the government enacted the Basic Environmental Law, which aimed to cope with a wide range of environmental problems and implement the outcomes of the UNCED. It also set up the National Action Plan for Agenda 21 in December 1993. Before the UNCED, South Korea stressed developed countries' historical responsibility for current environmental problems, seeking to exempt itself from the responsibility. However, the Korean government became aware of political realities associated with the international community's growing concern about environmental problems, and sought to play a mediator role by calling for practical and realistic compromises between the developed and developing groups (Yoon 2006: 78).

The evolved perception of environmental problems through the UNCED led to the launching of new multilateral institutions for environmental protection in 1992 and 1993. In October 1992, the first meeting of the Northeast Asian Conference on Environmental Cooperation (NEAC) was held in Niigata, Japan. The NEAC, which was formed among China, Japan, South Korea, Mongolia, and Russia, aimed to provide opportunities for information exchanges and policy dialogues among environmental experts from national government agencies, local governments, research institutes, and non-governmental organisations (NGOs). The acid rain problem became a major concern for the NEAC, and participants referred to the implementation of joint research and monitoring on acid rain at its first meeting. In August 1992, as a follow-up event to the UNCED, South Korea hosted the Seoul Symposium on UNCED and Prospects for the Environmental Regime in the 21st Century. The participants adopted a declaration calling for environmental cooperation in Northeast Asia (Yoon 2006: 81–82). In an effort to realise the declaration, the first meeting of the North-East Asian Subregional Programme of Environmental Cooperation (NEASPEC) was organised in Seoul in February 1993. The meeting was attended by six countries – South Korea, China, Japan, North Korea, Mongolia, and Russia –, and senior official meetings have, since then, been held every one or two years in order to implement activities regarding energy and air pollution, ecosystem management, and capacity-building (Takahashi 2002: 225).

The UNCED influenced environmental cooperation in Southeast Asia. Before the UNCED was held, ASEAN environmental ministers adopted the Singapore Resolution on Environment and Development at the fifth AMME meeting in February 1992. The resolution confirmed ASEAN's common stance on global environmental and developmental issues that would be addressed at the UNCED. In April 1994, the environmental ministers adopted the ASEAN Strategic Plan of Action on the Environment, and the first of its five objectives was 'to respond to specific recommendations of Agenda 21 requiring priority action in ASEAN'.[7] In the process of intensifying regional environmental cooperation, major countries in Southeast Asia fostered the recognition that measures to tackle transboundary atmospheric pollution problems should be implemented in Asia, following experiences in Europe (Hara 2009: 8).

In trends towards the formation of region-based environmental institutions in response to the UNCED, the Japanese Agency of the Environment (currently Ministry of the Environment, MOE) decided to launch a new institution to tackle transboundary air pollution problems in East Asia. The Agenda 21 suggested strengthening the capabilities of developing countries, to measure, model, and assess the fate and impacts of transboundary air pollution through exchange of information and training of experts.[8] The agency responded to this suggestion by organising a series of expert meetings in East Asia. The Japanese government proclaimed the EANET project in comprehensive UN-related initiatives. At the UN General Assembly Special Session for the overall review and appraisal of the implementation of Agenda 21 in June 1997, Prime Minister Ryutaro Hashimoto proposed establishing the EANET to assist the enhancement of monitoring capacity of relevant countries, the establishment of an information network on air pollution, and the transfer of environmental technologies.[9] The establishment of EANET was the first of four action programmes in the Initiatives for Sustainable Development that Japan launched in order to cooperate with the UN commitment to the preservation of the global environment.

In the 1980s the conservation of the global environment had gradually emerged as an important agenda item for the international community. However, multilateral institutions in addressing transboundary air pollution problems were not created in East Asia. The UNCED and Agenda 21 opened a window of opportunity for changing such a situation. While the UNCED generated a demand for establishing new institutional arrangements, Agenda 21 accentuated the European experience as a model for tackling transboundary air pollution. New enduring trajectories towards regional environmental cooperation were set out, and EANET was produced in such a developmental trajectory.

The parties' complicated stances

The UNCED surely provided an opportunity to move from an old path, where there was no institution to tackle acid deposition problems in East Asia, to a new path, where EANET exists as an institution for this objective. However, the initiation of EANET was accompanied by complicated interactions among participating countries with specific interests.

While East Asia as a whole exhibited steady increases in acid spills, China was deemed to make particular contributions to growth of SO_2 and NOx with its rapid industrialisation. Given China's dominant position in the emissions of air pollutants, its positive commitment was indispensable for the successful launching of EANET. However, China exhibited unstable and lukewarm attitudes towards EANET. China joined four sessions of expert meetings in

1993–97, but did not necessarily show a positive posture towards the resolution of acid deposition problems. The Design of the EANET, which was formulated at the fourth expert meeting, begins with the phrase 'acid rain is broadly recognised as one of the most serious air environmental problems and is collecting global-scale interests'. The original draft of this part was 'acid rain is one of the most serious global environmental problems'. The expression was changed to reflect China's assertion that 'acid rain is a domestic environmental problem, not a global environmental one' (Akimoto 2000: 45). Moreover, the Chinese delegate asserted at the fourth expert meeting that the monitoring should be carried out using a method that each country had adopted.[10] This assertion contradicted EANET's objective to establish a network with the standardised monitoring method.

The Chinese delegate announced that China could not participate in the EANET preparatory phase because it was in the process of drastic administrative reform and was not ready to prepare for the membership (Takahashi 2000: 112). After the start of the preparatory phase, China participated in the first IG meeting in March 1998 as an observer, not a full member. The issue of China's participation was later settled by political decision. When Jiang Zemin, president of China, made a formal visit to Tokyo in November 1998, he stressed the need to enhance bilateral environmental cooperation. Both governments issued a joint communiqué on environmental cooperation for the 21st century, which contained a phrase implying that both countries would jointly promote the establishment of EANET. Afterwards, China joined EANET as a full member.

China's cautious attitudes towards EANET sprang from two factors. First, the Chinese government tried to avoid a situation where China was regarded as a source country of acid rain that had transboundary effects. The government's formal stance was that air pollution and acid deposition were domestic issues. Indeed, the government recognised that local air pollution, including environmental degradation attributable to acid deposition, was getting worse, and that monitoring and relevant scientific activities were important for resolving domestic air pollution problems. However, it did not wish to be seen by other countries as a pollutant source that threatened environmental conditions in territories outside China (Takahashi 2000: 112). Second, the Chinese government paid attention to relative costs and benefits that participation in EANET would bring about. Participation in the network was expected to bring financial and technical assistance to tackle domestic acid rain problems. However, China was worried about financial burdens accompanying participation in EANET. If the EANET participation had invited a requirement to establish more monitoring spots to collect sufficient data, the Chinese government would have been forced to spend large funds on meeting such a requirement (Hara 2009: 8–9).

South Korea should have become the main supporter of EANET. Not only did the country, the sole developed country among EANET members except for Japan, have capabilities to make scientific evaluations of transboundary acid deposition, but it also stood in the same position as Japan in facing a risk of acid deposition originating in other countries, most notably China. However, South Korea was the main participant that put the brake on the EANET initiative. The country posed a question about a procedure to launch EANET, arguing that since the expert meetings were informal and unofficial gatherings made through non-diplomatic channels, decisions made at the meetings had no legal basis, and consequently, the results of the meetings could not be regarded as official conclusions (Takahashi 2000: 112).

South Korea's reluctance to advance the EANET initiative had much to do with rivalry sentiment against Japan. Seoul had a strong concern that the EANET initiative was advanced and controlled by Tokyo alone. This was because Japan dominated the initiation process by hosting all expert meetings, financing activities, and drafting the design of the network. In particular, Seoul believed that the functions of the network centre, which were totally assumed by Japan alone, should be divided among several subcentres following an example of the EMEP.[11] For instance, Japan should measure acid substances and operate as a comprehensive chemical analysis centre; South Korea should function as a centre for research on long distance transboundary air pollution; and China should install and operate an emission analysis centre (KEI 2005: xi). Accordingly, South Korea attempted to establish an additional network centre on its territory. But the attempt was unsuccessful, largely because Seoul did not have enough financial and technical capabilities to sustain a network (Brettell 2007: 97).

South Korea had a practical reason to be passive about the EANET initiative. The country took the lead in launching a transboundary air pollution programme in Northeast Asia – the Joint Research Project on Long-range Transboundary Air Pollutants in Northeast Asia (LTP) – which aimed to promote joint research and modelling to figure out source–receptor relationships regarding SO_2, NOx, ozone, and particulate matter (PM). The Korean National Institute of Environmental Research has, since 1995, hosted expert meetings on the LTP with experts and policymakers from South Korea, China, and Japan. EANET and LTP had complementary characters in that the former highlights measuring pollution of the broad region for long-term purposes, while the latter puts emphasis on modelling in a narrow area for short-term objectives (Kim 2007: 456). However, South Korea was apprehensive that the LTP would be merged with a part of EANET as the latter's geographical scope was larger.

Japan was the initiator of EANET. The four sessions of expert meetings in 1993–97 were crucial for providing common technical manuals and guidelines for monitoring acid deposition as well as designs of EANET. The meetings were organised under leadership by Japan that prepared for a blueprint for concrete cooperation and contributed all operational costs. After the launching of EANET, the Japanese government continuously provided financial and technical support. While the ACAP sent its experts to research centres in participating countries to help enhance technical levels and human resource capabilities, the Japan International Cooperation Agency (JICA) provided officials from participating countries with technical training and expertise in collaboration with sub-national governments such as Niigata, Hyogo, and Fukuoka, which retained genuine expertise in and experience of acid deposition monitoring (Miyazaki 2007: 28).

Japan's initiative in launching EANET derived from two interests. The first is its willingness to resolve acid rain problems of a transboundary nature. In Japan, acid deposition began to emerge as a serious environmental problem after the early 1990s. Although it was broadly recognised that substances causing acid deposition in Japan flew from China through circumpolar westerlies, scientific analyses indicated diverse results of the extent to which China contributed to acid deposition in Japan (Okimura 2012: 54). It was necessary to establish an objective scientific consensus involving neighbouring countries, especially China. The second is relevant to the leadership role. Japan had suffered from serious pollution problems in its industrialisation process and accumulated technologies, expertise, and experiences for resolving such problems. The Japanese government sought to take advantage of such accumulated assets for its leadership role in East Asia. Prime Minister Hashimoto, in his statement on the EANET establishment at the UN General Assembly Special Session in June 1997, referred to Japan's special position: 'There is perhaps no other country that can share both the suffering of a developing country and the concerns of a developed country to the extent that Japan can. This is why Japan makes it a national policy to cooperate in the promotion of sustainable development.'[12] Japan hoped to show leadership in mitigating air and water pollution to resolve environmental problems in developing countries, and the EANET initiative was produced from such a hope.

In addition to the above externally oriented factors, domestic political conditions had much to do with Japan's EANET initiative. The transboundary acid deposition was one of the newly emerging issues which tended to be a target of bureaucratic competition on jurisdiction, and two agencies proposed concrete programmes to deal with the issue. One was the Green Aid Plan that the Ministry of Economy, Trade and Industry (METI) launched in 1991 as a programme that would handle foreign policy for acid deposition.[13] Despite METI's earnest commitment, the plan did not make significant progress in China and other countries, largely because of the high costs of Japan's advanced technology and the lack of technical capacity for operation and maintenance (Wilkening 2004: 219). The other was the regional monitoring network programme pushed forward by MOE. The ministry had a long history of scientific momentum on the acid deposition issue. While the agency had been involved in acid deposition research since the Moist Air Pollution Investigation in 1974, it had been running an air pollution monitoring network since 1971 and a precipitation chemistry network since 1983 (Wilkening 2004: 200). The ministry successfully separated the issue from global warming, which was under the jurisdiction of METI, and formed alliances with the Ministries of Agriculture and of Health and Welfare (Matsumoto 2010: 59). Eventually, MOE's monitoring network programme became Japan's sole force in acid deposition diplomacy, which gave more leeway to MOE to advance flexible and decisive policies avoiding intervention from other government agencies.

Major concerns for Japan in launching the regional monitory network programme were reactions from China and South Korea. As already explained, China and South Korea adopted cautious postures towards the EANET initiative, and Japan adopted measures to mitigate such caution. In order to enhance monitoring capabilities in China, the Japanese government expanded bilateral cooperation for monitoring, targeting Jilin Province, Anhui Province, Tianjin, Chongqing, and Guiyang (Miyazaki 2007: 29). In order to remove South Korea's concern about the LTP, the government had a consultation with its Korean counterpart. Before the second IG meeting in 2000, the government sent a special mission to South Korea to forge a shared understanding that EANET and LTP would coexist by stressing the different roles played by the two institutions (Miyazaki 2007: 29).

In launching EANET, an important matter was the scope of membership. Japan hoped to expand the membership of EANET to the whole of East Asia including Southeast Asia. Since acid deposition was a concern for Northeast Asian countries, it was originally argued that membership of EANET should be limited to the countries of Northeast Asia, considering geographical and meteorological conditions (Miyazaki no year: 12). However, the inclusion of Southeast Asian countries was expected to mitigate the potential tensions, created by long-lasting political sensitivity, which existed between Japan on the one hand and China and South Korea on the other. More specifically, the broader membership was desirable to avoid likely bilateral tensions with China over the source of acid deposition and with South Korea over coordination between EANET and LTP.

As already explained, growing concerns over the global environment due to the UNCED encouraged Southeast Asian countries to make positive commitments to environmental issues. They responded positively to a request from Japan to join the expert meetings to discuss transboundary air pollution problems in East Asia. Since most Southeast Asian countries did not hold monitoring facilities and technologies to collect and evaluate data on air pollution, they expected that Japan would provide financial and technological assistance through the EANET initiative.

Southeast Asian countries had at least three concerns in joining EANET, and measures to mitigate such concerns were adopted. The first was relevant to the definition of a geographical area. At the third expert meeting in 1995, participants from Southeast Asia asserted that the expression of 'East and Southeast Asia' should be used to clarify the fact that EANET covers the geographical area of Southeast Asia. By defining 'East Asia' as a region combining 'Northeast Asia' and 'Southeast Asia', participants settled this issue (Akimoto 2000: 44–45). The second concern was a major interest in joining the network. Southeast Asian countries had an interest in acquiring a standardised method of gathering data to address urban pollution problems such as SO_2, NOx, and ozone, not transboundary acid deposition. In order to attract interest from Southeast Asian countries in EANET participation, it was proposed at the expert meetings to undertake dry deposition monitoring of SO_2, NOx, ozone, and PM, in addition to wet deposition monitoring (Akimoto 2000: 45).

Third, Southeast Asian countries had a suspicion that Japan hoped to dominate the EANET initiative in order to meet its own policy objective to tackle transboundary air pollution from China (Hara 2009: 6–7). In order to mitigate such a suspicion, Japan made efforts to phase out its dominant presence in EANET. Such efforts led to the transfer of the secretariat from the Japanese MOE to the UNEP RRC.AP in 2002. The managerial position of the secretariat was offered for public subscription with posts eventually being allocated to people from every country except Japan (Miyazaki no year: 18).[14] The transfer of the secretariat contributed to increasing the neutral nature and authority of EANET by fostering equal partnerships among participating countries, and reduced the suspicion about Japan's intention to dominate acid deposition problems in East Asia.

Japan provided material and intellectual resources that were necessary for initiating EANET. Such a dominant presence provoked relative gain concerns among other participants. They might obtain benefits from participation in EANET, but Japan's gain could be regarded as being larger than theirs as long as it dominated the management of EANET including the holding and analysis of collected data. Japan sought to resolve the relative gain concerns by enhancing equal partnerships among participants and responding to their specific concerns.

Scientific knowledge and the initiation of EANET

A critical feature in the process of the EANET initiation was that scientists were deeply involved in the process. In Japan, an idea to launch a programme for monitoring acid deposition in East Asia was fostered by scientists who were familiar with the scientific approach to regional acid deposition issues in Europe. By 1991, the scientists demonstrated that sulphate was being imported to Japan from mainland China and that SO_2 emissions in China were in worrisome future trajectories. Such demonstrations were delivered to MOE, and the idea of forming a regional monitoring network became a policy proposal to be pursued with the ministry's 1992 budget (Wilkening 2004: 210–11). The scientific knowledge provided the momentum to initiate a new institution to manage transboundary acid rain problems.

The scientists played a pivotal role in leading discussions at expert meetings that began in 1993. The expert meetings were unique in that at least one scientist and one administrative official from each country attended. The attendance of scientists helped to avoid unfruitful commitments under the limited budget by making it possible to check policies and measures from scientific standpoints. Moreover, the scientists' participation at the preparatory stage provided them with a significant responsibility for leading the institutionalisation of regional cooperation (Akimoto 2000: 44).

The major outcome of the experts' commitments was the formulation of guidelines and technical manuals, which provided the basis for a standardised method of monitoring acid deposition. The EANET Guideline was adopted at the second expert meeting, and the guideline on dry deposition monitoring was adopted at the fourth expert meeting. The three technical manuals for monitoring wet deposition, soil, and vegetation, as well as inland aquatic environments, were also adopted at this meeting. Importantly, experts had a perspective for the broader activities of EANET. The interpretation of the term 'acid precipitation' became a main agenda item at the second expert meeting, and experts reached an agreement that the term 'acid deposition', not 'acid precipitation', would be used to indicate the integrated focus on emissions, effects, and counter-measures (MOE 1997: 3–4). Moreover, the EANET Concept, which was adopted at the third expert meeting, presented valuable insights on the network's future direction. While it suggested the formulation of a guideline for an emission inventory and a need to develop statistical models to assess the impact of acid rain on the ecological system, it stressed efforts to advance surveys and research jointly implemented by actors at different levels, such as governments, universities, and private companies (MOE 1997: 70–71). Not only did scientists provide professional knowledge and insights for the design and operation of EANET, but they also exhibited the desirable direction of the EANET development from an objective and scientific standpoint. An additional role played by scientists was that they influenced concrete action by the government. As already explained, China's participation was one of the most critical issues in launching EANET. The Chinese government decided to participate in the first IG meeting at least as an observer, and this decision was influenced by a favourable assessment on the EANET programme by Chinese scientists who participated in the expert meetings (Lee 2011: 65).

However, while the scientists' group certainly established the foundation to launch EANET, it did not form a common front on causes, effects, and models of regional acid deposition. There were disagreements on the amount or origin of transboundary acid rain even within Japan, which led the launching of EANET. In 1996 a study completed by MOE found that most of the transboundary acid rain that was reaching Japan originated in South Korea. In contrast, a study by the privately owned Japanese Central Research Institute of Electric Power Industry concluded that South Korea was merely one of several sources (Brettell 2007: 96). There was discourse between individual scientists and information was presented by both groups at the same meetings and published in the same journals. However, at an institutional level, it was almost as if the other study did not exist (Wilkening 2004: 204). Differences in scientific estimation on transboundary air pollution were seen in different countries. As for calculation on Chinese-originated long-range air pollutants to Japan's overall acid deposition, Chinese and Japanese scientists presented different estimated results. While experts at the Chinese Academy of Science estimated that China accounted for only 3.5 per cent of Japan's total sulphur deposition, Japanese experts concluded that China was responsible for half of the anthropogenic wet sulphur deposition (Nam 2002: 187–88). Thus, uncertainties accompanying scientific evaluation on acid deposition constituted a critical impediment to establishing shared causal beliefs that constructed the foundation for the experts' collective identity and collective activities.

Stagnation in EANET development

Two challenges for EANET development

After the start of the regular phase in 2001, EANET produced cooperative results in several fields. The number of participants increased from 10 in 2000 to 13 by 2005, with three new members being accepted from Southeast Asia.[15] The number of monitoring sites increased from 69 (38 wet deposition and 31 dry deposition) in 2001 to 94 (52 wet deposition and 42 dry deposition) by 2008 (Toda 2000: 17; Nitta 2008). Moreover, the ecological monitoring of soil and forest vegetation was conducted in 29 sites in 21 areas and that of inland aquatic environments was done in 19 sites in 2008 (Nitta 2008). High-quality data sets were developed through the implementation of QA/QC activities at the national level and under the Inter-laboratory Comparison Project schemes. In order to develop technical capacity for developing members, various capacity-building activities were implemented, such as individual training and courses along with the dispatch of technical missions. The results of scientific activities were published in the EANET Science Bulletin and the Periodic Report on the State of Acid Deposition in East Asia.

There were two challenges that EANET had to meet to consolidate its foundation as a fully fledged institution. The first was the sharing of financial burdens among participating countries. The management and activities of EANET were financially supported by one country, Japan. In order to develop EANET as an equitable regional institution, it was necessary to establish a system to share necessary costs among participating countries. Moreover, insofar as the UNEP RRC.AP assumed the secretariat of EANET, it was desirable to show that the UN body's operation was sustained by funds shared by the broader membership, not those offered by a specific country (Kanie and Sodeno 2013: 39–40). At the fifth IG meeting in 2003, participants reached a common agreement on the financial issue to 'make effort on a voluntary basis to contribute to the budget to be directly spent by the secretariat using fully the latest UN assessment scale-based burden sharing' from the 2005 budget, and 'to review the possibility of developing an international agreement to provide a sound basis for financial contribution'.[16] Since participants stressed 'the voluntary nature' of the contribution, uneven sharing of costs continued even after 2005. Japan assumed nearly 90 per cent of costs for managing the secretariat with additional small contributions provided by China, South Korea, Malaysia, and Thailand (Table 7.1). It was agreed at the eighth IG meeting in 2006 that the core budget of the network centre would be contributed by participants on a voluntary basis from the 2008 budget (Yamashita 2009: 130). Even after this agreement, Japan contributed nearly 100 per cent of the budget since China and South Korea did not make any contributions to this budget.

The second and related challenge was the adoption of a foundation document of EANET. EANET began practical activities in 2001 and its operation was based on the Tentative Design of EANET. The network did not have a formal official document stipulating the principles, the scope of activities, and the functions of administrative organs. A foundation document that would clarify the legal status of EANET was also necessary for drawing financial contributions from participating governments. At the fifth IG meeting in 2003, participants agreed to set up the Working Group on Future Development (WGFD) of EANET to review the performance of the secretariat and network centre and develop guidelines on their administrative and financial management. At the seventh IG meeting in 2005 in Niigata, participants adopted the Niigata Decision, which decided that participating countries 'should begin a process to discuss an appropriate instrument and legal status to provide a sound basis for financial contribution to EANET'.[17] The result of discussions

Table 7.1 Members' contributions to the EANET secretariat budget (thousand $; %)

	2007		2008		2009	
Japan	300.0	87.2	367.4	89.9	382.2	90.3
South Korea	23.6	6.9	18.4	4.5	18.1	4.3
China	15.0	4.4	15.0	3.7	15.0	3.5
Thailand	2.7	0.8	3.8	0.9	3.8	0.9
Malaysia	2.6	0.8	3.8	0.9	3.8	0.9
Total	343.9	100.0	408.4	100.0	422.9	100.0

Source: Compiled by the author from budgetary data of the Japanese Ministry of the Environment.

would be reported to the tenth IG meeting in 2008. With the target year chosen, discussions on an appropriate instrument proceeded with at the WGFD and IG meetings.

Discussions on the instrument were confronted with great difficulty due to the members' diverse views on legal status, the scope of substances, and the scope of activities. The issue of legal status concerned whether the members would continue activities with a loose agreement as international networks or enhance the EANET consolidation with a formal framework agreement or a protocol. Some countries emphasised the need for a legal document in order to provide a solid foundation for strengthening the financial basis of EANET and for undertaking national activities on acid deposition smoothly. In particular, Russia, which had engaged in management of transboundary air pollution on legally binding treaties in Europe, strongly asserted that it would require a legally binding document for negotiations on financial arrangements with the legislative body.[18] These countries originally hoped to use the term 'agreement' with a stronger legal nature rather than 'instrument' for the foundation document. Others preferred a non-legally binding instrument on the grounds that it is inappropriate to adopt a legal document at a preliminary stage. As for the scope of substances, some countries gave support to a view that the scope should be expanded from 'acid deposition' to 'regional air pollution' because various polluted substances become the sources of acid rain through chemical reactions, and these substances needed to be monitored in the air in addition to deposited conditions. Others argued that since the instrument was originally designed to provide the basis for financial contribution to EANET, all discussions should be based on the present scope – acid deposition.[19] The scope of activities was another item of intense debate among the members. Some countries hoped that the instrument would have a broader scope of activities including emission inventory and simulation modelling in addition to monitoring. Others favoured a view that since many participating countries still had much room for improvement in monitoring capabilities, the scope of activities should not be extended until the network's monitoring activities improved further.[20]

At the tenth IG meeting in November 2008, the WGFD Progress Report on the Instrument to Provide a Sound Basis for Contribution to EANET was presented by the secretariat. The participants expressed diverse views and comments, failing to reach an agreement on conflicting matters. They eventually decided to task the WGFD to have further discussions on the instrument in accordance with the conclusions of the meeting. EANET members were unable to meet the original deadline due to a failure to coordinate diverse views on major agendas regarding the instrument.

The parties' complicated stances

China made complicated commitments to the development of EANET. On the one hand, the country exhibited willingness to sustain the network's activities. During the fourth IG meeting in 2002, the Chinese government proposed contributing US$15,000 voluntarily to the secretariat budget annually.[21] This amount was small compared with the UN assessment scale-based burden (US$24,560), a criterion agreed at the fifth IG meeting in 2003 (Hara 2009: 8). But this volunteer contribution had positive effects on the financial burden-sharing issue. Moreover, Dr. Jiang Wei, a Chinese expert, assumed the first headship of the secretariat. The Chinese government recommended him as the coordinator of the secretariat. On the other hand, China's engagement in the network's monitoring activities was far from positive. Despite its broad geographical area, deposition monitoring spots were located in only four cities – Xian, Chongqing, Xiamen, and Zhuhai – which were relatively affluent local cities that could conduct monitoring activities with their own capacities.[22] All of the cities are located in the southern part of China, and no monitoring sites existed in northern part. China had more monitoring spots for acid deposition. For instance, there were 34 spots where the JICA provided grant aid to install monitoring instruments.[23] The official reason for this small number of monitoring sites for EANET was that since the level of data accuracy was high in EANET monitoring, most sites in China could not meet this high level. However, it was also the Chinese government's unwillingness to undertake sufficient domestic monitoring that led to this small number of monitoring sites.

China showed a cautious posture towards the foundation document of EANET. This caution was typically exhibited in China's preferences for terminology regarding the document. At the seventh IG meeting in 2005, the Niigata Decision was adopted to begin a process to discuss an appropriate instrument and its legal status. In the Terms of Reference for WGFD presented at the sixth IG meeting in 2004, the term 'regional agreement' was used. One year later, this disappeared and a term 'appropriate instrument' with a weak legal nature was used. Moreover, 'Niigata *Mandate*' was used as the title of a document at the preparatory stage towards the seventh IG meeting. This term aimed to clarify the willingness of participants to reach a consensus within a fixed time frame. However, the title was changed to 'Niigata *Decision*' with an ambiguous and neutral meaning. These changes resulted from China's preferences for weakening the legal nature of EANET's founding document (Ando 2006: 182, 203–04). China's passive attitude continued at the following meetings. When the sixth WGFD was held in April 2008, China presented an original draft of a legally non-binding instrument that stipulated financial affairs with the existing scope of substances and activities. The Chinese government, by presenting this alternative option, demonstrated its position that it would not join discussions on other types of instrument (Kanie and Sodeno 2013: 44).

China's basic policy stances were that since EANET was established to tackle acid deposition problems, its activity should be limited to this area, and that since the formulation of the Instrument of EANET was originally intended to provide the basis for consolidating the network's finance, it was inappropriate to discuss the scope of substances and activities (Kanie and Sodeno 2013: 42, 47). There was a practical reason for China's opposition to the expansion of the network's scope. China considered it a priority matter to improve low-level monitoring capabilities under the existing framework. Certainly, given that only four cities were appointed as the EANET monitoring sites in the vast land area, the extension of activity from monitoring to emission inventory and simulation modelling was not easy.

China accepted EANET's engagement in emission inventory and simulation modelling as 'research activities'. However, it had a strong desire to limit the network's formal activity to monitoring alone. When China agreed to join EANET with its top leaders' agreement, this agreement was based on the recognition that EANET would undertake monitoring activities. It was difficult for the Chinese Ministry of Environmental Protection to accept EANET's new mandates, which might lead to the foundation of a regulatory regime. Under the highly centralised decision-making process, approval of EANET's new mandate required a decision at the vice-minister level because the Chinese government's decision to participate in the network was made at this level.[24] Moreover, the division of administrative operations made it extremely difficult for the Chinese government to accept the extension of EANET's activities. The monitoring activities were assumed by the China National Environmental Monitoring Centre (CNEMC), and emission inventory and simulation modelling would be undertaken by other administrative agencies, which would require intensive internal coordination.[25]

South Korea's position on the EANET development was complicated as well. Seoul sustained EANET activities by providing contributions to the secretariat budget. In 2007–09 it provided US$18,100–23,600, which was equivalent to 4.3–6.9 per cent of the total budget (Table 7.1). It was agreed that EANET members would contribute to the core budget of the network centre, but South Korea did not offer any contributions to the network centre budget. The Korean government considered that the ACAP lacked transparency in terms of administration and budget as a network centre of an international institution like EANET.[26] While all ACAP's senior executives except for a deputy director general were Japanese, EANET-related affairs in the centre's total budget were difficult to identify due to the integration with domestic air pollution affairs.[27]

As for the Instrument of EANET, South Korea was a major country that strongly asserted the maintenance of the existing scope, opposing the expansion of the network's scope of substances and activities. Some scholars argue that Seoul's opposition had much to do with the maintenance of the LTP (Kanie and Sodeno 2013: 48). The Korean government continuously sustained the LTP, providing huge financial contributions to the project: some US$600,000 annually between 2000 and the mid 2000s and US$1,000,000 after 2007 (Kim 2013). South Korea was apprehensive that the extension of

EANET's scope of substances and activities would broaden overlapping and duplication in objectives and activities between the LTP and EANET, and thereby undermine the LTP's existence. However, the relationships between the two institutions became more complicated. In 2009, the Korean government proposed the integration of the LTP with EANET, even accepting the LTP's position as a sub-scheme of EANET. This proposal derived from a policy change of the Korean government from confrontation to cooperation by accepting Japan's leadership on regional air pollution issues. However, Japan postponed the decision on this issue, fearing that the inclusion of the issue in negotiations on the instrument would further prolong ongoing negotiations.[28] The Korean government considered that the expansion of EANET's scope of activities would require the members to provide further financial contributions and that some members did not have enough capacity to implement the expanded activities.[29]

Southeast Asian countries were generally positive in strengthening EANET activity through the adoption of a foundation document. Some of them sought to contribute their assets, accumulated through environmental cooperation under ASEAN, to the process of deliberations on the instrument. For instance, Malaysia and Thailand proposed that the instrument should be 'simple, flexible and open for future development of EANET'. This phrase, being based on the experience of negotiations on the Agreement on Transboundary Haze Pollution, became a principle for drafting the instrument (Kanie and Sodeno 2013: 43). Notwithstanding such commitments, EANET did not necessarily attract keen interest from ASEAN's environment-related institutions. ASEAN members and three Northeast Asian countries have organised the ASEAN Plus Three (ASEAN+3) Environment Ministers Meeting since 2002. The EANET members confirmed the importance of disseminating information on EANET activities at the ASEAN+3 framework.[30] However, EANET has not been a topic at the ASEAN+3 meetings, largely because of ASEAN members' weak interest. This makes a contrast to Northeast Asian countries. China, Japan, and South Korea have referred to EANET in the joint communiqués issued at the Tripartite Environmental Ministers Meeting (TEMM).[31]

There are two reasons why Southeast Asian countries showed weak interest in the EANET development. The first is pertinent to geographical location in transboundary flow of acidic substances. The causal relationship in transboundary pollution by acidic substances in East Asia is basically determined by circumpolar westerlies, and scientific development demonstrates horizontal causal flows in which China is a source country and South Korea and Japan are the affected countries. In other words, the vertical line from Russia and Southeast Asia is less relevant to transboundary flows of acidic substances. Therefore, Southeast Asian countries had little incentive to make serious commitments to the EANET development and assume substantial financial burdens (Matsuoka 2010: 252–53). This is shown in the fact that

Singapore, a major promoter of regional cooperation in Southeast Asia, has not joined EANET despite its secretariat's encouragement.

The second reason is that Southeast Asian countries had their own transboundary air pollution problems. The most representative among these is transboundary haze pollution. In June 2002, ASEAN members signed the ASEAN Agreement on Transboundary Haze Pollution in order to cooperate in developing and implementing measures to prevent, monitor, and mitigate the pollution. The representation of transboundary acid deposition as the main regional environmental problem was disadvantageous for the ASEAN members who hoped to keep ASEAN's environmental issues as central agendas in East Asia. From such a baseline, Malaysia was concerned that the extension of EANET's scope of substances to regional air pollution would undermine the relative importance of the ASEAN Haze Agreement, and asserted that EANET would devote itself to the resolution of acid deposition problems alone.[32]

Japan, as the initiator of EANET, hoped to develop the network as a fully fledged institution with independent financial resources. Even after the secretariat was transferred to the UNEP RRC.AP in 2002, the Japanese government paid most of the costs for maintaining the secretariat. Japan expected to share burdens for managing the network in order to reduce its own financial burdens under overall pressure on reducing official development assistance (ODA) funds. The burden-sharing was also necessary for fostering ownership consciousness among participating countries.[33] The Japanese government hoped to foster EANET as an authentic Asian institution to provide regional public goods.

As for the legal status of the Instrument of EANET, Japan adopted a neutral stance, insisting that 'a discussion on legal status be made at a later stage, after completion of detailed discussion on content of the instrument'.[34] However, it had a strong desire to extend the scope of activities and substances. The Japanese government hoped to formulate a foundation document for EANET, which would be a kind of framework agreement that would provide the foundation for further protocols dealing with specific air pollution problems in East Asia.[35] Such an approach follows a model after the LRTAP, which has been extended by eight protocols regarding specific air pollutants such as sulphur, nitrogen oxides, and volatile organic compounds.

The Japanese MOE had an imperative need to extend EANET's scope of substances and activities in relation to bureaucratic politics. Although there was a long history of scientific research on the effect of acid rain on the Japanese vegetation, the real effects were still being researched. For instance, the destruction of forests in Japan, which is often raised as an example of bad effects of acid rain, was deemed to be caused by typhoons, pine weevils, and others. Accordingly, the Ministry of Finance posed a question about the rationale for spending large sums of money on the monitoring of acid deposition. The MOE hoped to extend the network's activities from monitoring alone to emission inventory and simulation modelling, covering not just acid deposition but regional air pollution as a whole.[36]

Japan made efforts to persuade China into a more positive posture towards the development of EANET. The Japanese government provided considerable amounts of financial aid to assist the development of acid rain monitoring networks in China. For instance, in December 2006 the Japanese government provided a grant of 793 million yen (US$6.82 million) to support China's project for the establishment of monitoring networks for acid deposition, dust, and sandstorm.[37] Moreover, the Japanese government has never formally accused China of responsibility for transboundary air pollution problems (Kim 2007: 451). The government also appealed to Chinese political leaders about the importance of the EANET development. When Japanese environmental ministers had a chance to talk with their Chinese counterparts, they asked for Chinese cooperation on the development of EANET. When Chinese Premier Wen Jiabao made a formal visit to Tokyo in April 2007, Wen and his counterpart, Shinzo Abe, issued a Joint Statement on the Further Enhancement of Cooperation for Environmental Protection. In this document, EANET was referred to as one mechanism that Japan and China would actively promote for regional cooperation. However, such commitments did not change China's fundamental position on regional environmental cooperation through EANET.

The adoption of the EANET instrument

Renewed cooperation through the EANET instrument?

Talks on the Instrument of EANET took a long time to reach a conclusion. It was agreed at the tenth IG meeting in 2008 that the instrument has a form of non-legally binding text, and it was confirmed at the following IG meeting that 'the word "agreed" in the last paragraph of the Preamble of the Instrument does not have legally-binding implication'.[38] The Instrument for Strengthening the EANET was finally adopted at the 12th IG meeting in November 2010. It took five years to realise the decision to adopt an appropriate Instrument of EANET.

Despite the long process of discussion on the instrument, its final text is short and simple with 17 items, containing main provisions regarding activities (Item 4–9) and administrative organs (Item 10–13). The instrument does not include items of a legally binding nature such as protocols, signatures, dispute settlement, decision-making of the IG meeting, ratification, acceptance, approval, or entry into force. The responsibilities of countries participating in the instrument are almost the same as those stipulated in the Tentative Design of EANET: the implementation of national monitoring activities and the reporting of monitoring data to the network centre; and voluntary financial contributions to support the administrative and operational costs of the network. The instrument spells out concrete tasks for the four organs, but does not provide their operational rules. The instrument does provide a stronger basis for member governments' obligations, including financial contributions through the signature of high-level officials of each government. But there were only meagre changes from the Tentative Design of EANET regarding provisions of the functions of administrative organs and obligations of participating countries. The instrument completely excluded any legally binding nature, becoming a proper document that confirmed EANET's ongoing activities formally.

As for the scope of substances and activities, it was finally agreed to 'monitor acid deposition' in East Asia. During discussions at the WGFD, phrases to extend the scope – 'monitor, prevent and control' and 'regional air pollution' – were presented, but the instrument did not adopt these phrases. As shown in engagements in other regions of the world, regional cooperation in managing transboundary air pollution needs to develop from monitoring to the examination of effects through modelling and the adoption of preventive measures. The EANET members were unable to follow such a developmental path through the instrument.

During the 12th IG meeting in November 2010, Cambodia, Japan, Mongolia, Myanmar, the Philippines, South Korea, and Thailand signed the instrument. China and Vietnam completed a signature in the following year, and the instrument became operational in January 2012. All members except for Indonesia completed a signature on the instrument by the end of 2012. The adoption of the instrument had positive effects on the sharing of financial burdens. As of October 2012, all participants except for Russia, Indonesia, the Philippines, and Myanmar provided their contributions to the secretariat budget.

The preferences of China, South Korea, and Japan for the instrument

The main factor that led to the adoption of a non-legalistic instrument with no changes in the scope of substances and activities was China's unwillingness. The Chinese government deepened the recognition that urban air pollution was one of the most serious environmental problems. For instance, the annual SO_2 emissions increased from 19.5 million tons in 2001 to 25.9 million tons in 2006 (SEPA 2007: 56). Thirty per cent of China's territory suffered from acid rain, which cost at least 110 billion yuan (US$13.3 billion) annually.[39] The cost associated with deteriorating environments imposed serious burdens on economic development, a primary policy goal for the Chinese authorities. Accordingly, the Chinese government set the target of reducing total SO_2 emissions by 10 per cent from the 2005 level by 2010 in the 11th Five-Year Plan (2006–10), and implemented various measures to achieve this target including the adoption of new rules on the promotion of local officials and performance standards for electric power plants (Cao et al. 2009). However, consideration of domestic air pollution problems did not necessarily lead to the acceptance of EANET's extending mandate and functions.

The fundamental reason for China's passive attitude towards the extension of EANET's scope of substances and activities lay in the avoidance of international responsibility. China is located in the upwind position of circumpolar westerlies and its rapid industrialisation has contributed to growing emissions of air pollutants. If the scope of substances had been extended, China would have been required to provide information as a pollutant source and to assume greater responsibility for reducing air pollution (Kanie and Sodeno 2013: 47–48). More generally, China was anxious about the negative impact of the EANET development on its economic growth. Given that Chinese leaders are obligated to exhibit high economic performance continuously, steady industrial growth and stable supply of electricity are indispensable policy goals. Beijing was apprehensive that the EANET development would lead to a regulatory regime that might require participants to implement mandatory emission reductions. Such a development was likely to threaten China's overarching economic development goals. The multilateral environment agreements create international obligations that a member has to assume in reducing emissions of air pollutants by taking into account the effects on neighbouring countries. The Chinese authorities hope to avoid such obligations that will constrain the sovereign right for environmental affairs. They are eager to retain policy autonomy to coordinate the pace of industrial growth and the protection of the environment by locating air pollution problems as purely domestic affairs.

As mentioned before, South Korea had a strong aspiration to establish a network centre, which derived from its rivalry sentiment against Japan and a belief in the appropriateness of dividing the network centre's functions. In the process of deliberating on the instrument, South Korea proposed the establishment of a sub-branch of the network centre in its territory, which would require a division of labour with the existing network centre in Japan. Since the network's scope of activities was not extended, Seoul's proposal was not realised.[40] However, the instrument contained a phrase that 'other entities could be designated as Network Centres for EANET by the decision of the IG, as the need arises' (Item 13, Section 3). This phrase was included in response to a request from South Korea, which successfully created the foundation to establish an additional network centre within its territory.[41]

Notwithstanding interest in establishing a network centre, South Korea did not necessarily have a keen interest in strengthening EANET through the instrument. In May 2012, the Korean Ministry of Environment announced a plan to launch its own geostationary orbit satellite by 2018 in order to monitor air pollution and climate change in Northeast Asia and the Korean Peninsula. As exemplified by this plan, Seoul sought to tackle regional air pollution problems with its own efforts, drawing on its long history of research on transboundary air pollution in Northeast Asia.

Japan failed to realise its preference for the extended scope of substances and activities in the instrument. A limited success was to include the phrase 'the scope of this Instrument may be extended, as decided by the IG' (Item 2, Section 2). The scope implies both the activities of EANET and substances targeted for monitoring. The extension of the scope became a major agenda at the IG meetings after 2011, and Japan took the lead in deepening debates on this agenda.

The procedural rules adopted by EANET members made it difficult to extend EANET's activities and targeted substances. According to the rules, decision-making is based on consensus and members are required to adopt a step-by-step approach on a voluntary basis. Under such rules, it was difficult to push forward matters on which member countries had different views. The difficulty of extending the scope of substances and activities had much to do with a 'prisoner's dilemma'. EANET is relevant to international environmental issues that contain some aspects of common pool resources (CPRs) that require cooperation from all relevant actors to mitigate a given problem. While cooperative efforts to reduce emissions of air pollutants could be made by individual members, emissions by one sufficiently important member can weaken any reduction undertaken by all others (DeSombre 2009: 148–49). The differences between the payoffs for cooperation and defection are much larger for CPRs than for public goods or club goods. China has produced the largest emissions of SO_2 and NOx in East Asia. Accordingly, China's defection from EANET would weaken any efforts for reduction by all other members, and thereby they were forced to respect its preferences to avoid such a defection.

Asia-wide moves to cooperation on air pollution

In the late 2000s, global environmental issues attracted much attention in the world. This was largely because the expiration of the Kyoto Protocol to the UN Framework Convention on Climate Change forced the international community to search for a new framework to manage greenhouse gas emissions. This issue became the main agenda at the Conference of the Parties (COP) 15 in 2009 and the COP 16 in 2010. Growing concern with climate change influences concrete approaches to air pollution problems. Transboundary air pollutants that cause acid rain are also regarded as main causes of global warming. This led to growing interest in the co-benefits approach as an effective integrated solution to both climate change and air pollution.[42] For instance, the 15th World Clean Air Congress held in Vancouver in September 2010 referred to a necessary paradigm shift in air quality policy that takes into account 'the integration of climate and pollution policies and the development of co-benefits strategies' in its Final Declaration.[43]

Linkages between climate change and acid rain as well as the co-benefits approach that takes into account the linkages were paid attention in EANET activities. The Second Periodic Report on the State of Acid Deposition in East Asia, which describes the outcome of EANET monitoring activities in 2005–09, contains the phrases 'air pollutants causing acid deposition (such as ozone and aerosols) contribute to climate change, while climate change affects acid deposition through influences such as precipitation variations', and 'it is also recommended that EANET consider the issue of co-benefits through activities such as discussions on how acid deposition and air quality relate to climate change' (EANET 2011: iii, 37). Moreover, the launching and activities of the Asian Co-benefits Partnership were presented at the IG meetings in 2010 and 2011.[44] However, EANET members as a group did not necessarily exhibit willingness to advance new initiatives in EANET operations in response to such new trends in global environmental issues. The positive consideration of these trends was likely to lead to some reformulations of EANET activities, and some members were reluctant to accept such changes.

On the regional scene, there was a crucial move to strengthen linkages among institutions to monitor transboundary air pollution in the late 2000s. In Asia, there are several sub-regional institutions to manage air pollution issues. The South Asian countries have promoted cooperation in air pollution since they adopted the Malé Declaration on Control and Prevention of Air Pollution and its Likely Transboundary Effects for South Asia in 1998. ASEAN members signed the Agreement on Transboundary Haze Pollution in 2002 in order to prevent, monitor, and mitigate transboundary haze pollution by controlling sources of land and/or forest fires. Furthermore, the Framework Convention on Environmental Protection for Sustainable Development in Central Asia was adopted in 2006. The formation of plural institutions with the same policy goal led to an initiative to strengthen cooperation among these institutions. The first joint meeting of intergovernmental institutions for regional air pollution in Asia was organised in Pathumthani, Thailand in March 2009 under UNEP auspices. The representatives from the Malé Declaration and EANET members, as well as from the secretariats of ASEAN, the Central Asian Environment Convention, the Pacific Regional Environment Programme, and the South Asia Cooperative Environment Programme joined the meeting. The participants agreed to develop this gathering as the 'Joint Forum on Atmospheric Environmental Issues in Asia and the Pacific' and to formulate a future plan for the activities of the joint forum by gathering comments from relevant intergovernmental meetings.[45] At the second meeting in Bangkok, Thailand in March 2010, participants adopted the Joint Plan for Joint Activities on Air Pollution in Asia and the Pacific. The plan lays out the vision, goals, scope, and activities of the forum. The vision was to achieve a clean atmospheric environment through collective and coherent actions, especially through enhanced cooperation and collaboration among regional and sub-regional networks. In July 2011, the first capacity-building workshop of the forum was held in Thailand.

The Asia-Pacific wide move to strengthen collaboration on air pollution issues did not have a significant impact on EANET members' engagement in regional cooperation. The joint forum has not implemented substantial activities for cooperation due to its short history. In its 2010–12 Work Plan, a priority was given to information-sharing, which would be promoted by building a clearing-house for air pollution information based on existing initiatives. EANET was one of the core participants in the forum, but not all EANET members joined its meetings. China and South Korea did not attend the meetings, and posed a question about EANET's positive commitment to the forum. When a UNEP representative formally introduced the forum at the 12th IG meeting in November 2010, some countries asserted that EANET's participation in the forum requires the consensus of all members, and that the scope of activities is different between the forum (atmospheric pollution) and EANET (acid deposition alone).[46]

In brief, new moves on air pollution issues on the global and regional scenes in the 2000s did not contribute to the strength of EANET. These moves emphasised the multiple nature of air pollution issues and the importance of the Asia-wide approach. Some member countries that adhered to EANET's narrow activity of acid deposition were unwilling to take such moves into account. Accordingly, the moves did not have a meaningful impact on the development of EANET. Thus, the new developments on air pollution issues did not function as a critical juncture elevating EANET cooperation to a new developmental path.

Scientific knowledge and the development of EANET

Scientists were deeply involved in the development of EANET. The SAC was formed as one of the four organs and its meeting has been held annually in parallel to the IG meeting. As already explained, three task forces were established under the SAC, and the Task Force on Monitoring Instrumentation and the Task Force on Research Coordination were organised later to deepen research activities. The SAC has published research outcomes from EANET operations and helped to facilitate monitoring activities. While the periodic report on the state of acid deposition was published in 2006 and 2011, new technical manuals for wet deposition monitoring, dry deposition flux estimation, soil and vegetation monitoring, and inland aquatic environment monitoring were produced in 2010. Thus, scientific expertise provided by professional networks in the SAC led to the production of objective, scientific data and facts that contributed to EANET operations.

The scientists also played a critical role in inducing the government to make a positive commitment to EANET development. This was the case in South Korea. The Korean government officials were unwilling to sign the Instrument of EANET largely because of awkward policy coordination with Japan on the content of the instrument. A Korean SAC member persuaded the officials to pay attention to the importance of the signature. This university professor, who was involved in the EANET development from its preparatory phase, gave priority to the success of EANET itself rather than the 'face' of the Korean government.[47] His persuasion successfully made South Korea one of seven members who signed the instrument during the 12th IG meeting.

Despite the solid presence of experts in the EANET development, their activities in the real policymaking were still limited. A fundamental problem is that EANET members have not established common monitoring methods ten years after the launching of the network. The adoption of common methods of monitoring necessary for a comparative survey and the employment of a single method of analysis are essential for development in monitoring networks of air pollution. The experts involved in EANET have produced the necessary monitoring guidelines and technical manuals. However, some members still adopted independent monitoring methods. At the 11th SAC meeting in October 2011, the following comment was presented:

> The monitoring method used in each country should be harmonized with each other to obtain comparable data, although each country may have their own policies on monitoring activities. It was suggested that appropriate common methods should be identified based on scientific review and common understanding, and then the selected method should be applied for the EANET monitoring.[48]

The experts' limited involvement in the real policymaking was revealed in the fact that some suggestions from experts on the basis of professional and scientific knowledge and insights were not reflected in actual policies adopted by policymakers. Such cases were relevant to EANET's scope of activities. The Periodic Report on the State of Acid Deposition in East Asia, published in November 2006, recommended that EANET's activities extend to emission inventory and simulation modelling in order to elucidate causal relationships pertinent to spatial distribution of pollutants and to facilitate a better understanding of regional air pollution and its effects on ecosystems (EANET 2006: 32). At the seventh SAC meeting in October 2007, members agreed to establish an expert group for the promotion of emission inventory and modelling and an expert group to review substances to be monitored in EANET.[49] However, this agreement was not accepted at the ninth IG meeting held one month later due to one country's reservations over establishing the expert groups.[50] Although the experts clearly showed the importance of extending the network's activities, the policymakers' final decision was to limit the activities to the monitoring of acid deposition.

Importantly, the experts' limited influence on the policymaking process had much to do with the real presence of experts at the SAC and the relationships between experts and government officials. The SAC originally intended to reflect objective, scientific views and knowledge on policymaking by inviting professional experts from each country. However, member countries such as Cambodia, Laos, and Myanmar were unable to send experts due to the shortage of human resources, and government officials joined the SAC meetings. The expert representatives from Japan, South Korea, Malaysia, and the Philippines included university professors who were able to maintain third-party status. However, experts from China and Vietnam came from government-affiliated research institutes. These diverse backgrounds discouraged the SAC members from deepening both relationality and common identity resulting from belonging to the scientific group. Significantly, Chinese experts from the CNEMC were reluctant to present opinions independent of the government's position, sometimes asserting that they had no way of discussing difficult matters without reference to the government or that decisions made at the SAC meetings needed to be further deliberated on at the IG meetings.[51] These assertions indicate that too close connections to governments undermine independence and the third-party status that professional experts were expected to represent.

The experts continued their efforts to increase the relevance of scientific and technical outcomes to the policymaking process. The Second Periodic Report on the State of Acid Deposition in East Asia, published in December 2011, contained the phrases 'as scientific understanding of the consequences and sources of such deposition becomes more reliable, EANET should consider ways to address the origins of harmful emissions by reaching out to policy developers and decision makers with scientific knowledge and policy advice' and

> a scientific review of the present status of the atmospheric environment in East Asia would also be worthwhile to support discussions on extending the scope of EANET. The promotion of research activities, including work on modeling and emission inventories, is another possible target for EANET toward further development of the network.
>
> (EANET 2011: iii)

At the 14th IG meeting in 2012, policymakers agreed to task the SAC with reviewing the status of air pollution in East Asia, to be used for the SAC's consideration in making recommendations to the 16th IG meeting for its decision on the future expansion of EANET's scope (Wangwongwatana 2012).

Experiences in Europe and North America indicate that scientific consensus on ecological, social, and economic impacts of air pollution on source and adjacent countries is crucial to overcome political impediments to the establishment of regional programmes (Nam 2002: 187). This is a substantive value of 'governance' in which non-state actors' involvement changes political configurations in which political actors formulate public policies. In East Asia, there were significant variations among countries in internal state capacities to hold human and technical resources, which disturbed the development of common understanding and the adoption of harmonised measures. At the same time, the highly state-centred governance system in some countries constrained the role of experts and the representation of objective and scientific insights in the policymaking process.

Conclusion

This chapter examined regional cooperation on environmental protection in East Asia. It focused on EANET, a representative institution to cope with transboundary air pollution problems, and traced its origin, development, and challenges. In particular, it analysed member countries' interests and stances on this multilateral institution, and the effects of their political interactions on its operations and development. The chapter also explored external impacts of global events and phenomena, as well as internal dynamics created through networks of scientists.

In launching EANET as a regional institution, Japan played a decisive role. It organised a series of expert meetings before launching the network and provided financial and technical support after its start. Other East Asian countries reacted to Japan's initiatives with diverse interests and motivations. China was cautious about likely impacts of the EANET initiative, adhering to a basic stance that acid deposition is a domestic environmental issue, not an international one. South Korea, which had its own institution for transboundary air pollution in Northeast Asia, was worried about the negative impacts of EANET on the institution. Southeast Asian countries joined the network as their concerns were settled at the expert meetings. Despite diverse interests and stances, EANET began its regular-phase activities with ten original members, and three Southeast Asian countries joined later.

EANET had two challenges for its development: the establishment of financial burden-sharing and the adoption of the Instrument of EANET. Japan hoped to achieve equitable burden-sharing in order to reduce its own contributions and to extend the network's activities through the enactment of the instrument. EANET members agreed to share financial burdens on the basis of the UN assessment in 2003. However, most countries did not assume their expected share of the burden as this commitment was voluntary, and Japan was forced to make dominant contributions to sustain the EANET management and activities. As for the Instrument of EANET, the instrument that was adopted in November 2010 could not extend the scope of substances and activities. While some participants gave support to Japan's stance to extend the scope, China and South Korea asserted that the existing scope should be maintained. Thus, a failure to coordinate diverse interests among participating countries became the main impediment to developing EANET as an institution that would create a regulatory regime for collective regional interests.

In launching EANET, there was an important global event: the UNCED. The conference constituted a critical juncture to change East Asian countries' perception of and commitments to transboundary air pollution. After this UN event, governmental actors in Northeast Asia organised cooperative institutions to protect the environment, and ASEAN members intensified collective commitments to the protection of regional environments. In this overall trend, Japan launched the EANET initiative. The UNCED changed a previous path of non-institution to the formation of multilateral institutions. In the late 2000s, debates on global environmental issues deepened but such moves did not produce a new impetus to deepen EANET cooperation. This may provide one background reason why the members failed to adopt a substantial Instrument of EANET.

EANET guaranteed the involvement of scientists in the policymaking process by institutionalising the SAC as one of its main organs. The scientists undertook research activities in various task forces under the SAC, helped to facilitate monitoring activities, and published research outcomes. However, their scientific insights were reflected in the policymaking process only to a limited extent, largely because government officials did not accept some of their important recommendations. The scientists' networks also had inherent weaknesses. Some countries were still in the process of enhancing experts' capabilities, and some experts paid respect to myopic national stances rather than universal scientific insights. In this sense, the SAC has not established a social learning network which would lead to the reinterpretation of national interests on the basis of shared causal beliefs and shared professional knowledge.

8
Conclusion

In the new millennium, states in East Asia intensified cooperation to advance collectively the overall interests of the region and respond to common challenges and risks. The previous chapters have examined the process of regional institution-building in specific policy fields: trade, agriculture, finance, energy, and the environment. In all cases policymakers in East Asia reached an agreement to launch formal institutions to tackle specific issues of a cross-national nature, and engaged in the subsequent development of these institutions. The original institutions were launched in the early 2000s and advanced institutions were created nearly ten years later in most cases. In the process of institution-building, four parties – China, Japan, South Korea, and Association of Southeast Asian Nations (ASEAN) – performed complicated political interactions in order to reflect their preferences and concerns on the genesis, design, and evolution of the institutions.

This concluding chapter shows the implications of the analysis of five empirical cases by confirming major features of the development and design of formal institutions and examining key factors that qualified their building processes. The first section identifies common patterns in the process of institution-building and common features in the design of institutions. The second section explores the implications of empirical analyses regarding the influence of key variables on the construction of regional institutions in East Asia. The third section presents the directions of future research.

The process of institution-building and design features

This research, which focuses on formal institutions to develop common interests in East Asia, is partially inspired by literature on the rational design of international institutions (Koremenos et al. 2001a; 2001b; Wendt 2001; Duffield 2003; Koremenos and Snidal 2003). The main interest of the research lies in 'causal mechanisms' that lead to institutional creation and evolution rather than design features of institutions or the 'correlation' between such features and the conditions underlying them. However, presenting major findings regarding the process of institution-building itself and design features of institutions provides implications for the study of regional institutions.

Common features in institutional development

In the policy fields examined in this research, four common features were identified regarding the process of institution-building. First, a similar pattern of institutional development was found. In each policy field, a new institution for regional cooperation was established in the early 2000s: bilateral/ minilateral free trade agreements (FTAs) in trade, the Chiang Mai Initiative (CMI) in finance, the East Asia Emergency Rice Reserve (EAERR) in food security, ASEAN Plus Three (ASEAN+3) cooperation in energy security, and the Acid Deposition Monitoring Network in East Asia (EANET) in the environment (Table 8.1). These initial institutions were functionally weak, with a narrow scope of issues and activities. Within a few years policymakers envisioned and pursued objectives and directions for further development of the institutions. Around 2010–12, except for energy, the second stage of regional cooperation was achieved with the launching of an advanced form of institution in each policy area: the Regional Comprehensive Economic Partnership (RCEP) as an East Asia-wide FTA in trade, the CMI multilateralisation (CMIM) in finance, the ASEAN+3 Emergency Rice Reserve (APTERR) in food security, and the Instrument of EANET in the environments. Thus, the common pattern that institutional development was achieved through the two-step process was identified in four out of five cases.

The second feature is slow progress in institutional development. It is not easy to assess the length of time required for creating an institution because it depends primarily on what kind of institution is envisioned by

Table 8.1 The two stages of institution-building in five policy fields

Policy field	First initiation stage		Second development stage	
Trade	Bilateral FTAs	Japan–Singapore EPA in 2002	RCEP	Launching of negotiations agreed in 2012
Finance	CMI	Agreed in 2000	CMIM	Came into force in 2010
Food security	EAERR	Pilot project began in 2004	APTERR	Came into force in 2012
Energy security	Five policy forums under EPGG	Began in 2003	OSRM	Formulated in 2010
Air pollution	EANET	Began in 2001	Instrument of EANET	Came into force in 2012

the members. In this regard, financial cooperation might provide a useful guide. The transition from the CMI to the CMIM took ten years, which could be regarded as too long. It took this length of time partly because the CMIM pursued substantial financial architectures including a joint decision-making mechanism for the first time in East Asia. In other policy fields it also took eight to ten years to reach the second stage. However, the new institutions in these areas did not necessarily make a significant departure from the original ones by achieving substantial transformations and/or developing intricate designs like the CMIM. In reality there were apparent causes for the long process. In food security cooperation the EAERR project was extended by three years longer than originally planned. In exploring the possibility of an East Asia-wide FTA through the East Asia Free Trade Area (EAFTA) and Comprehensive Economic Partnership Agreement in East Asia (CEPEA), the end of the expert group study did not lead to the launching of formal negotiations, but the holding of a phase-II study. As for environmental cooperation, there was a plan to present the result of discussions on the Instrument of EANET at the intergovernmental meeting in 2008, but it required two additional years to finalise discussions. These facts indicate that the progress of institutional development could be regarded as slow.

Thirdly, existing institutions provided the basis for new institutions. In the formation of a new institution, existing institutions often play a significant role. In this regard ASEAN played a crucial role in developing East Asia-wide institutions. The association had created multilateral institutions to prepare for an emergency event in the financial and agricultural sectors – the ASEAN Swap Agreement and the ASEAN Emergency Rice Reserve (AERR) –, and formed ASEAN+1 FTA networks in the trade sector.[1] Departing from these ASEAN-based institutions, new East Asia-wide institutions were created by involving the three Northeast Asian countries. In environmental cooperation ASEAN members joined EANET with an individual capacity, and no ASEAN-made institutions were relevant to the launching of EANET. This implied that transboundary acid deposition was basically a matter for Northeast Asia, not for Southeast Asia.

The fourth feature is the complicated relevance of ideational factors. Goldstein and Keohane (1993: 13–17) argue that ideas are expected to serve as guidelines or road maps, which are necessary to determine state actions especially under conditions of uncertainty. The ideas also increase the legitimacy and acceptance of particular policies, being regarded as 'focal points' to promote the harmonisation of policies and systems for the states concerned.[2] In the process of institution creation, the ASEAN Way became a set of procedural norms to guide the policy formation process among participants. For instance, cooperation on EANET and the Oil Stockpiling Roadmap (OSRM) incorporated the step-by-step approach as a guiding principle. The members' respect for this norm coupled with other normative principles such as informality and consultation resulted in a relatively long process of developing regional institutions. In contrast, substantive norms, constituting common goals to be pursued by participants who can develop collective identity in their achievements, were not presented or accentuated in the process of institution-creation. The primary objective of FTA formation is to attain market liberalisation for efficient functions. However, states in East Asia did not strictly adhere to this ideal, admitting exceptions to liberalisation for sensitive sectors. With regard to regional cooperation on emergency rice reserve, 'food security' was the key ideal, and additional ideals were not presented although programmes for poverty alleviation in rural areas were embedded in and implemented under this cooperation (Yoshimatsu 2008: 163). EANET neither raised specific normative ideals at its formal start in 2001 nor incorporated them in its subsequent development. The weak presence of ideational elements that help to foster collective identity among the members of institutions may have led to increasing the relative importance of material interests in the process of institution-building. The development of regional institutions was qualified by the pursuit of material interests, which served to make interest coordination among the member governments complicated and difficult.

The design features of achieved institutions

After the relatively long process of discussions on the strength of the existing institutions, advanced institutions were launched around 2010–12. A critical question is how design features of these institutions are assessed. Quite a few scholars have put forth various dimensions for evaluating the design of institutions (Abbott et al. 2000; Koremenos et al. 2001a; Camilleri 2003).[3] Since the institutions examined in this study remain primitive and underdeveloped, it is difficult to apply strictly defined dimensions. This study assesses the design of institutional structures in terms of three dimensions: scope, obligation, and control. 'Scope' means what issues and activities are covered by institutions, and extends from narrowly focused specific issues and activities to encompassing contingent ones. The institutions are created to guide and regulate the members' behaviour in specific areas of interest, and the scope of issues and activities targeted by the institutions is a crucial point for institutional design. 'Obligation' implies what kind of duties and responsibilities member states are required to carry out under the institutions. In this respect the dispute settlement mechanism (DSM) becomes a critical constituent of obligation, which provides the basis for compulsory coordination of divergent interests among the members and sustains the effective function of the institutions. 'Control' means to what extent collective systems for decisions are provided under the institutions. In this criterion, decision-making procedures and a standing secretariat's position in pursuing collective interests of the members are considered crucial components.

The scope of issues and activities covered by the institutions created in East Asia is relatively narrow compared with equivalent institutions in other parts of the world. In the trade field, the RCEP covers trade in goods, trade in services, investment, economic and technical cooperation, intellectual property, competition, dispute settlement, and other issues. The targeting of issues could be expanded through the category of 'other issues' in the negotiation process. However, this initial list is distinctly narrow in scope, which becomes apparent in comparison with other FTAs. For instance, the Trans-Pacific Partnership Agreement (TPP) covers 21 issue-areas including government procurement, environment, labour, e-commerce, and legal issues. The main objective of the strengthening of EANET was the expansion of its scopes of substances and activities. However, member countries were unable to achieve this objective at the adoption of the Instrument of EANET. Accordingly, EANET's scope of activities remained confined to monitoring, which is limited compared with other institutions that deal with transboundary air pollution, such as the Convention on Long-range Transboundary Air Pollution (LRTAP) in Europe and the Malé Declaration in South Asia, which cover impact assessment, emission inventory, and preventive measures. The APTERR aims to provide rice for a member country in an emergency shortage of food, and some members hoped to expand its scope by including other staple foods for broader consideration on price volatility. However, the member states have not achieved this objective yet, and the APTERR's scope of operations remains narrow. The CMI is a part of the East Asian financial architecture and its primary objective is to provide currency liquidity for a country in an emergency. Its development was accompanied by the integration of the surveillance system and expansion in the scope of activities by including crisis prevention facilities in response to the global financial crisis. In this sense, financial institutions had some 'flexibility' in that institutional rules and procedures accommodate new circumstances (Koremenos et al. 2001a: 773).

As for obligation, the duties and responsibilities the members assume under the institutions are qualified by the institutions' overall objectives and the relationships between the institutions and the members. In the process of enacting the Instrument of EANET, the clauses with a legally binding nature were removed from the text, and member governments just assume responsibilities for implementing national monitoring activities and reporting monitoring data. The instrument does not include any clauses regarding the DSM. The APTERR Agreement provides a few obligations for members: to earmark a certain quantity of rice; to provide information on policies and programmes for rice reserve; and make contributions to the APTERR Fund and the operational cost. It includes one clause regarding the DSM, which simply stipulates a peaceful settlement through bilateral consultation and a possible reference to the APTERR Council. The CMIM contains more detailed obligations. The member governments are obligated to meet conditions before voting for a swap request and to comply with covenants such as the submission of periodical surveillance reports and participation in economic review and policy dialogues. In sum, the main obligations for members under the institutions are the provision of information and financial contributions to support the operational cost, and obligations that require member governments to prescribe or proscribe some form of conduct are rare. This limited level of obligation implies that the institutions' presence as focal points to define members' behaviour towards collective policy goals is highly constrained.

As far as control is concerned, decision-making procedures are simple for the institutions. The CMIM adopts the weighted voting system and its decision-making follows a hybrid voting formula: consensus for fundamental issues and two-thirds majority for executive-level matters. The APTERR Council is responsible for the operation of the APTERR and its decision is made on the basis of consensus. While the intergovernmental meeting is stipulated to be 'the decision-making body of the EANET', there is no reference to its decision-making procedures. Although the consensus method does not necessarily require unanimous support for a policy proposal, not only does it grant veto power to block action to each member but it also tends to produce protracted bargaining and frequent failures of collective action (Fearon 1998). Accordingly, this method tends to produce the lowest common denominator, which results in a narrow scope of issues and activities as well as limited obligations of members in the design of institutions. One unique aspect of the control of the institutions is the division of representation between ASEAN and the +3 members. In both the CMIM and APTERR, one country from ASEAN members and the other from the +3 countries assume a co-chair role. While ASEAN+3 members formally adopted this system at the tenth finance ministers' meeting in 2007, Singapore adhered to its adoption in the launching of the APTERR. This system encourages individual ASEAN governments to voice concern first with one another and to speak as a unified group by enabling ASEAN to maintain ownership at every meeting (Ciorciari 2011: 931). The system also urges coordination among the +3 members through the chair country to harmonise their own policies as an entity *vis-à-vis* ASEAN. While EANET did not follow this system because not all ASEAN members joined the network, all +3 members had a right to represent in the OSRM in energy cooperation. The lack of this divisional representation system might have adverse effects on interest coordination among the members, particularly those in Northeast Asia.

The institutions examined in the study had some similarities in the structure of administrative systems. The APTERR and EANET hold each secretariat in Thailand, and the secretariats' functions are sustained by a technical office – the AFSIS and the Network Centre, respectively. In energy cooperation the ACE served as a coordinator, and its functions are sustained by technical organisations represented by the Institute of Energy Economics, Japan (IEEJ). In launching the CMIM the ASEAN+3 Macroeconomic

Research Office (AMRO) was established as an administrative body to sustain the operations of the CMIM as well as a technical centre to monitor and analyse regional economies. The negotiations on the RCEP are coordinated by the ASEAN Secretariat, and the ERIA provides technical support for the RCEP's development.

As for the position of standing secretariats, those of the APTERR and EANET are equipped with scant resources and weak capabilities. While the APTERR inherited a small, understaffed secretariat from the EAERR, EANET's standing secretariat remains weak with limited manpower and financial resources. Compared with these two institutions, the CMIM development has been accompanied by gradually increasing strength in the capabilities and authority of the AMRO. The AMRO, which began its operations in April 2011, still remains a small body, but member governments have explicit will to enhance its administrative capabilities and legal status to be a reliable and independent international organisation. Thus, member governments as the principals seek to retain strong control over institutions, eschewing significant constraints on their behaviour. The standing secretariats as the agents are delegated a very limited authority to make decisions and the restricted capabilities to undertake substantial tasks for collective interests.

Quite a few researchers have contended that multilateral institutions for regional cooperation remain shallow and thin in East Asia (Kahler 2010; Haggard 2011; Ravenhill 2013). For instance, Kahler (2010: 6) argues that 'Asian regional institutions appear to reflect preferences on the part of national governments for few restraints on their freedom of action and limited cooperative bargains'. Similarly, Ravenhill (2013) holds that the institutions in the Asia-Pacific are built on 'soft law' without precise legally binding obligations and mechanisms for enforcement, and a 'hardening' of law has seldom been experienced. This research underscores these views by confirming structurally weak institutions with limited obligations for members. Under such conditions the institutions have inherent limitations to making substantial commitments to both 'widening' (bringing in new issues and activities) and 'deepening' (developing formal rules and administrative systems for policy coordination) , except for the CMIM. In the 2000s, several scholars asserted that statements on the CMI were symbolic rather than substantial, assuring the international community that countries in East Asia continuously engaged in regional cooperation on the issue (Amyx 2008: 126; Sussangkarn 2011: 208). After 2010, the advanced CMIM began to shift from symbol to substance. The APTERR or even the ten-year lasting EANET still retain significant symbolic aspects for regional cooperation.

Four variables that qualify institution-building

This research has put forth independent variables that qualified the evolution of institution-building in East Asia through primary and supplementary pillars. The variable in the primary pillar is relative power distribution among states. The supplementary pillars comprise three variables; policymakers' preferences in the domestic political process, the involvement of research institutes in the policy formation process, and critical junctures in the historical trajectory. The following parts summarise findings across empirical cases and assess functions and influences of these variables, searching for their relevance to outcomes in institutional creation.

Relative power distribution in institution-building

Japan played a substantial role in initiating regional cooperation in five policy fields. The EAERR and EANET began with proposals from Japan that provided the original design of institutions and financial support for holding intergovernmental meetings. The ASEAN+3 energy cooperation was also initiated by Japan, which exhibited the design and direction of cooperation and offered financial support for concrete projects. In the trade sector, ASEAN members created the first multilateral FTA – the ASEAN Free Trade Area (AFTA) – in East Asia, but the formation of bilateral FTA networks in the region was initiated by the Japan–Singapore FTA. The CMI was formed after Japan's failed attempt to create the Asian Monetary Fund, and Japan became the key promoter of the initiative. Tokyo's initiatives were sustained by intellectual assets to conceptualise feasible institutions on the basis of long-term scientific research and international experiences as well as capabilities to provide financial resources to promote concrete activities under the institutions.

Certainly, Japan intended to play a leadership role in providing regional public goods to advance common interests of the region or to meet common challenges faced by the region. Such a leadership was expected to raise Japan's political and economic profile in East Asia. Importantly, a soft balancing factor became salient in Japan's regional strategies in the trade and financial fields. Japan's advocacy of the CEPEA and participation in TPP negotiations were exactly aimed at balancing against China's growing trade position in East Asia. In development towards the CMIM, Tokyo made efforts to maintain its regional influence *vis-à-vis* China, which had a growing interest in having its financial-power status accepted regionally and globally. Finance and trade are the two main vehicles to sustain states' economic power, and Tokyo certainly sought to counter Beijing's power maximisation in these fields.

While Japan was important as the initiator of regional institutions, its relative position declined during their development process. Tokyo was confronted with great difficulties in attaining several policy objectives such as a smooth transition from the pilot project to a permanent institution for food security, the adoption of the Asian Currency Unit as a regional currency unit, and the expansion of EANET's activities in the enactment of the Instrument of EANET. These difficulties derived from failure to convince other members of the necessity of advanced forms of institutions by coordinating their divergent interests. In most cases Japan was unable to get positive postures from China and South Korea, which had historically seeded antipathy and rivalry sentiments against it. Japan was also faced with difficulties in changing the perception of other countries that it initiated and sustained regional institutions for its own self-interest, which was typically seen in food security cooperation. Although Japan sought to play a role as a provider of regional public goods and a stabiliser of the regional economic order, it often failed to gain an acceptance of such a role from its regional neighbours.

China played a decisive role in the development process of regional institutions. In the trade field China made a bold proposal on the ASEAN–China FTA (ACFTA), and later converted its preference for the ASEAN+3 FTA into a new idea for an East Asia-wide FTA, which was then transformed into the ASEAN-initiated RCEP. In the agricultural sector, China's provision of the largest quantity of earmarked rice created a new impetus to promote regional cooperation on food security, which led to the launching of the APTERR. In the financial field, China was the main advocate of the multilateralisation of the CMI and made substantial commitments to realising it. In these cases, China's positive engagement constituted a main driver for realising the advanced form of regional institutions. The main factor underpinning China's successful engagements was bold and timely policy advocacies, typically seen in the trade and agricultural fields. In the environments and energy, China's position was crucial for regional institution-building in the negative sense. While China's passive attitude dampened initiatives to produce a foundation document for EANET with a legally binding nature and a broader scope of activities, its passive posture in regional energy cooperation constituted a crucial factor that disturbed the deepening of talks on development towards policy harmonisation.

China had strategic intentions in committing to the development of regional institutions. The trade initiative in an East Asia-wide FTA and support for the CMIM aimed to consolide an East Asian economic grouping that would dampen the influence of the United States. The proposal for the ACFTA and the generous offering of earmarked rice for the EAERR were designed to strengthen political linkages with ASEAN by combining them with other accommodating policies towards Southeast Asia. Moreover, Beijing intended to check and undermine Tokyo's influence in advancing its own regional initiatives. The ACFTA and the provision of the largest quantity of earmarked rice certainly eclipsed Japan's relative presence in Southeast Asia. In environmental cooperation, China sought to avoid the international responsibility that strengthened environmental institutions would impose. China's negativity in regional energy cooperation could be explained partly by its rivalry sentiment against Japan, and more fundamentally by the positioning of energy as a strategic issue to be pursued by bilateral, not multilateral, arrangements. In these two policy fields, China's passive posture had much to do with the weak strategic milieu: no need to balance against the US influence in East Asia and the weak or non-existent possibility of enhancing political linkages with ASEAN through positive engagements.

Past research stresses the importance of the Sino-Japanese relationship in advancing regional cooperation in East Asia (Dent ed. 2008; Nabers 2010). This study confirmed this point in all cases. In the financial field Sino-Japanese collaboration was the key to developing architectures for managing regional financial affairs. At the same time the two great powers were keen to maintain relative influence, which was prominently exhibited in battles over the largest contribution quota to the CMIM. In the trade field the main reason why East Asian countries were unable to advance an East Asia-wide FTA for a long time lay in rivalry between the two great powers. The two ideas of a regional FTA – China-induced EAFTA and Japan-proposed CEPEA – existed simultaneously, and both ASEAN and South Korea were unwilling and unable to coordinate the two great powers' confrontation. In the environmental field Japan's attempt to expand the scope of activities in enacting the Instrument of EANET was turned down by China, and the instrument could not incorporate this element explicitly. In the food security field China and Japan did not enter into sharp confrontation. However, the lack of commitment from China to strengthening the emergency rice reserve system was a main reason why Japan's hopes for the institutionalisation of the EAERR were not realised for a long time.

Significantly, regional power transition – a declining Japan and a rising China – had a crucial impact on the evolution of institution-building in trade, finance, and food security. While Japan initiated the formation of regional institutions and made serious efforts to upgrade the institutions, the player who exerted decisive power in realising the second stage of institution-building was China, which consolidated its position in regional institutions with bold policy advocacies underpinned by prudent regional strategies. Given past successful commitments mixed with growing economic capabilities, China's influence on the evolution of regional institutions in trade, finance, and food security – RCEP, CMIM, and APTERR – is likely to increase further.

As far as South Korea is concerned, it pursued two strategies in its commitments to regional institution-building in East Asia. The first is the check-and-accommodation strategy. Seoul did not show a clear leadership role in promoting regional cooperation in most policy fields examined in this study. It carefully checked Japan and China's initiatives and sought to maintain its interests by making commitments commensurate with its middle-power status and capabilities. In food security cooperation Seoul announced its contribution to earmarked rice reserve quickly after China's pledge of provision, contributing half as much as China. In fierce battles over the greater quota to the CMIM between China and Japan, South Korea secured half the contribution quota *vis-à-vis* the two states. The second strategy is harmonisation with its Northeast Asia-centred initiatives. In environmental cooperation South Korea launched and sustained the Joint Research Project on Long-range Transboundary Air Pollutants in Northeast Asia (LTP), an arrangement for transboundary air pollution in Northeast Asia. Seoul's passive posture towards EANET derived largely from its concern that the growing presence of EANET would undermine the presence of the LTP. In the trade field, Seoul exhibited more interest in the trilateral FTA rather than an East Asia-wide FTA because the former was important for gaining access to the huge market in China, its largest trading partner.

It is worth referring to South Korea's nuanced relationship with Japan in regional cooperation. Although South Korea could have behaved as a coordinator of interests between Japan and China in the environmental and trade fields, it did not play such a role largely because of rivalry against Japan. South Korea should have held common interests with Japan in resolving transboundary acid deposition problems by drawing positive postures from China. However, its commitments to EANET aimed partly to reduce Japan's influence, intending to attract a sub-branch of the Japan-located Network Centre to its territory. Seoul's crucial policy objective in regional FTA formation was directed towards securing an advantageous position for its manufacturing firms against their Japanese rivals. The energy case was unique because South Korea made positive commitments to regional cooperation by proposing new areas of cooperation and engaging intensively in capacity-building programmes. Such commitments were motivated to expand business chances, which were typically seen in the trade sector. At the same time, the identification of similarities in strategic milieu and energy structure with Japan allowed South Korea to show a positive posture towards Japan-initiated cooperative frameworks. The energy case might provide some insights on how South Korea and Japan can overcome antagonism in bilateral relations through increasing political and social relationality for the sake of broader strategic interests.

A salient feature in ASEAN's engagement in institution-building in East Asia was its keen interest in maintaining ASEAN centrality. While ASEAN officially maintained the pivotal position by making its neighbouring countries agree on its proposed trade arrangement, the association maintained collective power in contribution quotas in the CMIM and successfully lured the AMRO, a regional surveillance unit, to a city in Southeast Asia. Even in food security cooperation where ASEAN's overall presence and role were less prominent, an individual member – Singapore – made special commitments to preserving ASEAN's status and interests in East Asian cooperation. The adherence to ASEAN centrality was exhibited in cooperation on EANET in which not all ASEAN members participated. Indeed, Southeast Asian members did not push forward their collective interests on the basis of ASEAN, but an individual member – Malaysia – strove to make ASEAN's environmental issues the key concerns for the environments in East Asia.

ASEAN's commitments to preserving its central position in East Asian regionalism were sustained mainly by two strategies. The first is the indirect balancing strategy. In the trade field, ASEAN proposed its own initiative in a cohesive and timely manner in growing political complexities with great powers' interactions in re-engineering regional FTAs, and successfully had its own idea – the RCEP – accepted as the primary regional arrangement. The successful invitation of the AMRO to Singapore derived from an avoidance of strategic competition and the maintenance of balance between China and Japan. The second strategy is asset accumulation. ASEAN incorporated particular ideas, which have accumulated in its regional integration process, as guiding principles for promoting regional institution-building. The two-track approach and consideration to sensitivity became two of the RCEP's guiding principles, which encouraged Northeast Asian countries to support the ASEAN-induced RCEP. Singapore and Thailand have accumulated their experiences as a financial hub and a rice-cultivation centre, respectively, and such accumulations allowed them to attract the secretariats of the CMIM and APTERR.

Two broader implications of this study for regional power configuration should be noted. First, this study confirmed the importance of geographical position for the four parties' engagement in regional institution-building. This is a conventional insight in states' external relations and policies in strategic and security domains. Even in the economic and social policy spheres examined in this study, the geographical position played a significant role. China is the great power in Eurasia and shares national borders with 14 countries including those of East Asia, South Asia and Central Asia. Its commitments to regional institution-building are influenced by the broader geopolitical perspective, and due consideration to the US presence in advancing its regional strategies reflects such a perspective. Despite its still preponderant economic and technological capabilities in the world, Japan is a regional great power whose policy concern is directed towards the maintenance of political and economic influence in East Asia in evolving power transition. South Korea's geographical concern is narrower to establish a solid position in Northeast Asia where the country seeks to maintain its presence and interests between the two great powers. A unique feature is the position of ASEAN. Southeast Asia is bounded by India in the west: China, Japan, and Korea in the northeast; and the Oceania in the south. ASEAN intends to take advantage of the opportunities offered by this geographical position to be the hub of East Asia and the Indo-Pacific. ASEAN's commitments to the ASEAN Connectivity after 2009 aimed to take full advantage of the potential that this geographical advantage can provide.

The second implication is relevant to the rise of China. As this research demonstrated, China has shown growing presence in advancing cooperative institutions in individual policy fields in East Asia. An important challenge is how to direct China's dominant power towards regional institution-building in a harmonious way. This research found that the existence of a strategic milieu is important for drawing cooperative postures from China. For creating the strategic milieu internally, the presence of ASEAN is important. ASEAN has played a critical role in socialising China in regional relations (Ba 2006), and it is crucial to sustain ASEAN centrality in the building process of regional institutions. The maintenance of ASEAN centrality encourages China to forge stable political and economic relations with its southern grouping, sustaining the environments where Beijing exhibits benevolent postures by paying respect to the interests of small neighbouring countries.[4] Given that Japan has committed to the ASEAN centrality through its long-term support for ASEAN's consolidation and resiliency, South Korea's genuine commitment to regional cooperation in East Asia – not just checking China or Japan's behaviour – and the pursuit of closer ties with ASEAN in such commitments will be crucial for sustaining ASEAN's pivotal position. This implies that South Korea needs to expand its diplomatic concerns from the Korean peninsula to broader regional affairs with a long-term perspective (Oh 2012: 122–23). In order to establish the strategic milieu externally, it is vital to foster the meaningful presence of the United States and India in East Asian affairs.[5] In the late 1990s and early 2000s when China's economic power was rising quickly but its economic size was still moderate, there was a possibility that East Asian states could involve China in the regional community-building process primarily through their own efforts. However, after 2010 China became too capable politically and economically, and consequently the presence of the United States and India is indispensable for checking Chinese behaviour. Such a strategic milieu makes China adopt harmonious diplomatic postures to consolidate its presence in East Asia, an increasingly important region in the world.

The influence of China and Japan's domestic politics

The first supplementary variable is policymakers' preferences in the domestic political process. The four parties' political interactions at the systemic level created the fundamental configuration for institution-building in East Asia. However, China and Japan, two prominent powers in the region, had material capabilities to reflect domestic political conditions in the development of regional cooperation in East Asia.

In Japan's commitments to regional institution-building, preferences of individual government agencies, not the government as a whole, mattered. The government ministries initiated specific regional institutions and such initiations had much to do with the maintenance of core interests of the ministries. In the agricultural field, the Ministry of Agriculture, Forestry and Fisheries (MAFF) sought to utilise the formation of the regional rice reserve system in East Asia as a way to mitigate the negative impact of World Trade Organization (WTO) obligations on the domestic rice market. In the environmental field, the Ministry of the Environment (MOE) initiated EANET as an institution to take advantage of its accumulated scientific expertise on air pollution for resolving transboundary acid rain problems that affected Japan. While the Ministry of Economy, Trade and Industry (METI) advocated the CEPEA in order to secure regional production networks created by manufacturing companies under its jurisdiction, it pushed forward ASEAN+3 energy cooperation as a platform to enhance Japan's energy security in the evolving energy environments. MOF intended to promote the internationalisation of the yen in advancing regional financial cooperation. Importantly, inter-ministerial rivalry or conflict had much to do with the initiation of regional institutions. MOE proposed EANET as a programme for acid deposition diplomacy applied to East Asia in competition against METI, which also pushed forward another programme for the diplomacy. METI's proposal for the CEPEA was confronted with chilly responses from other ministries such as MAFF and the Ministry of Foreign Affairs, which worried about the concept's unfavourable effects on the domestic agricultural market and the alliance with the United States, respectively.

The Japanese political system has been characterised by a weak cabinet and strong bureaucracy. The prime minister and the cabinet have limited power to coordinate interests among ministries, which hold a high-level freedom to pursue specific policy objectives (Mulgan 2000: 189–93; Shinoda 2000). The Japanese ministries, in committing to regional institution-building, had high autonomy which allowed them to determine policy objectives, secure budget and personnel, and implement concrete measures to realise the objectives. The politicians did not find much interest in taking advantage of external policies to increase the political legitimacy of their reign, partly because all policy areas examined in the study were relevant to economic and social fields, not political and security ones that constitute the core areas of political manoeuvring. Accordingly, the ministries were not confronted with substantial veto points. A series of such conditions enabled the ministries to formulate and implement regional initiatives in order to maintain interests under their jurisdictions, secure their budgets and prestige, and thereby enhance their political legitimacy.

Certainly, it is possible to find some developments in Japan's recent external policies. The FTA policy has become more strategic and cohesive, combining 'economic-security' elements such as 'resource security' and economic statecraft for soft balancing. The Japanese government under the returned Liberal Democratic Party (LDP) began to formulate prudent trade policies and decided to join TPP negotiations despite adamant domestic opposition. Notwithstanding these developments, Japanese policymaking is characterised as 'policy fragmentation': weak top-down decisions and strong ministerial autonomy under the decentralised system. This policy fragmentation tends to create indecisiveness and inconsistency in Japan's external relations and policies, preventing the government from formulating integrated and strategic policies towards East Asia from a long-term perspective.

Given that frequent changes of prime minister have created regime vulnerability in Japan, the establishment of a stable government and the effective division of labour between politicians and bureaucrats will provide the foundation for formulating consistent, far-sighted external policies.

In China's commitments to regional institution-building, the preferences of senior leaders, not individual government agencies, mattered. As is widely known, the Chinese bureaucratic system is highly fragmented with duplication of the mandate among plural bureaucratic agencies.[6] This bureaucratic fragmentation was seen in China's commitments to regional cooperation examined in this study. In the fields of environment and agriculture, the administrative agencies concerned could not agree on the enhancement of regional cooperation partly because expanded cooperative activities required coordination with other administrative agencies. In the energy sector, the fragmentation of energy-related policies among diverse bureaucratic apparatuses impeded the main administrative agency from holding the authority and capabilities to formulate a cohesive energy policy. Under such a bureaucratic fragmentation, top-down decision-making played a crucial role. In agricultural cooperation, senior leaders suddenly decided to provide the largest quantity of earmarked rice, which propelled the formation of the APTERR. The top-down initiative was apparent in trade policy. While China's astonishing proposal for the ACFTA derived from Primer Zhu's leadership, senior leaders changed China's regional FTA policy, abandoning its previous adherence to the EAFTA. Importantly, senior leaders paid due attention to likely effects of regional initiatives on domestic political and economic conditions. On the one hand, China has made substantial commitments to advancing regional financial cooperation in order to prevent the proliferation of a financial crisis to its territory, which had the potential to provoke economic and social unrest internally. On the other hand, China has maintained cautious postures in environmental cooperation. The senior leaders' decision paved the way for China's participation in EANET. But, they were cautious about the expansion of the EANET mandate, fearing that the strengthened EANET might force China to accept interference in domestic affairs and constrain policy autonomy to advance economic growth.

The Chinese political system has been sustained by party-state dominance under the Chinese Communist Party's (CCP) single-party regime. The CCP's legitimacy as China's single ruling party is based on steady economic development and a rise in international status (Lai 2010). The party-state authorities make decisions on public policies and check their implementation by paying due attention to the policies' influences on the domestic economy and society. The Chinese government supports a regional initiative that will be conducive to the growth of the domestic economy and thereby raise the CCP's political legitimacy. On the other hand, it opposes the development of a regional institution that might have negative effects on the stability of the domestic society and the CCP's political reign.

Thus, the fragmentation and porosity of functional bureaucracies and the strong control of policymaking by senior leaders created 'policy centralisation' on China's commitment to regional cooperation. Government agencies with jurisdiction over a specific policy field were unable to pursue autonomous policies for regional cooperation due to constraints from domestic politics. In particular, senior leaders' prudent calculations on how specific regional policies would influence the CCP's domestic political legitimacy constituted the baseline for China's regional policies.

An increasing number of studies highlights the pluralisation of Chinese policymaking through the growing involvement of various actors outside the government (Mertha 2009; Jakobson and Knox 2010; Christensen 2011). This study confirmed this observation in several cases. In promoting the energy policy, national oil companies had strong autonomous power and China's commitments to regional energy cooperation were influenced by their corporate strategies. Some industrial groups gradually raised concerns about likely negative influences of trade liberalisation on their activities and interests. The National Development and Reform Commission (NDRC), a powerful administrative agency with a conservation position on reform and opening, played a critical role in reflecting such concerns on Chinese trade policymaking. The integration of the Chinese economy into globalisation increases the direct impact of global forces on the domestic society. Such a development will increase the possibility of appeals from some segments of the society for governmental action, which will undermine both policy centralisation and policy cohesion.

The relevance of research institutes to institution-building

This research paid particular attention to the presence and role of researchers and research institutes in the process of institution-building in East Asia. The main task of research institutes is to offer professional interpretation and advice on the development of specific policy affairs. Various research institutes fulfilled this function in the initiation and development of regional institutions examined in this study. Researchers and research institutes provided a basic design for new regional initiatives. Before launching EANET, scientists undertook intensive discussions on transboundary atmospheric issues in East Asia, and formulated guidelines and technical manuals, which became fundamental instruments for operating EANET. Before the start of regional energy cooperation, the IEEJ confirmed challenges with which ASEAN members were confronted in energy security, and provided guiding ideas for enabling the Japanese government to assist them to meet the challenges. In the process of institutional development, researchers and research institutes played a role in agenda-setting for the direction of deepening cooperation. In the development of financial cooperation, research networks – the Asian Policy Forum (APF), the ASEAN+3 Research Group, and the Network of East Asian Think-tanks (NEAT) working group – provided new ideas and insights to flesh out regional financial cooperation, and these ideas and insights were realised in the development of financial cooperation. In the trade field, researchers and research institutes in each of the four parties undertook surveys and analyses of the FTA formation, and their results became important references for the governments' FTA strategies. Moreover, some research institutes indicated feasible routes to overcome specific hurdles to advancing regional cooperation. The Economic Research Institute for ASEAN and East Asia (ERIA) sought to resolve technical problems in developing the existing ASEAN+1 FTA networks into the East Asia-wide FTA by providing a comprehensive mapping of the existing ASEAN+1 FTAs.

Another important role played by research institutes is the formation of a transnational network of professionals and experts. The transnational networks were formed as organs affiliated to regional institutions. In the financial sector the ASEAN+3 Research Group was organised as a gathering affiliated to the ASEAN+3 finance ministers' meeting. Various research institutes and individual economists were involved in specific research regarding regional financial and monetary affairs, which was commissioned by finance ministers. In environmental cooperation, the Scientific Advisory Committee (SAC), a formal network of scientists from 13 member countries, functioned as one of four main organs for EANET. Moreover, transnational networks of research institutes were formed under the initiative of standing regional research institutes. While the Asian Development Bank Institute organised the APF as a transnational networking of 17 research institutes all located in Asia, the ERIA established the Research Institute Networks (RIN), comprised of 16 research institutes in the Asia-Pacific region.

The expected tasks of a transnational network are to foster common identity among participants to pursue collective objectives, deepen social relationality through intensive discussions, and propose innovative ideas and methodologies to meet regional challenges on the basis of shared scientific beliefs. The transnational networks mentioned above still had limitations in performing these tasks adequately. This was the case with the SAC, which had the most solid institutional foundation for its activities. In promoting environmental cooperation, the committee did not establish shared beliefs on the causes, effects, and models of regional acid deposition largely because scientific knowledge still fell short of removing uncertainties of a complex nature in transboundary atmospheric issues in East Asia. Uncertainty normally has a positive correlation to the influence of expert groups (Haas 1992: 14–16); however, high uncertainty has a negative correlation to such influence by undermining internal cohesion within the experts' group and legitimacy of their expertise for policymakers. An additional factor was that some countries had not reached the stage of having human resources with sufficient research capabilities, which disturbed the formation of a cohesive network of experts.

The research institutes and researchers are non-state actors who are expected to provide a venue to promote policymakers' social learning through the objective interpretation of facts on politically sensitive issues and the provision of innovative solutions to problems in defined areas. Such expectations were best met by EANET, where the scientists' group was institutionally embedded into the policymaking process. However, recommendations on the basis of objective interpretation of facts and scientific views were sometimes rejected by government officials who gave priority to political concerns rather than professional expertise or scientific research. Fundamentally, there is a distinction between decisions on technical issues and those on political issues. While experts might dominate governmental decision-making regarding technical issues, it is questionable to what extent policymakers employ the understanding of technical details in relation to basic issues of international relations (Krebs 2001: 225). The environmental case exhibits the experts' limitations in influencing policymaking when technical issues are linked to political considerations and in making policymakers pay respect to scientific, tactical details by reinterpreting national interests and overcoming political constraints.

As a fundamental problem, the research groups have not established members' cohesion sufficiently on the basis of shared causal beliefs and professional knowledge, for fulfilling the function of social learning. In environmental cooperation the impact of research expertise on real policies was limited partly because scientists from some countries played the role of spokesmen for government positions, not sticking to providing professional proposals with objective and scientific values. The lack of internal harmonisation was also seen in financial cooperation where research institutes were intensively involved in policy development. The ASEAN+3 Research Group, which had direct access to the policymaking process, did not have prior coordination on research outcomes from several research institutes to produce cohesive views on the development of regional financial cooperation. Cross (2013) argues that the more internally cohesive an epistemic community, the more likely it is to achieve a high degree of influence on policy outcomes. In particular, 'when a group of professionals with recognised expertise is able to speak with one voice, that voice is often seen as more legitimate because it is based on a well-reasoned consensus among those in the best position to know' (Cross 2013: 147). The research groups in East Asia have not developed enough to be networks of cohesion to develop one voice, which is crucial for performing the function of social learning and for influencing the governments' actions or policies.

It is worth referring to the presence and role of the NEAT, which was relevant to research activities in three policy fields – financial cooperation, food security, and energy security – examined in this study. The NEAT has a critical value as the sole comprehensive research network involving all

ASEAN+3 members. The network collects experts' professional views and expertise on key issues and major potential areas for East Asian cooperation through the operations of field-specific working groups, and its recommendations are delivered to and acknowledged at the annual ASEAN+3 summit meetings. At the same time, the NEAT's operations have at least two inherent weaknesses. First, the involvement of the NEAT track II bodies in the intergovernmental track I process is far from deep and effective. As confirmed in this study, government officials have been confronted with practical hurdles to flesh out cooperative initiatives in various policy fields. Yet, the NEAT's research activities have not presented effective ideas to overcome such hurdles by forging direct linkages with government officials who engage in concrete cooperative activities or institutionalised mechanisms for ongoing, two-way dialogues for feedback and further deliberations. Second, the NEAT research networks do not include effective mechanisms to develop networks of researchers and think-tanks. Indeed, its membership is open to all think-tanks and their scholars in the 10+3 countries. In reality, however, one research institute or think-tank, which was designated the coordinating body by the foreign ministry of each country, has maintained a dominant position in the NEAT process. The network of these research bodies tends to be static, just holding a few formal meetings annually (Wong 2012: 94). There is, however, a possibility of deepening the network of knowledge and expertise by forging close linkages with various research communities at the regional and domestic levels, helping to develop capacity-building of experts in developing countries, and exploring linkages with private companies and civil society groups.

The involvement of experts – non-state actors – in the policymaking process is important for fostering regional governance. Past research has confirmed this importance in the development of European integration and governance. While Zito (2001b) examined the influence of expert groups and scientific communities in the European Union (EU) policymaking process in increasing technical complexity and scientific uncertainty, Verdun (1999) confirmed that a specific group of monetary experts contributed to the creation of the Economic and Monetary Union. In East Asia, the process towards regional governance is highly managed by state actors' interests and preferences. The research institutes and researchers that have vested connections to the government could be involved in the policymaking process by giving professional input in the formation of regional policies. This point is important because the members of research institutes need to become part of the bureaucratic apparatus by acquiring regulatory and policymaking responsibility if they hope to have real influence on policymaking (Adler and Haas 1992: 374). However, greater access to policymaking tends to lead to less influence on policy decisions themselves. The relationship between state actors and researchers remained vertical and hierarchical at least for some states, and close connections with the government discouraged researchers from playing a role independent from the government's strategies or actions. The essence of governance lies in the incorporation of diverse views and ideas from various independent actors who stand in a horizontal, non-hierarchical position. In this line of insight, regional governance in East Asia remains at a preliminary stage, and has a long way to go for its development.

Critical juncture in institution-building

In analysing the genesis and evolution of regional institutions in East Asia, this study employed the idea of critical juncture, a key concept for historical institutionalism, which 'works best at delineating the origins and development of institutional structures over time' (Schmidt 2006: 105). In the policy areas examined in this study, exogenous shocks and events had positive effects on the progress of regional institution-building.

A crisis became a catalyst in changing the institutional path of a historical trajectory, which was typically seen in the financial field. The 1997–98 Asian financial crisis became a catalyst in making regional leaders recognise their collective identity living in a region vulnerable to financial instability. The political leaders in crisis-stricken countries and China recognised the devastating effects of the financial crisis and its contagious nature, and intensified their willingness to construct regional financial architectures to prevent financial turmoil. The global financial crisis of 2008 revealed the shortcomings of the existing financial architectures, and urged political leaders to finalise their decision to elevate the CMI to the CMIM as the most effective option to respond to an enormous challenge like a global financial crisis. A similar pattern of institutional development was seen in the agricultural sector. The food crisis in 1998, which caused increases in the prices of major foodstuffs, increased policymakers' interest in establishing a feasible regional institution to ensure food supply in an emergency. The food crisis of 2007–08 created a similar pattern to raise the policymakers' sense of urgency about food emergencies in their societies. They sought to take advantage of the EAERR as a pivotal mechanism to react to an urgent food need, and this renewed interest in food security underpinned a transition from the EAERR pilot project to the launching of the APTERR. In the energy sector, volatile oil prices coupled with the fear of a US attack on Iraq made policymakers in East Asia more concerned about energy security. Under such conditions, an informal ASEAN+3 energy ministers' meeting on the sidelines of an international meeting became a direct catalyst in creating a new institutional path to hold a regional forum for periodical talks on energy security.

For a long time, ASEAN has existed as the sole intergovernmental organisation with substantial experience of regional cooperation in East Asia. The association had created regional institutions to prepare for a time of emergency in finance and food security. The external shocks articulated the inherent weaknesses of these ASEAN-made institutions, which were then strengthened through the involvement of economically more powerful Northeast Asian countries. The external upheavals urged the transformation of nominal institutions into substantial ones, creating East Asia-wide institutions that have more resiliency against emergency circumstances.

International events or trends provided critical stimuli to initiate a new institutional path in trade and the environment. In the trade field, moves to promote FTAs in other parts of the world combined with stagnated progress in trade liberalisation under multilateralism encouraged major states in East Asia to reconsider the multilateral-oriented trade policy and find more value in a discriminatory FTA policy. The emergence of the US-induced TPP as a main trade arrangement in the Asia-Pacific region became a direct impetus to converge diverse views on an East Asia-wide FTA into a new idea of the RCEP. The US drive for the TPP encouraged China to advance an East Asia-wide FTA that excludes the United States, and ASEAN sought to maintain its political status in response to such moves by presenting its own design for trade cooperation. Regarding the environment, the 1992 United Nations Conference on Environment and Development (UNCED) became a catalyst in awakening interest in tackling global environmental problems, urging the diffusion of European experience of managing transboundary air pollution. After this UN event, region-based institutions for managing transboundary atmospheric issues were created in East Asia, and EANET was one such institution. In these cases, there were historical points when multiple institutions with similar policy objectives began to emerge in global and regional settings, forming complicated structures of overlapping institutions or nesting institutions. Under such conditions, major states in East Asia changed their views on the evolving reality and examined carefully what was a feasible option to attain their policy objectives. Through such examination, common interests in developing East Asia-specific institutions were fostered.

It is worth examining the relationship between external events or moves and institutional development in the environmental sector. In enacting the Instrument of EANET, there were neither prominent events that urged the deepening of existing level of institution-building nor scientific progress to show that acid deposition caused serious and urgent problems in East Asia. On the contrary, new international initiatives on the basis of scientific advances reduced the relative importance of EANET as an independent cooperative institution. Such initiatives urged more collaboration with similar institutions in other parts of Asia and encouraged the integration of an acid deposition issue with other environmental problems such as climate change. Although EANET started with relatively solid institutional frameworks, it failed to strengthen institutional structures and functions by producing a foundation document that holds legalistic power and the broader scope of activities. The lack of exogenous shocks provides one reason for this result.

In the development of regional institutions, an adherence to maintaining sovereign rights and domestic regime autonomy as well as collective norms in the region such as incrementalism and informality hindered the steady progress of regional institution-building. Moreover, the four parties were concerned about relative gains and costs associated with the development of regional institutions, producing complicated views on the institutions' functions and policy directions. Such complexities created 'institutional inertia' – the parallel existence of two ideas for a regional FTA, continuous talks on the CMIM, prolonged implementation of the EAERR pilot project, the repetition of meetings for information exchange in energy affairs, and long-lasting dialogues on the Instrument of EANET. In the first three cases, the inertia was punctuated by exogenous shocks and events, which increased policymakers' sense of urgency about the insufficiency of existing institutions, encouraging them to make political compromises on controversial issues for breaking the institutional status quo and creating an advanced form of institutions. The external upheavals and events played a significant role in articulating opportunity costs regarding the unresolved coordination games, overcoming institutional inertia resulting from political deadlocks, and paving the way for elevating the institutional path to an enhanced stage.

A major feature of critical junctures is contingency, which makes it impossible to predict in advance what historical events will become critical junctures (Arthur 1994; Pempel 2012). However, it might be possible to identify some conditions under which a particular kind of historical event constitutes a critical juncture. The insights from the empirical cases of this study suggest four conditions. First, a historical event reveals the functional limitation of an existing institution. The existing institution cannot resist and absorb shocks from the critical event. Second, costs associated with the malfunction of the existing institution are deeply perceived by the policymakers concerned. The policymakers who worry about the negative impacts of the shocks on the domestic economy and society increase their willingness to transform the existing institution into a new one. Third, a particular actor initiates the transformation process by proposing ideas and designs of the new institution. This kind of leadership becomes a catalyst in assisting the institution's members to gain clear ideas about the objective, design, and function of the new institution. Fourth, a new institutional path is created after this critical event, and this new path reproduces itself in a path-dependent process, making it difficult to return to the initial point. When a series of these evolutions occurs in a particular historical period, this period could be regarded as a historical breakpoint of institutional change – a critical juncture. An important factor in these conditions is the combination of historical, structural factors and actors' perceptions and purposeful behaviour (Calder 2008: 17; Chin and Stubbs 2011).

Future directions of research

There are three areas of future research that are drawn from this study. The first is the deepening of research on commonality in institution-building in East Asia through comparative and historical analyses. This research found common features in the process of institution-building and concrete designs in achieved institutions in different policy areas. These commonalities are likely to be influenced by the political milieu and sociopolitical cultures in East Asia. It will be useful to explore the implications of these features from comparative and historical perspectives by undertaking similar research in other policy areas such as health, transport, science and technology, and human rights, and integrating the essence of the commonalities in the broader political and social textures in the region.

The second area concerns complicated structures of regional institutions. In East Asia, various institutions with different memberships coexist, creating the structures of institutional overlapping and institutional nesting. In this study, marked influence from nested institutional structures under the ASEAN+3 and EAS was found in trade and energy, and East Asian cooperation in finance and air pollution is connected to institutions in the broader Asia-Pacific and Asia. It will be crucial to explore how these institutions interact with each other in the practical process of regional cooperation and how the complex configurations of institutional structures affect the overall development of regionalism in East Asia.

The third area is relevant to the governance perspective. This research highlighted research institutes as the critical non-state actors involved in the formation of regional institution-building. The research found that the limited presence of research institutes derived partly from close linkages with governments. This insight implies that research on the involvement of more independent non-state actors such as business groups and NGOs in regional institution-building needs to be undertaken. The governance perspective is also important in exploring how a set of sociopolitical norms with universal character is incorporated into the building of regional institutions.

Lastly, there are two policy suggestions for advancing regional cooperation in East Asia. The first is the creation of a 'learning loop' for regional cooperation. In the new millennium, an impetus for regional cooperation gained momentum in various policy fields in East Asia, and the advance of formal institutions is a major method of promoting regional cooperation. In the process of institution-building, a particularly important challenge is how to coordinate divergent interests of participating members, and policymakers have made various commitments to meeting this challenge. It is useful to establish systems for learning from experiences in various policy fields, searching for the possible best practices for institution-building. The second is pertinent to the importance of policy responses in a critical period.

As this research confirms, institutional development takes a significant step forward during the critical period. While the critical period normally implies a crisis or risk, it also has the potential to overcome political stalemate in regional institution-building. It is necessary to foster decisive political will to take advantage of a critical time as a valuable opportunity for advancing collective regional interests.

Notes

1 Introduction

1. Grimes (2009) analyses regional financial challenges and cooperation in East Asia in terms of strategic power relations among the United States, Japan, and China. Particularly important was that Japan's proposal to set up the Asian Monetary Fund during the Asian currency crisis in 1997–98 was not realised, largely because of opposition from the United States (Amyx 2002). The US opposition constituted a major impediment to the development of Malaysian proposal for establishing an East Asian collaborative body (EAEC) (Lim 2001).
2. The ASEAN Way consists of behavioural norms encapsulated in a code of conduct as well as procedural norms (Acharya 1997: 328–29). The former entail well known international principles such as respect for sovereignty and territorial integrity, non-interference in domestic affairs, and pacific settlement of disputes. The latter is a set of norms that expect ASEAN members to undertake decision-making by following the principles of consultation and consensus with a high degree of informality, flexible incrementalism, and non-confrontational bargaining styles.

2 Frameworks for Analysing Institution-Building in East Asia

1. The US approach to East Asia formed a sharp contrast to its approach to Western Europe. The US government considered that the integration of West Germany with Europe would lead to the prosperity and stability of the region, and West Germany was embedded into regional frameworks of the North Atlantic Treaty Organisation (NATO) and European Community (EC) (Hemmer and Katzenstein 2002).
2. 'Balancing' means a state's strategy to form alliances with other states with similar concerns (external balancing) and/or to mobilise its national resources to increase its own defence and economic capabilities (internal balancing). The balancing concept has long meant 'hard balancing' – countervailing alliances and military build-ups –, which has been directed towards explaining security affairs in general, a state's motivations for alliance formation in particular (Walt 1987). After the end of the Cold War, scholars articulated different contexts in the balancing notion by developing the concept of soft balancing.
3. A well-known example is the substantial commitment of the eighth President, Kim Dae-jung, who proposed the establishment of the East Asian Vision Group and the East Asian Study Group.
4. For instance, the Chinese government studied the history of Japan's industry policy implemented by the Ministry of Economy, Trade and Industry.
5. The summit comprises the China Council for the Promotion of International Trade (CCPIT) of China, Japan Business Federation (*Nippon Keidanren*) of Japan, and Federation of Korean Industries (FKI) of South Korea.
6. In addition to the previously mentioned business groups, transgovernmental network of regulators, judges, and legislators, transnational advocacy networks, and communities of practices are included in these actors (Cross 2013: 139–41).

7. While the logic of consequentialism is relevant to the rational choice approach that treats the interests and preferences of actors as constant during the process of interaction, the logic of appropriateness relates to rule-guided and deliberative behaviour that is associated with particular identities in particular situations (Risse 2000).
8. Representatives of such think-tanks are the Japan Research Institute and the Sejong Institute in South Korea.
9. In China, the Chinese Academy of Social Sciences (CASS), China Institute of International Studies (CIIS), China Institute of Contemporary International Relations (CICIR), Development Research Center of the State Council (DRC), and Chinese People's Institute of Foreign Affairs (CPIFA) are just a few examples. In Japan, the National Institute for Research Advancement is a liaison institute, and government agencies have quite a few affiliated research institutes. The Japan Institute of International Affairs (JIIA), Research Institute of Economy, Trade and Industry (RIETI) are typical examples. In South Korea, the Korea Institute for International Economic Policy (KIEP), Korea Institute for Industrial Economics and Trade (KIET), and Korea Development Institute (KDI) are typical examples. In Southeast Asia, the ASEAN-Institutes of Strategic and International Studies (ASEAN-ISIS), a gathering of ten institutes specialising in strategic research from across the ASEAN region, is a representative research network. For a concise summary of these think-tanks, see http://www.nira.or.jp/past/ice/nwdtt/2005/index.html.
10. The track II framework is based on 'activities or discussions involving academics and intellectuals, journalists, business elites and others as well as officials "acting in their private capacity" ' (Nesadurai and Stone 2000: 192).
11. Positive feedback occurs when the choice of multiple individuals generates positive externalities such as network and condition effects (Fioretos 2011: 377). 'Self-reinforcing' implies that 'initial steps in a particular direction induce further movement in the same direction such that over time it becomes difficult or impossible to reverse direction' (Mahoney 2000: 512).
12. Contingency is defined as 'the inability of theory to predict or explain, either deterministically or probabilistically, the occurrence of a specific outcome' (Mahoney 2000: 513).
13. Learning is defined as a change of beliefs or the development of new beliefs as a result of the observation and interpretation of experience (Levy 1994: 283). Many theorists hold that learning takes place at two levels: 'simple learning' involves a change of means, but not in ends; and 'complex learning' involves a change of behaviour due to recognition of conflicts among underlying values, and a redefinition of end, not just means (Haas 1990: 26).
14. This insight is particularly applicable to a within-case design. This research adopts the within-case design – two cases in the initiation and development of institutions in each policy field.

3 Promoting Trade Liberalisation through Free Trade Agreements

1. These sectors are environmental goods and services, energy-related products and services, fish and fish products, toys, forest products, gems and jewellery, medical equipment and instruments, chemicals, telecommunications, food, rubber, fertiliser, automotive standards, oilseeds, and aircraft. The first nine belong to the priority sectors.

2. For the Statement on Bold Measures, see http://www.aseansec.org/8756.htm.
3. The leaders of ASEAN and Japan signed the Framework for the AJCEP during the Bali Summit in October 2003. The two parties commenced formal negotiations on the AJCEP in April 2005, and reached a general agreement on merchandise trade in August 2007 after nine rounds of negotiations.
4. The EHP, proposed by China and included in the Framework Agreement, committed ASEAN and China to reduce their respective tariffs for certain products from January 2004. Some 600 products covered by the EHP are those in the first eight chapters of the Harmonised System of Tariffs code, which basically belong to the agricultural sector.
5. This format calls for the progressive signing of agreements in situations in which common objectives among contracting parties have been established but no specific agreements regarding the details of the parties' rights and obligations have been reached within a short period (Chen 2006: 137).
6. For instance, per capita GDP of Guangxi and Yunnan in 2005 was 8,788 yuan and 7,835 yuan, 37 per cent and 44 per cent below the national average (14,040 yuan), respectively (*China Statistical Yearbook 2006*: 66).
7. The Guangxi Zhuang Autonomous Region was allowed to join the GMS Programme at the GMS summit in 2005 although the region geographically is not a part of the Mekong River basin.
8. The mission, headed by Hiroshi Okuda, President of Toyota Motor Corp. and Chairman of *Nikkeiren* (Japan Federation of Employers' Associations), visited six Asian countries in August–September 1999 in order to formulate the mission's report. For details of the mission and its report, see http://www.mofa.go.jp/mofaj/area/asiakeizai/saisei/index.html.
9. According to the Asian Development Bank's firm-level survey in 2007–08, around 28 per cent of the 841 Asian firms surveyed used FTA preferences and 25 per cent had plans to do so (Kawai and Wignaraja 2011: 7).
10. 'Towards an East Asia FTA: Modality and Road Map, A Report by Joint Expert Group for Feasibility Study on EAFTA, July 22, 2006'. Available at http://www.thaifta.com/thaifta/Portals/0/eafta_report.pdf.
11. 'The 12th AEM Plus Three Consultation: Joint Media Statement' http://www.aseansec.org/JMS-12th-AEM-Plus-Three.pdf and 'The AEM+6 Working Lunch: Joint Media Statement' http://www.aseansec.org/JMS-AEM+6-Working-Lunch.pdf.
12. 'Chairman's Statement of the 12th ASEAN Plus Three Summit' http://www.aseansec.org/23594.htm and 'Chairman's Statement of the 4th East Asia Summit' http://www.aseansec.org/23609.htm.
13. *Asahi Shimbun*, August 27, 2006.
14. 'Press Conference by Shoichi Nakagawa, Minister of Agriculture, Forestry and Fisheries, April 7, 2006'. Available at http://www.kanbou.maff.go.jp/kouhou/060407daijin.htm.
15. Both governments were forced to rush through FTA negotiations to conclude them by March 2007 because the US government's Trade Promotion Authority (TPA) would expire in July 2007.
16. The two parties signed the Korea–EU FTA in October 2010 after eight rounds of negotiations.
17. *Kyodo News*, August 28, 2012.
18. For instance, the TPP covers a wide range of areas including government procurement, environment, labour, e-commerce, legal issues, and so on.

19. *Nihon Keizai Shimbun*, November 2, 2011.
20. In 2011, trade with countries in the RCEP accounted for 47.5 per cent of Japan's total trade. This ratio was far larger than 26.4 per cent of trade with the TPP partners.
21. *People's Daily*, November 9, 2011.
22. 'Remarks at the G20 Ministerial by Hillary Rodham Clinton'. Available at http://www.state.gov/secretary/rm/2012/02/184623.htm.
23. 'TPP Negotiation Updates, Round 9: Lima'. Available at http://www.ustr.gov/trade-agreements/free-trade-agreements/trans-pacific-partnership/tpp-negotiation-updates/round-9-lim.
24. *Asahi Shimbun*, November 10, 2011.
25. 'Wen Jiabao Attends the 14th ASEAN Plus Three Summit and Delivers Speech'. Available at http://www.fmprc.gov.cn/eng/topics/wjbdyldrhy/t879362.shtml.
26. *Jakarta Post*, November 18, 2011.
27. 'Remarks by H. E. Wen Jiabao Premier of the State Council of the People's Republic of China at the Lunch Meeting of the Third Trilateral Business Summit'. Available at http://www.fmprc.gov.cn/eng/topics/wenzonglichuxizhongrihanhuiyi/t825297.htm.
28. 'Joint Media Statement on the ASEAN Roadshow to Japan'. Available at http://www.meti.go.jp/policy/trade_policy/east_asia/dl/120428asean_road_show.pdf.
29. As of December 2010, South Korea ratified FTAs with five countries and regions and concluded negotiations on FTAs with three additional partners. Since the FTA partners include three regional groupings, the total number of countries with FTAs becomes 45, containing major trading partners such as the United States and the EU.
30. This preference was clearly stated by senior government officials. Bark Taeho, Korean Trade Minister, clearly made this point, stating that 'bilateral discussions and agreements should be carried out and reached at first, then the trilateral consensus can be made' and 'compared with the free-trade area among the three countries, the South Korea–China free-trade area is a more "natural" phenomenon' (*Xinhua News Agency*, November 29, 2012).
31. *Yomiuri Shimbun*, May 15, 2012.
32. The CEFP was established in January 2001 within the Cabinet Office as a consultative body to facilitate Prime Minister's leadership in economic and fiscal policy formation. The council comprises the Chief Cabinet Secretary, the Minister of State for Economic and Fiscal Policy, other relevant ministers (Ministers for Internal Affairs and Communications, Finance, and Economy, Trade and Industry), Governor of the Bank of Japan, and four private-sector experts.
33. 'The Basic Policies for Economic and Fiscal Management and Structural Reform 2006', July 7, 2006, Cabinet Decision. Available at http://www5.cao.go.jp/keizai-shimon/cabinet/2006/decision060707.pdf.
34. The Japanese METI revealed the idea of the ERIA in the *Global Economic Strategy* published in April 2006, and its establishment was formally proposed at the second EAS meeting in January 2007, and was agreed at the third EAS meeting in November 2007.
35. The ERIA-RIN members comprise the CASS, the Institute of Developing Economies (IDE/JETRO) of Japan, the Korea Institute for International Economic Policy (KIEP), the Thailand Development Research Institute (TDRI), the Centre for Strategic and International Studies (CSIS) of Indonesia, and so on. For details of the ERIA-RIN, see http://www.eria.org/about_eria/organization/16rin.html.

4 Developing Institutions for Regional Financial Stability

1. 'Joint Statement on East Asia Cooperation, 28 November 1999'. Available at http://www.mofa.go.jp/region/asia-paci/asean/pmv9911/joint.html.
2. The initiative, which was announced by then Finance Minister Miyazawa in October 1998, aimed at providing packages of support measures totalling US$30 billion, of which US$15 billion would be made available for mid- and long-term development while another US$15 billion would be used for the short-term capital needed during the process of implementing economic reform.
3. In July 2001, the office was further strengthened as the Regional Financial Cooperation Division.
4. *Nikkei Kinyu Shimbun*, May 12, 2000: *Asahi Shimbun*, May 24, 2000.
5. Speech by His Excellency Zhu Rongji, Premier of the State Council of The People's Republic of China, At the Fourth Meeting of Heads of State/Government of ASEAN, China, Japan and the Republic of Korea (10+3). Available at http://www.fmprc.gov.cn/eng/topics/zgcydyhz/dsiczgdm/t25976.htm.
6. South Korea's GDP growth rose from minus 6.7 per cent in 1998 to 10.9 per cent in 1999.
7. 'Report Summary of Studies on Toward a Regional Financial Architecture for East Asia, March 29, 2004, Institute for International Monetary Affairs'. Available at http://www.mof.go.jp/english/international_policy/convention/asean_plus_3/ASEAN_plus_3research-1-1.pdf.
8. 'ASEAN+3 Research Group Studies 2004–2005'. Available at http://www.asean.org/news/item/asean3-research-group-studies-2004-2005.
9. The Japanese MOF set up the ADB Institute in December 1997. The institute, located in Tokyo, aimed to provide intellectual bases for pursuing the appropriate development paradigms for Asia, which were composed of a balanced combination of the role of markets, institutions, and the government.
10. 'ADB Institute Review 2000'. Available at http://www.adbi.org/files/adbi_review_2000.pdf.
11. Interview, Institute for International Monetary Affairs, Tokyo, June 2013.
12. Interview, Institute for International Monetary Affairs, Tokyo, June 2013.
13. *The Nation*, December 16, 2002.
14. 'The Joint Ministerial Statement of the 10th ASEAN+3 Finance Ministers' Meeting (5 May 2007, Kyoto)'. Available at http://www.mof.go.jp/english/international_policy/convention/asean_plus_3/20070505.htm.
15. 'Joint Ministerial Statement of the 11th ASEAN Plus Three ASEAN Ministers Meeting Madrid, Spain, 4 May 2008'. Available at http://www.asean.org/news/item/joint-ministerial-statement-of-the-11th-asean-plus-three-asean-ministers-meeting-madrid-spain-4-may-2008.
16. 'The Joint Ministerial Statement of the 8th ASEAN+3 Finance Ministers' Meeting Istanbul, Turkey, 4 May 2005'. Available at http://www.asean.org/news/item/the-joint-ministerial-statement-of-the-8th-asean3-finance-ministers-meeting-istanbul-turkey-4-may-2005.
17. 'The Purpose of AMU and AMU Deviation Indicators for East Asian Currencies'. Available at http://www.rieti.go.jp/users/amu/en/detail.html.
18. 'The Joint Media Statement of the 12th ASEAN Plus Three Finance Ministers' Meeting Bali, Indonesia, 3 May 2009'. Available at http://www.asean.org/news/item/the-joint-media-statement-of-the-12th-asean-plus-three-finance-ministers-meeting-bali-indonesia-3-may-2009-2.

19. For the AMRO, see its home page, http://www.amro-asia.org/.
20. *Asahi Shimbun*, March 10, 2009.
21. 'Japan-China-ROK Trilateral Summit, Joint Statement on the International Finance and Economy'. Available at http://www.mofa.go.jp/region/asia-paci/jck/summit0812/economy.html.
22. 'Joint Media Statement of the 13th ASEAN Finance Ministers' Meeting Pattaya, Thailand, 9 April 2009'. Available at http://www.asean.org/news/item/joint-media-statement-of-the-13th-asean-finance-ministers-meeting-pattaya-thailand-9-april-2009-2.
23. *Asahi Shimbun*, August 2, 2009.
24. *China Daily*, August 17, 2011.
25. Those swaps included Hong Kong (RMB 200 billion), Indonesia (RMB 100 billion), South Korea (RMB 180 billion), Malaysia (RMB 80 billion), Argentina (RMB 70 billion), and Belarus (RMB 20 billion).
26. After the 2010 reform in IMF quota, China's quota increased dramatically from 3.99 per cent to 6.39 per cent while that of South Korea increased from 1.41 per cent to 1.80 per cent.
27. For instance, the three countries organised a workshop on macroeconomic and financial stability in November 2008. The finance ministers, central bankers, and financial supervisory authorities from the three countries attended this gathering.
28. For the NEAT's operations and research activities, see its home page, http://www2.pids.gov.ph/neat/.
29. The projects are 'Toward Greater Financial Stability in the Asian Region: Exploring Steps to Create Regional Monetary Units' (2006/07) and Toward Greater Financial Stability in the Asian Region: Measures for Possible Use of Regional Monetary Units for Surveillance and Transaction (2007/08).

5 Food Security Cooperation through Emergency Rice Reserve

1. 'The Joint Press Statement of the First Meeting of the ASEAN Agriculture and Forestry Ministers and the Ministers of the People's Republic of China Japan and Republic of Korea (AMAF+3)'. Available at http://www.asean.org/news/item/the-first-meeting-of-the-asean-agriculture-and-forestry-ministers-and-the-ministers-of-the-peoples-republic-of-china-japan-and-republic-of-korea-amaf-plus-three-5-october-2001-medan-north-sumatera-indonesia.
2. For the details of the AFSIS, see its home page, http://afsis.oae.go.th/.
3. The initial earmarked stock was 50,000 tonnes. The stock of each country was as follows: 15,000 tonnes for Thailand; 12,000 tonnes for Indonesia; 12,000 tonnes for the Philippines; 6,000 tonnes for Malaysia; and 5,000 tonnes for Singapore.
4. 'Strategic Plan of Action on ASEAN Cooperation in Food, Agriculture and Forestry'. Available at http://www.asean.org/communities/asean-economic-community/item/strategic-plan-of-action-on-asean-cooperation-in-food-agriculture-and-forestry.
5. 'Joint Statement on East Asia Cooperation'. Available at http://www.mofa.go.jp/region/asia-paci/asean/pmv9911/joint.html.
6. 'Negotiating Proposal by Japan on WTO Agricultural Negotiations, 21 December 2000'. Available at http://www.mofa.go.jp/policy/economy/wto/agri0012.html.

7. 'The Report of the Study Group of the International Food Stockholding Concept, 30 October 2001'. Available at http://www.maff.go.jp/j/kokusai/kousyo/wto/w_14_kanren/bitiku/02_kenkyu/pdf/houkoku_02.pdf.
8. Interview, former coordinator of the EAERR Secretariat, Fukushima, Japan, February 2013.
9. The provision of stockpiled rice was mainly implemented as Japan's rice offer to the Philippines (950 tonnes), Cambodia (380 tonnes), Indonesia (180 tonnes), and Laos (350 tonnes).
10. Interview, Japanese Ministry of Agriculture, Forestry and Fisheries, Tokyo, March 2007.
11. 'Joint Press Statement of the Fifth Meeting of the ASEAN Agriculture and Forestry Ministers and the Ministers of the People's Republic of China, Japan and Republic of Korea (5th AMAF Plus Three), Tagaytay City, Philippines, September 30, 2005'. Available at http://www.asean.org/news/asean-statement-communiques/item/joint-press-statement-of-the-fifth-meeting-of-the-asean-agriculture-and-forestry-ministers-and-the-ministers-of-the-people-s-republic-of-china-japan-and-republic-of-korea-5th-amaf-plus-three-tagaytay-city-philippines.
12. The stock quantity of the MAV rice increased from 310,000 tonnes in 1996 to 950,000 tonnes in 2002, which required considerable costs for reserve (MAFF 2009: 19).
13. The government paid US$5.75 million for the pilot project in 2004–10.
14. Interview, former coordinator of the EAERR Secretariat, Fukushima, Japan, February 2013.
15. APTERR Home page, Current Issues on EAERR, 'April 2005 – 4th Project Steering Committee EAEER Meeting has successfully conducted'. Available at http://www.apterr.org/index.php/current-issues/38-year-2005/64-april-2005-4th-project-steering-committee-eaerr-meeting-has-successfully-conducted (accessed on August 18, 2013).
16. Interview, former coordinator of the EAERR Secretariat, Fukushima, Japan, February 2013.
17. 'Joint Press Statement of the Ninth Meeting of the ASEAN Ministers on Agriculture and Forestry and the Ministers of Agriculture of the People's Republic of China, Japan and the Republic of Korea (9th AMAF Plus Three) Bandar Seri Begawan, 11 November 2009'. Available at http://www.asean.org/news/item/joint-press-statement-of-the-ninth-meeting-of-the-asean-ministers-on-agriculture-and-forestry-and-the-ministers-of-agriculture-of-the-people-s-republic-of-china-japan-and-the-republic-of-korea-9th-amaf-plus-three-bandar-seri-begawan-11-november-2009-2.
18. Interview, former coordinator of the EAERR Secretariat, Fukushima, Japan, February 2013.
19. 'The Eleventh Meeting of the ASEAN Ministers on Agriculture and Forestry and the Ministers of Agriculture of the People's Republic of China, Japan and the Republic of Korea (11th AMAF Plus Three) 7 October 2011, Jakarta'. Available at http://www.asean.org/images/archive/documents/Joint_Press_Statement%2011th%20AMAF3%20_final%2011.pdf.
20. 'Remarks by H.E. Wen Jiabao Premier of the State Council of the People's Republic of China At the 13th ASEAN Plus Three Summit'. Available at http://www.fmprc.gov.cn/eng/wjdt/zyjh/t765939.htm.
21. Interview, Japanese Ministry of Agriculture, Forestry and Fisheries, Tokyo, June 2012.

22. 'Strengthen Cooperation for Global Food Security: Address by H.E. Hui Liangyu, Vice Premier of the State Council of the People's Republic of China, at the World Food Summit, 16 November 2009'. Available at http://www.fmprc.gov.cn/eng/wjb/zzjg/gjs/gjsxw/t628178.shtml.
23. *Asia Pulse*, September 25, 2009.
24. *Financial Times*, February 27, 2008.
25. *Xinhua Net*, April 13, 2008.
26. 'ASEAN Integrated Food Security (AIFS) Framework and the Strategic Plan of Action on Food Security in the ASEAN Region (SPA-FS) (2009–2013)'. Available at http://www.asean.org/images/archive/22338.pdf.
27. 'Cha-am Hua Hin Statement on ASEAN Plus Three Cooperation on Food Security and Bio-Energy Development'. Available at http://www.mofa.go.jp/region/asia-paci/asean/conference/asean3/state0910-2.pdf.
28. Interview, former coordinator of the EAERR Secretariat, Fukushima, Japan, February 2013.
29. *Antara (Indonesia)*, 'ASEAN ready to tackle soaring food prices', April 29, 2008.
30. For details of the forum, see its home page, http://www.fanea.org/.
31. At the meeting, three ministers had in-depth discussions on food security and agreed to foster trilateral cooperation on food security issues through regional institutions such as the AFSIS, APTERR, and APIP (Asia-Pacific Information Platform on Food Security).
32. *Rice Today*, (January–March, 2009), Vol.8 No.1. Available at http://www.scribd.com/doc/34622848/Rice-Today-Vol-8-No-1.
33. 'NEAT Working Group on East Asian Food Security: Final Report, Tokyo, 2 July 2009'. Available at http://www.ceac.jp/e/pdf/neat_07wg01.pdf.
34. 'NEAT Working Group on East Asian Food Security: Final Report, Tokyo, 9 July 2010'. Available at http://www.ceac.jp/e/pdf/neat_08wg01.pdf.
35. Interview, Chairman of the NEAT Working Group on East Asian Food Security, June 2012, Tokyo.

6 Energy Security Cooperation under ASEAN+3

1. 'Joint Ministerial Statement ASEAN, China, Japan and Korea Energy Ministers Meeting (Manila AMEM+3) Makati City, Metro Manila, Philippines, 9 June 2004 "Forging Closer ASEAN+3 Energy Partnership" '. Available at http://www.asean.org/news/item/joint-ministerial-statement-asean-china-japan-and-korea-energy-ministers-meeting-manila-amem3-makati-city-metro-manila-philippines-9-june-2004-forging-closer-asean3-energy-partnership.
2. The IEA was established in 1974 within the OECD, after the lesson of the first oil shock in 1973. Under the International Energy Program agreement, the IEA members are required to maintain emergency oil reserves equivalent to at least 90 days of net oil imports, and to have an effective plan to use their strategic petroleum reserve through IEA-coordinated action (Mukherjee 2011: 18–19).
3. 'ASEAN Petroleum Security Agreement, Manila, 24 June 1986'. Available at http://www.asean.org/communities/asean-economic-community/item/asean-petroleum-security-agreement-manila-24-june-1986.
4. The project aimed to construct highways, railroads, and other facilities as part of integrated transport and communication systems in the southern seaboard of the country.

5. The IEF was organised in 1991 as a dialogue meeting of oil producers and consumers to promote mutual understanding. The IEF has held a biennial gathering since 1996.
6. 'Joint Press Statement Nineteenth ASEAN Ministers on Energy Meeting (19th AMEM) 5 July 2001, Bandar Seri Begawan, Brunei Darussalam'. Available at http://www.asean.org/news/item/joint-press-statement-nineteenth-asean-ministers-on-energy-meeting-19th-amem-5-july-2001-bandar-seri-begawan-brunei-darussalam.
7. 'Joint Press Statement 21st ASEAN Ministers on Energy Meeting (21st AMEM) 3 July 2003, Langkawi Island, Malaysia'. Available at http://www.asean.org/news/item/joint-press-statement-21st-asean-ministers-on-energy-meeting-21st-amem-3-july-2003-langkawi-island-malaysia.
8. *Financial Times*, July 3, 2003.
9. Japan has continuously relied on external sources for 96 per cent of its energy resources.
10. The low energy efficiency is shown in total primary energy supply (TPES) per thousand US dollars of gross domestic product (GDP). The TPES per GDP was 0.59 for Asia and 0.72 for China in 2009. These figures were more than double compared with the world average (0.31) (International Energy Agency, *Key World Energy Statistics 2011*: 49).
11. For instance, CNOOC acquired nine Repsol subsidiaries from a Spanish firm, Repsol-YPF, for US$585 million in 2002, and the subsidiaries owned working interests in five oil and gas properties in Indonesia. In July 2006, CNOOC signed an agreement with a Malaysian oil company, Petronas, to purchase LNG over 25 years. These are just a few examples of China's bilateral energy commitments to the countries in East Asia.
12. *Financial Times*, July 3, 2003.
13. Interview, Institute of Energy Economics, Japan, Tokyo, June 2013.
14. The member countries could choose either category A or B according to their preference. The countries that belonged to category A were Indonesia, Thailand, Singapore, the Philippines, and Vietnam, while those in category B were Brunei, Malaysia, Cambodia, Laos, and Myanmar.
15. The development of oil stockpiling has become a challenging issue within ASEAN. The new APSA signed in February 2009 stipulates that oil stockpiling, whether individually or jointly by members, shall be on a voluntary and commercial basis (3.3.1(f)). The 'voluntary' provision invariably makes oil stockpiling an option instead of a stipulation to ensure energy security in times of emergency, and this shortcoming derives from a host of complications such as disputes over where stocks would be located, which nations would take responsibility for securing them, and what would be the exact purpose of stocks (Nicolas 2009: 28; Youngho and Koh 2009).
16. 'Cebu Declaration on East Asian Energy Security Cebu, Philippines, 15 January 2007'. Available at http://www.asean.org/news/item/cebu-declaration-on-east-asian-energy-security-cebu-philippines-15-january-2007-2.
17. Interview, Japanese Ministry of Economy, Trade and Industry, Tokyo, June 2013.
18. The EAS originally had special importance for Japan. Japan was the main supporter of the EAS, which includes Australia, New Zealand, and India, as an institution to balance against growing Chinese influence centred on the ASEAN+3. As discussed in Chapter 3, Japan sustained the development of the

EAS by proposing the Comprehensive Economic Partnership Agreement in East Asia (CEPEA) and the ERIA.

19. 'Joint Ministerial Statement of the Fifth East Asian Summit Energy Ministers Meeting Jerudong, Brunei Darussalam, 20 September 2011'. Available at http://www.asean.org/news/item/joint-ministerial-statement-of-the-fifth-east-asian-summit-energy-ministers-meeting-jerudong-brunei-darussalam-20-september-2011-2.
20. The first China-Japan energy policy dialogue was held in 1996. The eighth dialogue was held in Tokyo in September 2006.
21. 'Report of the First Working Group Meeting on the Development of Oil Stockpiling Roadmap for the ASEAN+3', November 28, 2008, Available at http://aseanenergy.org/download/reports/energy_organisastion/asean+3/FINAL%20Report%20of%20the%201st%20WG%20%20Meeting%20OSRM.pdf.
22. Interview, Institute of Energy Economics, Japan, Tokyo, June 2013.
23. *People's Daily*, November 20, 2007.
24. Tozai Boeki Tsushinsha, *Chugoku no Sekiyu Sangyo to Sekiyu Kagaku Kogyo* [The petroleum industry and the petro-chemical industry in China], various years.
25. Interview, Japanese Ministry of Economy, Trade and Industry, Tokyo, February 2010.
26. After both governments reached an agreement on joint development in the East China Sea in June 2008, further talks were not undertaken for two years. In July 2010, the first formal talk to discuss a treaty concerning the joint development had been held at the director-general level.
27. *Yonhap News*, August 8, 2008.
28. For instance, Indonesia planned to set up a nuclear power plant by 2018 and Thailand by 2020, and Malaysia announced a plan to set up Southeast Asia's first nuclear monitoring laboratory (*Kyodo News*, August 23, 2007).
29. 'ASEAN Plan of Action on Energy Cooperation (APAEC) 2010–2015'. Available at http://www.asean.org/images/archive/22675.pdf.
30. Interview, Japanese Ministry of Economy, Trade and Industry, Tokyo, February 2010.
31. In October 2009, ASEAN leaders adopted the Statement on ASEAN Connectivity at the 15th summit. One year later, they agreed on the Master Plan on ASEAN Connectivity, which comprises three pillars: physical, institutional, and people-to-people linkages.
32. 'Joint Ministerial Statement of the 5th ASEAN+3 (China, Japan and Korea) Ministers on Energy Meeting Thailand, 7 August 2008'. Available at http://www.asean.org/news/item/joint-ministerial-statement-of-the-5th-asean3-china-japan-and-korea-ministers-on-energy-meeting-thailand-7-august-2008.
33. Interview, Institute of Energy Economics, Japan, Tokyo, June 2013.

7 Environmental Cooperation: The Monitoring of Transboundary Air Pollution

1. The member countries are Cambodia, China, Indonesia, Japan, Laos, Malaysia, Mongolia, Myanmar, the Philippines, South Korea, Russia, Thailand, and Vietnam.
2. The Design of EANET, which was formulated at the fourth expert meeting, was further discussed at the IG meetings, and was finally named as the Tentative Design of EANET.

3. The major tasks of the network centre are to compile, evaluate, and store the EANET monitoring data, provide data upon request by the participating countries, and prepare data reports. In addition, the centre plays a role in promoting QA/QC activities in member countries by giving technical assistance.
4. The ASEAN+3 environment ministers' meeting has been organised since 2002. The major activities of the meeting are the exchange of information and the introduction of cases on environmental cooperation.
5. The UNCED, which is also known as the Earth Summit, brought together representatives of 172 countries, including 108 heads of state or government. The UNCED produced important documents such as the Rio Declaration on Environment and Development, the Statement of Forest Principles, the UN Framework Convention on Climate Change, and the UN Convention on Biological Diversity.
6. Agenda 21, Chapter 9, Protection of the Atmosphere, 9.26.
7. 'Resolution on Environment and Development, Bandar Seri Begawan, 26 April 1994'. Available at http://environment.asean.org/resolution-on-environment-and-development/.
8. The Agenda 21, Chapter 9, Protection of the Atmosphere, 9.27.
9. 'Statement by Prime Minister of Japan Ryutaro Hashimoto at the Special Session of the General Assembly for the Overall Review and Appraisal of the Implementation of Agenda 21, June 23, 1997, New York'. Available at http://www.mofa.go.jp/announce/announce/archive_3/agenda21.html.
10. *Asahi Shimbun*, February 23, 1997.
11. The EMEP is managed by five centres: the Centre on Emission Inventories and Projections; the Chemical Coordinating Centre; the Meteorological Synthesizing Centre-West; the Meteorological Synthesizing Centre-East; and the Centre for Integrated Assessment Modelling.
12. 'Statement by Prime Minister of Japan Ryutaro Hashimoto at the Special Session of the General Assembly for the Overall Review and Appraisal of the Implementation of Agenda 21, June 23, 1997, New York'. Available at http://www.mofa.go.jp/announce/announce/archive_3/agenda21.html.
13. For the Green Aid Plan, see Evans (1999).
14. The nationalities of the secretariat's original three staff members were Chinese (coordinator), Filipino (program officer), and Thai (assistant officer) (Yamashita 2009: 124).
15. Cambodia, Laos, and Myanmar joined EANET in 2001, 2002, and 2005, respectively.
16. The Fifth Session of Intergovernmental Meeting. Available at http://www.eanet.asia/event/ig/ig05.pdf.
17. The Seventh Session of Intergovernmental Meeting. Available at http://www.eanet.asia/event/ig/ig07.pdf.
18. Interview, Japanese Ministry of the Environment, Tokyo, January 2013.
19. The Third Special Session of the Working Group on Future Development. Available at http://www.eanet.asia/event/wgfd/wgfds3.pdf.
20. The Tenth Session of Intergovernmental Meeting. Available at http://www.eanet.asia/event/ig/ig10.pdf.
21. The Fourth Session of Intergovernmental Meeting. Available at http://www.eanet.asia/event/ig/ig04.pdf.
22. Interview, Asia Centre for Air Pollution Research, Niigata, Japan, June 2012.
23. Interview, Japanese Ministry of the Environment, Tokyo, January 2013.
24. Interview, Asia Centre for Air Pollution Research, Niigata, Japan, June 2012.
25. Interview, Japanese Ministry of the Environment, Tokyo, January 2013.

26. Interview, National Institute of Environmental Research, Incheon, South Korea, September 2013.
27. The ACAP undertakes tasks as the Network Centre for EANET and as the National Centre for Japan, to prepare for drafting national monitoring plans and collect and evaluate national monitoring data.
28. Interview, National Institute of Environmental Research, Incheon, South Korea, September 2013.
29. Interview, National Institute of Environmental Research, Incheon, South Korea, September 2013.
30. The Fifth Session of Intergovernmental Meeting. Available at http://www.eanet.asia/event/ig/ig05.pdf.
31. The TEMM is an intergovernmental institution comprising China, Japan, and South Korea, whose first meeting was held in 1999. The TEMM has functioned as a forum to confirm a common front on global environmental issues and the necessity of joint efforts to protect the regional environment, and a joint communiqué has been issued at every annual meeting.
32. Interview, Japanese Ministry of the Environment, Tokyo, January 2013.
33. Interview, Japanese Ministry of the Environment, Tokyo, January 2013.
34. The Ninth Session of the Intergovernmental Meeting. Available at http://www.eanet.asia/event/ig/ig09.pdf, p. 2.
35. Interview, Japanese Ministry of the Environment, Tokyo, January 2013.
36. Interview, Asia Centre for Air Pollution Research, Niigata, Japan, June 2012.
37. 'The implementation of grant aid for "the project for the Establishment of the Monitoring Network for Acid Deposition, Dust and Sandstorm" in China, December 20, 2006'. Available at http://www.mofa.go.jp/mofaj/press/release/18/rls_1220b.html.
38. The 11th Session of the Intergovernmental Meeting. Available at http://www.eanet.asia/event/ig/ig11.pdf.
39. *The People's Daily*, March 25, 2004.
40. Interview, Japanese Ministry of the Environment, Tokyo, January 2013.
41. Interview, Asia Centre for Air Pollution Research, Niigata, Japan, June 2012.
42. The co-benefits approach normally means integrated efforts to address climate change mitigation concerns and development needs of developing countries in a sustainable manner. The co-benefits approach here implies integrated efforts to address climate change mitigation concerns and air pollution abatement.
43. 'One Atmosphere: Final Declaration of the XVth World Clean Air Congress Vancouver, September 2010'. Available at http://www.iuappa.org/newsletters/VancouverDeclaration.pdf.
44. The Asian Co-benefits Partnership was launched in 2010 in order to support the mainstreaming of co-benefits into sectoral development plans, policies, and projects in Asia.
45. 'Stockholm Environment Institute, Global Atmospheric Pollution Forum, International Cooperation'. Available at http://www.sei-international.org/rapidc/gapforum/html/regions.php.
46. The 12th Session of the Intergovernmental Meeting. Available at http://www.eanet.asia/event/ig/ig12.pdf.
47. Interview, National Institute of Environmental Research, Incheon, South Korea, September 2013.
48. The 11th Session of the Scientific Advisory Committee. Available at http://www.eanet.asia/event/sac/sac11.pdf.

49. The Seventh Session of the Scientific Advisory Committee. Available at http://www.eanet.asia/event/sac/sac07.pdf.
50. The Ninth Session of the Intergovernmental Meeting. Available at http://www.eanet.asia/event/ig/ig09.pdf.
51. Interview, Japanese Ministry of the Environment, Tokyo, January 2013.

8 Conclusion

1. This was also the case in oil stockpiling. ASEAN members had set up the ASEAN Petroleum Security Agreement (APSA), which provided oil-sharing systems.
2. The concept of 'focal point' was originally introduced by Schelling. It is referred to as the 'point for each person's expectation of what the other expects him to expect to be expected to do' (Schelling 1960: 57).
3. Abbott et al. (2000) focus on three dimensions: obligation (being bound by a rule or commitment or by a set of rules or commitments); precision (unambiguously defined rules for the conduct requited, authorised, and proscribed); and delegation (granted authority to third parties to implement, interpret, and apply the rules). Koremenos et al. (2001a) highlight the dimensions of membership, scope, centralisation, control, and flexibility. Camilleri (2003) also presents five dimensions for a typology of regional institutional forms: membership, structure, function, external orientation, and architecture.
4. After 2009, Chinese diplomatic behaviour became increasingly aggressive, which was typically shown in the maritime security field. While it is difficult to expect China's cooperative postures in policy issues pertinent to China's vital interests, it is more likely that China pays respect to ASEAN members' interests in the economic and social fields.
5. In this respect, the presence and role of the expanded East Asia Summit, which includes the United States and Russia, is crucial.
6. For instance, the report of the International Crisis Group identifies as many as 11 administrative agencies that were involved in affairs in the South China Sea (ICG 2010).

References

Abbott, Kenneth W., Keohane, Robert O., Moravcsik, Andrew, Slaughter, Anne-Marie, and Snidal, Duncan. 2000. 'The concept of legalization', *International Organization* 54 (3): 401–19.

Acharya, Amitav. 1997. 'Ideas, identity, and institution-building: From the "ASEAN Way" to the "Asia-Pacific Way"?', *Pacific Review* 10 (3): 319–46.

Acharya, Amitav. 2001. *Constructing a Security Community in Southeast Asia: ASEAN and the Problem of Regional Order*. London: Routledge.

Acharya, Amitav. 2003. 'Regional institutions and Asian security order: Norms, power, and prospects for peaceful change', in Muthiah Alagappa (ed.) *Asian Security Order Instrumental and Normative Features*. Stanford, C.A.: Stanford University Press.

Acharya, Amitav. 2004. 'How ideas spread: Whose norms matter? Norm localization and institutional change in Asian regionalism', *International Organization* 58 (2): 239–75.

ADB Institute. 2000. *Policy Recommendations for Preventing another Capital Account Crisis*. Tokyo: ADB Institute. Available at http://www.adbi.org/files/2000.7.7.apf002.capital.account.pdf.

ADB Institute. 2009. *Recommendations of Policy Responses to the Global Financial and Economic Crisis for East Asian Leaders*. Tokyo: ADB Institute. Available at http://www.adbi.org/files/2009.03.18.keydocs.policy.recommend.global.financial.crisis.east.asian.leaders.pdf.

ADB Institute. 2010. *Policy Recommendations to Secure Balanced and Sustainable Growth in Asia*. Tokyo: ADB Institute. Available at http://www.adbi.org/files/2010.10.25.keydocs.policy.recommendations.sustainable.growth.asia.pdf.

Adler, Emanuel and Haas, Peter M. 1992. 'Conclusion: Epistemic communities, world order, and the creation of a reflective research program', *International Organization* 46 (1): 367–90.

AFSIS (ASEAN Food Security Information System). 2008. *ASEAN Agricultural Commodity Outlook No.1*. Bangkok: AFSIS.

Aggarwal, Vinod K. and Koo, Min Gyo. 2008. 'Asia's new institutional architecture: Evolving structures for managing trade, financial, and security relations', in Vinod K. Aggarwal and Min Gyo Koo (eds) *Asia's New Institutional Architecture: Evolving Structures for Managing Trade, Financial, and Security Relations*. Berlin: Springer.

Akimoto, Hajime. 2000. 'Higashi ajia no sanseiu heno torikumi' [Engaging in acid rain problems in East Asia], *Gaiko Foramu* (October): 42–46.

Amyx, Jennifer. 2002. 'Moving beyond bilateralism?: Japan and the Asian Monetary Fund', Pacific Economic Paper 331, Australia Japan Research Centre, Australian National University, Canberra.

Amyx, Jennifer. 2005. 'What motivates regional financial cooperation in East Asia today?', *Asia Pacific Issues* 76: 1–8.

Amyx, Jennifer. 2008. 'Regional financial cooperation in East Asia since the Asian financial crisis', in Andrew MacIntyre, T. J. Pempel, and John Revenhill (eds) *Crisis as Catalyst: Asia's Dynamic Political Economy*. Ithaca, N.Y.: Cornell University Press.

Ando, Horoshi. 2006. 'EANET: "Higashi ajia kyodotai" no senkuteki rentai' [EANET: A pioneering linkage for an East Asian community], in Tokai Daigaku Heiwa

Senryaku Kokusai Kenkyujo (ed.) *Higashi Ajia ni 'Kyodotai' wa Dekiruka [Searching for the Possibility of a 'Community' in East Asia]*. Tokyo: Shakai Hyoronsha.

Andrews-Speed, Philip. 2012. *The Governance of Energy in China: Transition to a Low-Carbon Economy*. Basingstoke: Palgrave Macmillan.

Antoniades, Andreas. 2003. 'Epistemic communities, epistemes and the construction of (world) politics', *Global Society* 17 (1): 21–38.

APTERR. no year. *20 Frequently Asked Questions about APTERR*. Bangkok: APTERR Secretariat.

Arnst Randall. 2009. 'Business as usual: Responses within ASEAN to the food crisis', Focus on the Global South Occasional Papers 4.

Arthur, W. Brian. 1994. *Increasing Returns and Path Dependence in the Economy*. Ann Arbor: University of Michigan Press.

Asami Tadahiro. 2002. 'Japan's strong leadership urged to promote regional economic cooperation in East Asia', *IIMA Newsletter* 2 (May 15).

ASEAN. 2009a. 'East Asia Emergency Rice Reserve (EAERR) Pilot Project, Fact Sheet', Available at http://www.asean.org/archive/Fact%20Sheet/AEC/2009-AEC-016.pdf.

ASEAN. 2009b. 'ASEAN Food Security Information System (AFSIS) Project, Fact Sheet', Available at http://www.asean.org/archive/Fact%20Sheet/AEC/2009-AEC-015.pdf.

ASEAN. 2009c. *ASEAN Plus Three Cooperation*. Jakarta: ASEAN Secretariat.

ASEAN. 2010. *Roadmap for an ASEAN Community 2009–2015*. Jakarta: ASEAN.

ASEAN. 2011. *Master Plan on ASEAN Connectivity*. Jakarta: ASEAN Secretariat. Available at http://www.aseansec.org/wp-content/uploads/2013/06/MPAC.pdf.

Ba, Alice D. 2006. 'Who's socializing whom? Complex engagement in Sino-ASEAN relations', *Pacific Review* 19 (2): 157–79.

Ba, Alice D. 2009. *(Re)Negotiating East and Southeast Asia: Region, Regionalism, and the Association of Southeast Asian Nations*. Stanford, C.A.: Stanford University Press.

Beeson, Mark. 2007. *Regionalism and Globalization in East Asia: Politics, Security and Economic Development*. Basingstoke: Palgrave Macmillan.

Beeson, Mark and Berger, Mark T. 2003. 'The paradoxes of paramountcy: Regional rivalries and the dynamics of American hegemony in East Asia', *Global Change, Peace & Security* 15 (1): 27–42.

Beeson, Mark and Higgott, Richard. 2005. 'Hegemony, institutionalism and US foreign policy: Theory and practice in comparative historical perspective', *Third World Quarterly* 26 (7): 1173–88.

Bluth, Christoph and Dent, Christopher M. 2008. 'A shrimp among the whales? Korea in the Northeast and East Asia regional system', in Christopher M. Dent (ed.) *China, Japan and Regional Leadership in East Asia*. Cheltenham: Edward Elgar.

Bowles, Paul. 2002. 'Asia's post-crisis regionalism: Bringing the state back in, keeping the (United) States out', *Review of International Political Economy* 9 (2): 244–70.

Brettell, Anna. 2007. 'Security, energy, and the environment: The atmospheric link', in In-Taek Hyun and Miranda A. Schreurs (eds) *The Environmental Dimension of Asian Security: Conflict and Cooperation over Energy, Resources, and Pollution*. Washington, D.C.: United States Institute of Peace Press.

Briones, Roehlano M. 2011. 'Regional cooperation for food security: The case of emergency rice reserves in the ASEAN Plus Three', ADB Sustainable Development Working Paper Series 18.

Buchanan, James M. 1977. 'Why does government grow?', in Thomas E. Borcherding (ed.) *Budgets and Bureaucrats: The Sources of Government Growth*. Durham: Duke University Press.

Bustelo, Pablo. 2008. 'Energy security with a high external dependence: The strategies of Japan and South Korea', MPRA Paper, 8323.

Cáceres, Sigfrido Burgos and Ear, Sophal. 2012. 'The geopolitics of China's global resources quest', *Geopolitics* 17 (1): 47–79.

Calder, Kent. 2008. 'Critical junctures and the contours of Northeast Asian regionalism', in Kent Calder and Francis Fukuyama (eds) *East Asian Multilateralism: Prospects for Regional Stability*. Baltimore: The John's Hopkins University Press.

Calder, Kent and Ye, Min. 2004. 'Regionalism and critical junctures: Explaining the "organization gap" in Northeast Asia', *Journal of East Asian Studies* 4 (2): 191–226.

Calder, Kent and Ye, Min. 2010. *The Making of Northeast Asia*. Stanford, C.A.: Stanford University Press.

Camilleri, Joseph A. 2003. *Regionalism in the New Asia-Pacific Order*. Cheltenham: Edward Elgar.

Cao, Jing, Garbaccio, Richard, and Ho, Mun S. 2009. 'China's 11th five-year plan and the environment: Reducing SO_2 emissions', *Review of Environmental Economics and Policy* 3 (2): 231–50.

Capie, David and Evans, Paul. 2002. *The Asia-Pacific Security Lexicon*. Singapore: Institute of Southeast Asian Studies.

Capoccia, Giovanni and Kelemen, R. Daniel. 2007. 'The study of critical junctures: Theory, narrative, and counterfactuals in historical institutionalism', *World Politics* 59 (3): 341–69.

CDRI (Cambodia Development Resource Institute). 2008. *Impact of High Food Prices in Cambodia: Survey Report*. Phnon Penh: CDRI.

CEAC (Council on East Asian Community). 2010. *Higashi Ajia Kenkyujo Rengo (NEAT) Dai 8-kai Sokai (AC), Dai 13-kai Kunibetsu Daihyosha Kaigi (CCM) Hokokusho* [*Report on the 8th Annual Conference (AC) and the 13th Country Coordinators Meeting (CCM)*]. Tokyo: CEAC. Available at http://www.ceac.jp/j/pdf/neat-008.pdf.

Chan, Gerald. 2012. 'China's response to the global financial crisis and its regional leadership in East Asia', *Asia Europe Journal* 9 (2–4): 197–209.

Chandra, Alexander C. and Lontoh, Lucky A. 2010. 'Regional food security and trade policy in Southeast Asia: The role of ASEAN', Series on Trade and the Food Security – Policy Report 3.

Checkel, Jeffrey T. 2001. 'Why comply? Social learning and European identity change', *International Organization* 55 (3): 553–88.

Chen, Huiping. 2006. 'China-ASEAN FTA: An investment perspective', in John Wong, Zou Keyuan, and Zeng Huaqun (eds) *China-ASEAN Relations: Economic and Legal Dimensions*. Singapore: World Scientific.

Chey, Hyoung-kyu. 2009. 'The changing political dynamics of East Asian financial cooperation: The Chiang Mai initiative', *Asian Survey* 49 (3): 450–67.

Chia, Siow Yue. 2006. 'The economic rise of China: Challenges and opportunities for ASEAN', *Asian Economic Policy Review* 1 (1): 102–28.

Chia, Siow Yue. 2010. 'Regional trade policy cooperation and architecture in East Asia', ADBI Working Paper Series 191 (February).

Chin, Gregory and Stubbs, Richard. 2011. 'China, regional institution-building and the China-ASEAN Free Trade Area', *Review of International Political Economy* 18 (3): 277–98.

Cho, Youngwon. 2011. 'The limits of financial and monetary cooperation in East Asia', paper presented at the International Studies Association Annual Convention 2011, Montreal Canada, March 16–19.

Choo, Jaewoo. 2006. 'Energy cooperation problems in Northeast Asia: Unfolding the reality', *East Asia: An International Quarterly* 23 (3): 91–106.

Christensen, Thomas J. 2011. 'The advantages of an assertive China', *Foreign Affairs* 90 (2): 54–67.

Christoffersen, Gaye. 2009. 'Energy security cooperation in Asia and the role of the United States', in Christopher Len and Alvin Chew (eds) *Energy and Security Cooperation in Asia: Challenges and Prospects*. Stockholm-Nacka: Institute for Security and Development Policy.

Chung, Jae Ho. 2012. 'Korean views of Korea-China relations: Evolving perceptions and upcoming challenges', *Asian Perspective* 36 (2): 219–36.

Ciorciari, John D. 2009. 'The balance of great-power influence in contemporary Southeast Asia', *International Relations of the Asia-Pacific* 9 (1): 157–96.

Ciorciari, John D. 2011. 'Chiang Mai initiative multilateralization: International politics and institution-building in Asia', *Asian Survey* 51 (5): 926–52.

Cohen, Benjamin J. 2010. 'Finance and Security in East Asia'. Department of Political Science, University of California. Santa Barbara. Available at www.polsci.ucsb.edu/faculty/cohen/working/pdfs/East_Asia_Rev_2.pdf.

Collier, Ruth Berins and Collier, David. 1991 *Shaping the Political Arena*. Princeton, N.J.: Princeton University Press.

Collier, David, Henry E. Brady, and Jason, Seawright. 2004. 'Sources of leverage in causal inference: Toward an alternative view of methodology', in Henry E. Brady and David Collier (eds) *Rethinking Social Inquiry: Diverse Tools, Shared Standards*. Lanham: Rowman & Littlefied.

Cowles, Maria Green. 1995. 'Setting the agenda for a new Europe: The ERT and EC 1992', *Journal of Common Market Studies* 33 (4): 501–26.

Cross, Mai'a K. Davis. 2013. 'Rethinking epistemic communities twenty years later', *Review of International Studies* 39: 137–60.

Danõ, Elenita. 2006. 'ASEAN's emergency rice reserve schemes: Current developments and prospects for engagement', *Women in Action* 3: 35–45.

Danõ, Elenita and Peria, Elpidio. 2006. 'Emergency or expediency? A study of emergency rice reserve schemes in Asia', A Joint Publication of AFA and Asia DHRRA.

Davidson, Paul J. 2002. *ASEAN: The Evolving Legal Framework for Economic Cooperation*. Singapore: Times Academic Press.

Deng, Yong. 2008. *China's Struggle for Status: The Realignment of International Relations*. Cambridge: Cambridge University Press.

Dent, Christopher M. 2005. 'Taiwan and the new regional political economy of East Asia', *China Quarterly* 182: 385–406.

Dent, Christopher M. 2008. *East Asian Regionalism*. London: Routledge.

Dent, Christopher M. (ed.) 2008. *China, Japan, and Regional Leadership in East Asia*. Northampton, MA: Edward Elgar.

DeSombre, Elizabeth R. 2009. 'Power, interdependence, and domestic politics in international environmental cooperation', in Helen V. Milner and Andrew Moravcsik (eds) *Power, Interdependence, and Nonstate Actors in World Politics*. Princeton, N.J.: Princeton University Press.

Dickson, Bruce. 2008. *Wealth into Power: The Communist Party's Embrace of China's Private Sector*. Cambridge: Cambridge University Press.

Dieter, Heribert. 2008. 'ASEAN and the emerging monetary regionalism: A case of limited contribution', *Pacific Review* 21 (4): 489–506.

Downs, Anthony. 1967. *Inside Bureaucracy*. New York: Harper Collins.

Downs, Erica. 2006. 'China: The Brookings foreign policy studies energy security series', *The Brookings Institution*. Available at http://www.brookings.edu/~/media/research/files/reports/2006/12/china/12china.pdf.

Downs, Erica. 2008. 'China's "new" energy administration', *China Business Review*, November–December: 42–45.

Duffield, John S. 2003. 'The limits of "rational design" ', *International Organization* 57 (2): 411–30.

EANET. 2006. 'Periodic report on the state of acid deposition in East Asia: Executive summary', *EANET*. Available at http://www.eanet.asia/product/PRSAD/1_PRSAD/1_ex.pdf.

EANET. 2011. 'Second periodic report on the state of acid deposition in East Asia: Part III executive summary', *EANET*. Available at http://www.eanet.asia/product/PRSAD/2_PRSAD/2_ex.pdf.

Ehara, Norio. 2005. 'Chugoku, indo, ASEAN ni yoru senryaku bichiku no sosetsu no ugoki to IEA ni yoru kyoryoku' [Moves to create strategic stockpiling in China, India and ASEAN, and cooperation from IEA], *Sekiyu Tenne Gasu Rebyu* 39 (3): 39–48.

Emmers, Ralf and Ravenhill, John. 2011. 'The Asian and global financial crises: Consequences for East Asian regionalism', *Contemporary Politics* 17 (2): 133–49.

Evans, Peter C. 1999. 'Japan's green aid plan: The limits of state-led technology transfer', *Asian Survey* 39 (6): 825–44.

Fallon, Karla S. 2006. 'Promoting an energy partnership in Northeast Asia', *Pacific Focus* 21 (1): 175–200.

FAO (Food and Agriculture Organisation). 2011. *China and FAO: Achievements and Success Stories*. Beijing: FAO Representation in China.

Fearon, James D. 1998. 'Bargaining, enforcement and international cooperation', *International Organization* 52 (2): 269–305.

Fergusson, Ian F., Cooper, William H., Jurenas, Remy, and Williams, Brock R. 2013. 'The Trans-Pacific partnership negotiations and issues for Congress', *Congressional Research Service* 7–5700.

Fioretos, Orfeo. 2011. 'Historical institutionalism in international relations', *International Organization* 65 (2): 367–99.

Frieden, Jeffry A. 1999. 'Actors and preferences in international relations', in David A. Lake and Robert Powell (eds) *Strategic Choice and International Relations*. Princeton, N.J.: Princeton University Press.

Fritz-Morgenthal, Sebastian, Greenwood, Chris, Menzel, Carola, Mironjuk, Marija, and Sonntag-O'Brien, Virginia. 2009. 'The global financial crisis and its impact on renewable energy finance', Paris, France: UNEP Sustainable Energy Finance Initiative, New Energy Finance, Frankfurt School of Finance & Management.

Funabashi, Yoichi. 1995. *Asia-Pacific Fusion: Japan's Role in APEC*. Washington D.C.: Institute for International Economics.

Gal, John and Bargal, David. 2002. 'Critical junctures, labour movements and the development of occupational welfare in Israel', *Social Problems* 49 (3): 432–54.

Garrett, Geoffrey and Lange, Peter. 1996. 'Internationalization, institutions, and political change', in Robert O. Keohane and Helen V. Milner (eds) *Internationalization and Domestic Politics*. Cambridge: Cambridge University Press.

Godement, Francois. 2011. 'The United States and Asia in 2010', *Asian Survey* 51 (1): 5–17.

Goh, Evelyn. 2009. 'Southeast Asian responses to China's rise: Managing the "elephants" ', in Kevin J. Cooney and Yoichiro Sato (eds) *The Rise of China and International Security: America and Asia Respond*. London: Routledge.

Goh, Evelyn. 2011. 'Institutions and the great power bargain in East Asia: ASEAN's limited "brokerage" role', *International Relations of the Asia-Pacific* 11 (3): 373–401.
Goldstein, Judith. 1988. 'Ideas, institutions, and American trade policy', *International Organization* 42 (1): 179–217.
Goldestein, Judith and Keohane, Robert. 1993. 'Ideas and foreign policy: An analytical framework', in Judith Goldestein and Robert Keohane (eds) *Ideas and Foreign Policy: Beliefs, Institutions, and Political Change*. Ithaca, N.Y.: Cornell University Press.
Goto, Yasuhiro. 2004. 'Ajia no keizai togo to enerugi kyoryoku' [Economic integration and energy cooperation in Asia], in Yasuo Tanabe (ed.) *Ajia Enerugi Patonashippu* [Energy partnership in Asia]. Tokyo: Enerugi Foramu.
Grieco, Joseph M. 1988. 'Anarchy and the limits of cooperation: A realist critique of the newest liberal institutionalism', *International Organization* 42 (2): 485–507.
Grieco, Joseph M. 1999. 'Realism and regionalism: American power and German and Japanese institutional strategies during and after the Cold War', in Ethan B. Kapstein and Michael Mastanduno (eds) *Unipolar Politics: Realism and State Strategies After the Cold War*. New York: Columbia University Press.
Grimes, William W. 2006. 'East Asian financial regionalism in support of the global financial architecture? The political economy of regional nesting', *Journal of East Asian Studies* 6 (3): 353–80.
Grimes, William W. 2009. *Currency and Contest in East Asia: The Great Power Politics of Financial Regionalism*. Ithaca, N.Y.: Cornell University Press.
Haas, Ernst B. 1990. *When Knowledge is Power: Three Models of Change in International Organizations*. Berkeley: University of California Press.
Haas, Peter M. 1992. 'Introduction: Epistemic communities and international policy coordination', *International Organization* 46 (1): 1–35.
Hagan, Joe D. 1993. *Political Opposition and Foreign Policy in Comparative Perspective*. Boulder, C.O.: Lynne Rienner.
Haggard, Stephan. 2011. 'The organizational architecture of the Asia-Pacific insights from the new institutionalism', ADB Working Paper Series on Regional Economic Integration 71.
Hamanaka, Shintaro. 2008. 'Comparing summitry, financial and trade regionalisms in East Asia: From the Japanese perspective', in Christopher M. Dent (ed.) *China, Japan and Regional Leadership in East Asia*. Cheltenham: Edward Elgar.
Hamilton-Hart, Natasha. 2003. 'Asia's new regionalism: Government capacity and cooperation in the Western Pacific', *Review of International Political Economy* 10 (2): 222–45.
Hara, Takuya. 2009. 'Higashi ajia ni okeru kankyo kyoryoku ni kansuru ichi kosatsu' [Environmental cooperation in East Asia], *Hokuto Ajia Chiiki Kenkyu* 15: 1–14.
Hasenclever, Andreas, Mayer, Peter, and Rittberger, Volker. 1996. 'Interests, power, knowledge: The study of international regimes', *Mershon International Studies Review* 40 (2): 177–228.
Hatakeyama, Noboru. 2002. 'A short history of Japan's movement to FTAs', *Journal of Japanese Trade and Industry* (November/December).
He, Kai. 2009. *Institutional Balancing in the Asia Pacific: Economic Interdependence and China's Rise*. Abingdon: Routledge.
Hemmer, Christopher and Katzenstein, Peter J. 2002. 'Why is there no NATO in Asia? Collective identity, regionalism, and the origins of multilateralism', *International Organization* 56 (3): 575–607.
Henning, C. Randall. 2009. 'The future of the Chiang Mai initiative: An Asian Monetary Fund?', *Policy Brief* PB09–5.

Hew, Denis and Soesastro, Hadi. 2003. 'Realizing the ASEAN economic community by 2020', *ASEAN Economic Bulletin* 20 (3): 292–96.
Higgott, Richard. 1998. 'The Asian economic crisis: A study in the politics of resentment', *New Political Economy* 3 (3): 333–56.
Higgott, Richard. 2000. 'Back from the brink: The theory and practice of globalisation at century's end', in Mely C. Anthony and Mohamed Jawhar Hassan (eds) *Beyond the Crisis: Challenges and Opportunities*. Kuala Lumpur: Institute of Strategic and International Studies.
Higgott, Richard. 2005. 'The theory and practice of region: The changing global context', in Bertrand Fort and Douglas Webber (eds) *Regional Integration in East Asia and Europe: Convergence or Divergence?* New York: Routledge.
Higgott, Richard and Timmermann, Martina. 2008. 'Institutionalizing East Asia: Learning lessons from Europe on regionalism, regionalization, identity and leadership', in Martina Timmermann and Jitsuo Tsuchiyama (eds) *Institutionalizing Northeast Asia: Regional Steps towards Global Governance*. Tokyo: United Nations University Press.
Hiwatari, Nobuhiro. 2003. 'Embedded policy preferences and the formation of international arrangements after the Asian financial crisis', *Pacific Review* 16 (3): 331–59.
Hogan, John and Doyle, David. 2007. The importance of ideas: An a priori critical juncture framework, *Canadian Journal of Political Science* 40 (4): 883–910.
Holt-Giménez, Eric and Peabody, Loren. 2008. 'From food rebellions to food sovereignty: Urgent call to fix a broken food system', *Food First Backgrounder* 14 (1): 1–6.
Horii, Nobuhiro. 2006. 'Higashi ajia no enerugi kyoryoku: Sono senzaiteki koka to tenbo' [Energy cooperation in East Asia: Potential, and prospects], in Daisuke Hiratsuka (ed.) *Higashi Ajia no Chosen: Keizai Togo, Kozo Kaikaku, Seido Kochiku [Challenges for East Asia: Economic Integration, Structural Reform, and Institution Building]*. Chiba: Institute of Developing Economies.
Horiuchi, Kenji. 2007. 'Hokuto ajia no enerugi shigen gaiko' [Energy/resource diplomacy in Nortehast Asia], in Takehiko Yamamoto and Satoshi Amako (eds) *Higashi Ajia Kyodo tai no Kochiku: Aratana Chiiki Keisei [Designing an East Asian Community: Forming a New Region]* Tokyo: Iwanami Shoten.
Hundt, David and Kim, Jaechun. 2011, 'Competing notions of regionalism in South Korean politics', *Japanese Journal of Political Science* 12 (2): 251–66.
Huotari, Mikko. 2012. 'Practices of financial regionalism and the negotiation of community in East Asia', Southeast Asian Studies at the University of Freiburg, Occasional Paper Series 8.
ICG (International Crisis Group). 2010. 'Stirring up the South China Sea (I)', Crisis Group Asia Report 223, (April 23).
ICSEAD. 2000. 'Recent trends and prospects for major Asian economies', *East Asian Economic Perspectives* 11: 1–177.
IIMA (Institute for International Monetary Affairs). 2006. 'Research papers and policy recommendations on regional coordination of policy measures forward: Financial market liberalization and capital market development', (March), Tokyo: IIMA. Available at http://www.mof.go.jp/english/international_policy/convention/asean_plus_3/ASEAN_plus_3research05-1-2.pdf.
Ikenberry, G. John and Mastanduno, Michael. 2003. 'Introduction: International relations theory and the search for regional stability', in G. John Ikenberry and Michael Mastanduno (eds) *International Relations Theory and the Asia-Pacific*. New York: Columbia University Press.

Ishida, Hiroyuki. 2012. 'The security of energy and regional cooperation in Asia', paper presented at the Third International Association for Energy Economics (IAEE) Asian Conference, Kyoto, February 20–22.

Ishikawa, Koichi. 2005. 'Shido suru ASEAN-Chugoku FTA (ACFTA)' [ASEAN-China FTA (ACFTA) in Start-up], *Kokusai Boeki to Toshi* 61: 34–46.

Ivanov, Igor. 2013. 'Globalization and the quest for a "smart" foreign policy', *Chinese Journal of International Politics* 6 (1): 49–57.

Jain, Purnendra and Mito, Takamichi. 2014. 'The institutionalisation of energy cooperation in Asia', in Saadia M. Pekkanen (ed.) *Asian Designs: Rising Powers and the Shaping of International Governance* (forthcoming).

Jakobson, Linda. 2008. 'Does China have an "energy diplomacy": Reflections on China's energy security and its international dimensions', in Antonio Marquina (ed.) *Energy Security: Visions from Asia and Europe*. Basingstoke: Palgrave Macmillan.

Jakobson, Linda and Knox, Dean. 2010. 'New foreign policy actors in China', *SIPRI Policy Paper* 26.

Jayasuriya, Kanishka. 2004. 'Introduction: The vicissitudes of Asian regional governance', in K. Jayasuriya (ed.) *Asian Regional Governance: Crisis and Change*. New York: Routledge.

Jiang, Yang. 2010a. 'Changing patterns of Chinese policy-making on regionalism', *Copenhagen Journal of Asian Studies* 28 (1): 109–30.

Jiang, Yang. 2010b. 'China's pursuit of free trade agreements: Is China exceptional?', *Review of International Political Economy* 17 (2): 238–61.

Jiang, Yang. 2010c. 'Response and responsibility: China in East Asian financial cooperation', *Pacific Review* 23 (5): 603–23.

Jiang, Yang. 2011. 'Rethinking the Beijing consensus: How China responds to crises', *Pacific Review* 24 (3): 337–56.

Johnson, Chalmers. 1982. *MITI and the Japanese Miracle: The Growth of Industrial Policy 1925–1975*. Stanford, C.A.: Stanford University Press.

Johnson, Chalmers. 1995. *Japan: Who Governs? The Rise of the Developmental State*. New York: Norton.

Kahler, Miles. 2010. 'Regional institutions in the era of globalization and crisis: Asia in comparative context', paper presented at the 2010 Annual Meeting of the American Political Science Association September 2–5.

Kanekiyo, Kensuke and Kobayashi, Yoshikazu. 2013. 'Oil price volatility: A threat to sustainable development in East Asia', in Daojiong Zha (ed.) *Managing Regional Energy Vulnerabilities in East Asia: Case Studies*. London: Routledge.

Kang, David C. 2003/04. 'Hierarchy, balancing and empirical puzzles in Asian international relations', *International Security* 28 (3): 165–80.

Kang, David C. 2005. 'Hierarchy in Asian international relations: 1300–1900', *Asian Security* 1 (1): 53–79.

Kang, David C. 2009. 'Between balancing and bandwagoning: South Korea's response to China', *Journal of East Asian Studies* 9 (1): 1–28.

Kanie, Norichika and Sodeno, Reiko. 2013. 'Ajia ni okeru kokusai kankyo rejimu keisei no kadai [Challenges for creating an international environmental regime in Asia]', in Shunji Matsuoka (ed.) *Ajia no Kankyo Gabanansu* [*Environmental Governance in Asia*]. Tokyo: Keiso Shobo.

Katada, N. Saori. 2011. 'Seeking a place for East Asian regionalism: Challenges and opportunities under the global financial crisis', *Pacific Review* 24 (3): 273–90.

Katzenstein, Peter J. 2005. *A World of Regions: Asia and Europe in the American Imperium*. Ithaca, N.Y.: Cornell University Press.

Katzenstein, Peter J. and Sil, Rudra. 2004. 'Rethinking Asian Security: A case for analytical eclecticism', in J. J. Suh, Peter J. Katzenstein, and Allen Carlson (eds) *Rethinking Security in East Asia: Identity, Power, and Efficiency*. Stanford, C.A.: Stanford University Press.

Kawai, Masahiro. 2010. 'Kinyu kyoryoku' [Financial cooperation], in Council on East Asian Community (ed.) *Higashi Ajia Kyodotai Hakusho 2010* [*White paper on an East Asian community 2010*]. Tokyo: Tachibana Shuppan.

Kawai, Masahiro and Houser, Cindy. 2007. 'Evolving ASEAN+3 ERPD: Toward peer reviews or due diligence?', ADBI Discussion paper 79.

Kawai, Masahiro and Wignaraja, Ganeshan. 2008. 'EAFTA or CEPEA: Which way forward?', *ASEAN Economic Bulletin* 25 (2):113–39.

Kawai, Masahiro and Wignaraja, Ganeshan. 2011. 'Asian FTAs: Trends, prospects and challenges', *Journal of Asian Economics* 22 (1): 1–22.

KEI (Korea Environment Institute). 2005. *Dongbuka Hwangkyung Hyupryukchagea Hyoryulwha Bangan Yeongu* [*The Environmental Cooperation System in Northeast Asia: The Study for Effective Programme*]. Seoul: Korea Environment Institute.

Keohane, Robert O. 1989. *International Institutions and State Power: Essays in International Relations Theory*. Boulder, C.O.: Westview Press.

Khong, Yuan Foong and Nesadurai, Helen E. S. 2007. 'Hanging together, institutional design and cooperation in Southeast Asia: AFTA and the ARF', in Amitav Acharya and Alastair Iain Johnston (eds) *Crafting Cooperation: Regional International Institutions in Comparative Perspective*. Cambridge: Cambridge University Press.

Kim, Hoseok, Shin, Eui-soon, and Chung, Woo-jin. 2011. 'Energy demand and supply, energy policies, and energy security in the Republic of Korea', *Energy Policy* 39: 6882–97.

Kim, Inkyoung. 2007. 'Environmental cooperation of Northeast Asia: Transboundary air pollution', *International Relations of the Asia-Pacific* 7 (3): 439–62.

Kim, Inkyoung. 2013. 'Messages from a middle power: Participation by the Republic of Korea in regional environmental cooperation on transboundary air pollution issues', *International Environmental Agreements: Politics, Law and Economics* 13: 1–16 (published online March 30).

Kim, Jin-Young. 2008. 'Financial cooperation within the ASEAN+3: Viability and prospects', in Jehoon Park, T. J. Pempel, and Gérard Roland (eds) *Political Economy of Northeast Asian Regionalism: Political Conflict and Economic Integration*. Cheltenham: Edward Elgar.

Kim, Soyoung and Yang, Doo Yong. 2011. 'Financial and monetary cooperation in Asia: Challenges after the global financial crisis', *International Economic Journal* 25 (4): 574–87.

King, Gary, Keohane, Robert O., and Verba, Sidney. 1994. *Designing Social Inquiry: Scientific Inference in Qualitative Research*. Princeton, N.J.: Princeton University Press.

Kokusai Keizai Koryu Zaidan. 2011. *CO_2 Haishutsu-ken Torihiki Kokusai Shijo Kakudai heno Wagakuni Sangyokai no Taio ni Kansuru Chosa Hokokusho* [*Survey Report on the Japanese Industry's Responses to the Expansion of the International Emission Trading Market*]. Tokyo: Kokusai Keizai Koryu Zaidan.

Koo, Min Gyo. 2006. 'From multilateralism to bilateralism? A shift in South Korea's trade strategy', in Vinod K. Aggarwal and Shujiro Urata (eds) *Bilateral Trade Agreements in the Asia-Pacific: Origins, Evolution, and Implications*. London: Routledge.

Koo, Min Gyo. 2009. 'South Korea's FTAs: Moving from an emulative to a competitive strategy', in Mireya Solís, Barbara Stallings, and Saori N. Katada (eds) *Competitive Regionalism: FTA Diffusion in the Pacific Rim*. Basingstoke: Palgrave Macmillan.

Koremenos, Barbara, Lipson, Charles, and Snidal, Duncan. 2001a. 'The rational design of international institutions', *International Organization* 55 (4): 761–800.

Koremenos, Barbara, Lipson, Charles, and Snidal, Duncan. 2001b. 'Rational design: Looking back to move forward', *International Organization* 55 (4): 1051–82.

Koremenos, Barbara and Snidal, Duncan. 2003. 'Moving forward, one step at a time', *International Organization* 57 (2): 431–44.

Koyama, Ken. 2001. 'ASEAN shokoku no enerugi sekyuriti seisaku to waga kuni heno inpurikeishon [The energy security policies of ASEAN countries and implications for Japan], *Enerugi Keizai* 27 (4): 55–74.

Koyama, Ken. 2002. 'Kokusai sekiyu shijo to ASEAN enerugi sekyuriti' [The international oil market and ASEAN energy security], *Enerugi Keizai* 28 (3): 22–36.

Koyama, Ken and Koide, Takaaki. 2004. 'The report for the energy cooperation among ASEAN+3 countries for 2003–2004', *IEEJ Research Paper* (September): 1–4.

Krebs, Ronald R. 2001. 'The limits of alliance: Conflict, cooperation, and collective identity', in Anthony Lake and David Ochmanek (eds) *The Real and the Ideal*. Lanham: Rowman & Littlefield.

Kuik, Cheng-Chwee. 2008. 'The essence of hedging: Malaysia and Singapore's response to a rising China', *Contemporary Southeast Asia* 30 (2): 159–85.

Kuramochi, Kazuo. 2012. 'Kankoku no kome jukyu doko to kome seisaku wo meguru shomondai' [Supply/demand trends and various issues regarding rice policies in South Korea], in Nihon Noygo Kenkyujo (ed.) *Sekai no Kome Jyukyu Doko to Shuyo Shokoku no Kanren Seisaku* [*Supply/Demand Trends in World Rice and Relevant Policies of Major Countries*]. Tokyo: Nihon Nogyo Kenkyujo. Available at http://www.nohken.or.jp/18sekai-kome/18-4-3kuramoti2012.pdf.

Kurihara, Tsuyoshi. 2011. 'ASEAN+3 chiiki kinyu kyoryoku' [Regional financial cooperation under ASEAN+3], *Kokusai Kinyu* 1229: 14–26.

Kurlantzick, Joshua. 2007. *Charm Offensive: How China's Soft Power is Transforming the World*. New Haven: Yale University Press.

Lai, Hongyi. (ed.) 2009. *Asian Energy Security: The Maritime Dimension*. New York: Palgrave Macmillan.

Lai, Hongyi. 2009. 'China's oil diplomacy in Asia', in Hongyi Lai (ed.) *Asian Energy Security: The Maritime Dimension*. New York: Palgrave Macmillan.

Lai, Hongyi. 2010. *The Domestic Sources of China's Foreign Policy*. New York: Routledge.

Larson, Deborah Welch and Shevchenko, Alexei. 2010. 'Status seekers: Chinese and Russian responses to U.S. primacy', *International Security* 34 (4): 63–95.

Lee, Alice Park. 2011 'Critical juncture in path dependence of Asian regional environmental institutions', *Journal of the Graduate School of Asia-Pacific Studies* 22: 55–69.

Lee, Seungjoo and Moon, Chung-In. 2009. 'South Korea's regional economic cooperation policy: The evolution of an adaptive strategy', in Vinod K. Aggarwal, Min Gyo Koo, Seungjoo Lee, and Chung-In Moon (eds) *Northeast Asia: Ripe for integration?* Berlin: Springer.

Levy, Jack S. 1994. 'Learning and foreign policy: Sweeping a conceptual minefield', *International Organization* 48 (2): 279–312.

Lim, Kian Tick. 2001. 'Competing regionalism: APEC and EAEG, 1989–1990', in Andrew T. H. Tan and J. D. Kenneth Boutin (eds) *Non-Traditional Security Issues in Southeast Asia*. Singapore: Select Publishing.

Liu, Fu-Kuo. 2003. 'East Asian regionalism: Theoretical perspectives', in Fu-Kuo Liu and Philippe Regnier (eds) *Regionalism in East Asia: Paradigm Shifting?* London: Routledge Curzon.

Lye, Liang Fook. 2013. 'NEAT working group on energy security cooperation', in Daojiong Zha (ed.) *Managing Regional Energy Vulnerabilities in East Asia: Case Studies*. London: Routledge.

Lynch, Julia. 2006. *Age in the Welfare State*. Cambridge: Cambridge University Press.

MacIntyre, Andrew, Pempel, T. J., and Revenhill, John (eds) 2008. *Crisis as Catalyst: Asia's Dynamic Political Economy*. Ithaca, N.Y.: Cornell University Press.

MAFF (Ministry of Agriculture, Forestry and Fisheries). no year. *Toward a World Free of Starvation and Poverty: Introductory Information on the International Food Stockholding Scheme and East Asia Emergency Rice Reserve*. Tokyo: MAFF.

MAFF (Ministry of Agriculture, Forestry and Fisheries). 2009. *Minimamu Akusesu Mai ni Kansuru Hokokusho* [*Report on Minimum Access Rice*]. Tokyo: MAFF.

Mahoney, James. 2000. 'Path dependence in historical sociology', *Theory and Society* 29 (4): 507–48.

Mahoney, James. 2001. 'Path-dependent explanation of regime change: Central America and comparative perspective', *Studies in Comparative International Development* 36 (1): 111–41.

Malik, Mohan. 2006. 'The East Asia Summit', *Australian Journal of International Affairs* 60 (2): 207–11.

Matsumoto, Naoko. 2010. 'Case study on Japan: Japan's domestic policy process towards regional cooperation on air quality management', proceedings of International Experts Workshop on International Framework and Cobenefit Approach to Promote Air Pollution Control Countermeasures in East Asia 2010, January 23–24, Hayama, Japan.

Matsuoka, Shunji. 2010. 'Ajia kankyo ron' [The environmental issues of Asia], in Takashi Terada (ed.) *Ajia-gaku no Susume 1: Ajia-Seiji Keizai Ron* [*The Exhortation of Asian Studies 1: The Politics and Economy of Asia*]. Tokyo: Kobundo.

Mendoza, Maria Nimfa F. 2012. 'The socioeconomic impact of energy security in Southeast Asia', in Mely Caballero-Anthony, Youngho Chang, and Nur Azha Putra (eds) *Energy and Non-Traditional Security (NTS) in Asia*. Berlin: Springer.

Mertha, Andrew. 2009. ' "Fragmented Authoritarianism 2.0": Political pluralisation in the Chinese policy process', *China Quarterly* 200: 995–1012.

METI (Ministry of Economy, Trade and Industry). 1999. *1999 White Paper on International Economy and Trade*. Tokyo: Okurasho Insatsukyoku.

METI (Ministry of Economy, Trade and Industry). 2001. *Sogo Shigen Enerugi Chosakai Sogo Bukai Enerugi Sekyuriti Wakingu Gurupu Hokokusho* [*Report by the Energy Security Working Group, Advisory Committee for Natural Resources and Energy*]. Tokyo: METI.

METI (Ministry of Economy, Trade and Industry). 2006. *Gurobaru Keizai Senryaku: Higashi Ajia Keizai Togo to Nihon no Sentaku* [*Global Economic Strategy: Economic Integration in East Asia and Japan's Choice*]. Tokyo: Gyosei.

METI (Ministry of Economy, Trade and Industry). 2008. *2008 White Paper on International Economy and Trade*. Tokyo: Nikkei Insatsu.

METI (Ministry of Economy, Trade and Industry). 2009. *2009-nen Enerugi Hakusho* [*White Paper on Energy 2009*]. Tokyo: Enerugi Foramu.

METI (Ministry of Economy, Trade and Industry). 2011. *2011 White Paper on International Economy and Trade*. Tokyo: Yamaura Insatsu.

Meunier, Sophie. 2003. 'Trade policy and political legitimacy in the European Union', *Comparative European Politics* 1 (1): 67–90.

Milner, Helen V. 1997. *Interests, Institutions, and Information: Domestic Politics and International Relations*. Princeton, N.J.: Princeton University Press.

Ministry of the Environment (MOE). 1997. *Higashi Ajia Sanseiu Monitaringu Nettowaaku: Senmonka Kaigo no Seika* [*The Acid Deposition Monitoring Network in East Asia: The Outcomes of Expert Group Meetings*]. Tokyo: MOE.

Miyazaki, Asami. no year. 'Judiciousness of networks in environmental governance? A case study of the Acid Deposition Monitoring Network in East Asia (EANET)'. Available at http://userpage.fu-berlin.de/ffu/akumwelt/bc2008/papers/bc2008_404_Miyazaki.pdf.

Miyazaki, Asami. 2007. 'Kankyo gabanansu ni okeru "nettowaku" no igi' ['The implications of "network" in environmental governance'], *Koeki-gaku Kenkyu* 9 (1): 24–36.

MOFA (Ministry of Foreign Affairs). 2007. 'Nihon no keizai renkei kyotei (EPA) kosho: Genjo to kadai' [Japan's EPA negotiations: Current states and problems], (March), Tokyo: MOFA.

Mols, Manfred. 2000. 'Asia-Pacific: Why theory and what type of it? A view from political science', in Jörn Dosch and Manfred Mols (eds) *International Relations in the Asia-Pacific: New Patterns of Power, Interest, and Cooperation*. New York: St. Martin's Press.

Moon, Chung-In and Chun, Chaesung. 2003. 'Sovereignty: Dominance of the Westphalian concept and implications for regional security', in Muthiah Alagappa (ed.) *Asian Security Order: Instrumental and Normative Features*. Stanford, C.A.: Stanford University Press.

Morton, Katherine. 2012. 'Learning by doing: China's role in the global governance of food security', Indiana University Research Center for Chinese Politics & Business Working Paper 30.

Mukherjee, Saptarshi. 2011. 'Joint strategic oil stocks in Asia: An analysis', *Energy Security Insights* 3 (2): 18–22.

Mulgan, Aurelia George. 2000. 'Japan's political leadership deficit', *Australian Journal of Political Science* 35 (2): 183–202.

Munakata, Naoko. 2001. 'Nihon no chiiki keizai togo seisaku no keisei' [The formation of Japan's regional economic integration policy], in Naoko Munakata (ed.) *Nicchu Kankei no Tenki* [*A Turning Point of Japan-China Relations*]. Tokyo: Toyo Keizai Shinposha.

Munakata, Naoko. 2006. *Transforming East Asia: The Evolution of Regional Economic Integration*. Washington D.C.: Brooking Institution Press.

Munck, Gerard L. 2004. 'Tools for quantitative research', in Henry E. Brady and David Collier (eds) *Rethinking Social Inquiry: Diverse Tools, Shared Standards*. Lanham: Rowman & Littlefied.

Nabers, Dirk. 2003. 'The social construction of international institutions: The case of ASEAN+3', *International Relations of the Asia-Pacific* 3 (1): 113–36.

Nabers, Dirk. 2010. 'Power, leadership, and hegemony in international politics: The case of East Asia', *Review of International Studies* 36 (3): 931–49.

Nakai, Tsuyoshi. 2009. 'A way forward to enhance ASEAN+3 energy security', paper presented at Petrostock 2009: Stockpiling in New Market Realities, February 9–11, 2009, Huston Texas, USA.

Nakatsuji, Keiji. 2009. Higashi ajia kinyu togo no kokusai seiji ['International politics of financial integration in East Asia'], *Kokusai Seiji* 158: 57–74.

Nam, Sangmin. 2002. 'Ecological interdependence and environmental governance in Northeast Asia: Politics versus cooperation', in Paul G. Harris (ed.) *International Environmental Cooperation: Politics and Diplomacy in Pacific Asia*. Boulder, C.O.: University Press of Colorado.

Narine, Shaun. 2004. 'State sovereignty, political legitimacy and regional institutionalism in the Asia-Pacific', *Pacific Review* 17 (3): 423–50.

Nesadurai, Helen and Stone, Diane. 2000. 'Southeast Asian research institutes and regional cooperation', in Diane Stone (ed.) *Banking on Knowledge: The Genesis of the Global Development Network*. London: Routledge.

Nicolas, Françoise. 2009. 'ASEAN energy cooperation: An increasingly daunting challenge'. Paper from Institut Francais des Relations Internationles (IFRI). Available at http://www.nst.or.th/n-power/Asean-energy-IFRI_fnicolas.pdf.

Nishimura, Hidetoshi. 2013. 'The progress report of the ERIA (Economic Research Institute for ASEAN and East Asia), As of May 30, 2013'.

Nitta, Akira. 2008. 'Recent progress of Acid Deposition Monitoring Network in East Asia (EANET)', presentation at International Conference on Transboundary Air Pollution, December 17–19, Tokyo.

North, Douglass C. 2005. *Understanding the Process of Economic Change*. Princeton, N.J.: Princeton University Press.

Oba, Mie. 2003. 'Tsuka kinyu kyoryoku to FTA ni miru nihon no higashi ajia chiiki keisei senryaku' [Japan's strategies for regional formation in East Asia in light of currency/financial cooperation and FTAs], in Susumu Yamakage (ed.) *Higashi Ajia Chiiki Shugi to Nihon Gaiko* [*Regionalism in East Asia and Japanese Diplomacy*]. Tokyo: Nihon Kokusai Mondai Kenkyujo.

Oba, Mie. 2004. 'Higashi ajia ni okeru shokuryo anzen hosho kyoryoku no shinten' [The evolution of cooperation on food security in East Asia], *Kokusai Seiji* 135: 24–42.

Oh, Chong Jin. 2012. 'Security conditions and regional competition in East Asia after the new millennium: A South Korean perspective', *Perceptions: Journal of International Affairs* 17 (4): 105–28.

Oike, Atsuyuki. 2006. 'Nihon no EPA kosho no tenkai to tenbo' [The evolution and prospect of Japan's EPA negotiations], *Boeki to Kanzei* 54 (12): 24–39.

Okimura, Satoshi. 2012. 'Hokuto ajia ni okeru kokusai kankyo mondai to kokusai kankyo seido' [International environmental issues and international environmental institutions in Northeast Asia], *Hokuto Ajia Kenkyu* 23: 47–58.

Onis, Ziya. 1991. 'The logic of the developmental state', *Comparative Politics* 24 (1): 109–26.

Onishi, Yasuo. 2007. 'Chugoku no FTA senryaku to kaigai chokusetsu toshi' [China's FTA strategy and FDI], in Chiharu Tamamura (ed.) *Higashi Ajia FTA to Nicchu Boeki* [*East Asian FTAs and Japan-China Trade*]. Chiba: Ajia Keizai Kenkyujo.

Oyane, Satoshi. 2004. 'Higashi ajia FTA: Nihon no seisaku tenkan to chiiki koso' [East Asian FTA: Japan's policy change and regional concept], *Kokusai Mondai* 528: 52–66.

Oyane, Satoshi. 2012. *Kokusai Rejimu to Nichibei no Gaiko Koso* [*International Regimes and the Diplomatic Concepts of Japan and the United States*]. Tokyo: Yuhikaku.

Pacific Consultant International. 2002. *Taikoku Higasi Ajia Shokuryo Anzen Hosho oyobi Kome Bichiku Shisutemu Keikaku Chosa: Saishu Hokokusho* [*Thailand: Survey on East Asian Food Security and Rice Reserve System: The Final Report*]. Tokyo: Pacific Consultants International.

Pape, Robert A. 2005. 'Soft balancing against the United States', *International Security* 30 (1): 7–45.

Pearson, Margaret M. 2010. 'Domestic institutional constraints on China's leadership in East Asian economic cooperation mechanisms', *Journal of Contemporary China* 19 (66): 621–33.

Pekkanen, Saadia M. and Tsai, Kellee S. 2005. 'Introduction: Late liberalizers: Comparative perspectives on Japan and China', in Saadia M. Pekkanen and Kellee S. Tsai (eds) *Japan and China in the World Political Economy*. New York: Routledge.

Pempel, T. J. 2005a. 'Introduction: Emerging webs of regional connectedness', in T. J. Pemple (ed.) *Remapping East Asia: The Construction of a Region*. Ithaca, N.Y.: Cornell University Press.

Pempel, T. J. 2005b. 'Conclusion: Tentativeness and tensions in the construction of an Asian region', in T. J. Pempel (ed.) *Remapping East Asia: The Construction of a Region*. Ithaca, N.Y.: Cornell University Press.

Pempel, T. J. 2012. 'Book reviews, the making of Northeast Asia,' *International Relations of Asia-Pacific* 12 (1): 193–96.

Pierre, Jon and Peters, B. Guy. 2000. *Governance, Politics, and the State*. New York: St. Martin's Press.

Pierson, Paul. 2004. *Politics in Time: History, Institution, and Social Analysis*. Princeton, N.J.: Princeton University Press.

Qin, Yaqing. 2008. 'International factors and China's external behaviour: Power, interdependence, and institutions', in Pauline Kerr, Stuart Harris, and Qin Yaqing (eds) *China's New Diplomacy: Tactical or Fundamental Change?* New York: Palgrave Macmillan.

Rajan, Ramkishen S., Sen, Rahul, and Siregar, Reza. 2001. *Singapore and Free Trade Agreements: Economic Relations with Japan and the United States*. Singapore: Institute of Southeast Asian Studies.

Rathus, Joel. 2011. *Japan, China and Networked Regionalism in East Asia*. Basingstoke: Palgrave Macmillan.

Ravenhill, John. 2003. 'The new bilateralism in the Asia Pacific', *Third World Quarterly* 24 (2): 299–317.

Ravenhill, John. 2010. 'The "new East Asian regionalism": A political domino effect', *Review of International Political Economy* 17 (2): 178–208.

Ravenhill, John. 2013. 'Resource insecurity and international institutions in the Asia-Pacific region', *Pacific Review* 26 (1): 39–64.

Ravenhill, John and Jiang, Yang. 2009. 'China's move to preferential trading: A new direction in China's diplomacy', *Journal of Contemporary China* 18 (58): 27–46.

Risse, Thomas. 2000. ' "Let's argue!": Communicative action in world politics', *International Organization* 54 (1): 1–39.

Rose, Gideon. 1998. 'Neoclassical realism and theories of foreign policy', *World Politics* 51 (1): 144–72.

Ross, Robert S. 2006. 'Balance of power politics and the rise of China: Accommodation and balancing in East Asia', *Security Studies* 15 (3): 355–95.

Rozman, Gilbert. 2007. 'South Korea and Sino-Japanese rivalry: A middle power's options within the East Asian core triangle', *Pacific Review* 20 (2): 197–220.

Rüland, Jürgen. 2012. 'The limits of democratizing interest representation: ASEAN's regional corporatism and normative challenges', *European Journal of International Relations*, published online July 16, 2012, DOI: 10.1177/1354066112445289.

Sakakibara, Eisuke. 1999. 'Mister yen's message on the financial crisis', *Japan Echo* 26 (5): 45–9.

Schelling, Thomas C. 1960. *The Strategy of Conflict*. Cambridge: Harvard University Press.

Schmidt, Vivien. 2006. 'Institutionalism and the state', in Colin Hay, Michael Lister, and David Marsh (eds) *The State: Theories and Issues*. Basingstoke: Palgrave Macmillan.

Searight, Amy. 2009. 'Emerging economic architecture in Asia: Opening or insulating the region?', in Michael J. Green and Bates Gill (eds) *Asia's New Multilateralism: Cooperation, Competition and the Search for Community*. New York: Columbia University Press.

Severino, Rodolfo C. 2006. *Southeast Asia in Search of an ASEAN Community: Insights from the Former ASEAN Secretary-General*. Singapore: Institute of Southeast Asian Studies.

Severino, Rodolfo C. 2007. 'ASEAN beyond forty: Towards political and economic integration', *Contemporary Southeast Asia* 29 (3): 406–23.

Shekhar, Vibhanshu. 2012. 'ASEAN's response to the rise of China: Deploying a hedging strategy', *China Report* 48 (3): 253–68.

Shih, Chih-yu and Yin, Jiwu. 2013. 'Between core national interest and a harmonious world: Reconciling self-role conceptions in Chinese foreign policy', *Chinese Journal of International Politics* 6 (1): 59–84.

Shimura, Noriko. 2004. 'Higashi ajia ni okeru chiiki kinyu kyoryoku no shinten' [The development of regional financial cooperation in East Asia], Institute for International Monetary Affairs, *International Economic and Financial Review* 6: 1–8.

Shin, Eui-soon and Savage, Tim. 2011. 'Joint stock piling and emergency sharing of oil: Arrangements for regional cooperation in East Asia', *Energy Policy* 39: 2817–23.

Shinoda, Tomohito. 2000. *Leading Japan: The Role of the Prime Minister.* Westport, C.T.: Praeger.

Sidik, Mulyo. 2004. 'Indonesia rice policy in view of trade liberalisation', paper presented at the FAO Rice Conference, February 12–13, Rome Italy.

Sohn, Injoo. 2008. 'Learning to co-operate: China's multilateral approach to Asian financial co-operation', *China Quarterly* 194: 309–26.

Sohn, Injoo. 2012. 'Toward normative fragmentation: An East Asian financial architecture in the post-global crisis world', *Review of International Political Economy* 19 (4): 586–608.

Solingen, Etel. 2008. 'The genesis, design and effects of regional institutions: Lessons from East Asia and the Middle East', *International Studies Quarterly*, 52 (2): 261–94.

Solís, Mireya. 2009. 'Japan's competitive FTA strategy: Commercial opportunity versus political rivalry', in Mireya Solís, Barbara Stallings, and Saori N. Katada (eds) *Competitive Regionalism: FTA Diffusion in the Pacific Rim*. Basingstoke: Palgrave Macmillan.

Solís, Mireya. 2011. 'Global economic crisis: Boon or bust for East Asian trade integration?', *Pacific Review* 24 (3): 311–36.

Song, Guoyou and Yuan, Wen Jin. 2012. 'China's free trade agreement strategies', *Washington Quarterly* 35 (4): 107–19.

Stallings, Barbara and Katada, Saori N. 2009. 'Conclusion: FTAs in a competitive world', in Mireya Solís, Barbara Stallings, and Saori N. Katada (eds) *Competitive Regionalism: FTA Diffusion in the Pacific Rim*. Basingstoke: Palgrave Macmillan.

State Environmental Protection Administration (SEPA). 2007. *2006 Report on the State of the Environment in China*. SEPA: Beijing.

Stone, Diane. 2002. 'Introduction: Global knowledge and advocacy networks', *Global Networks* 2 (1): 1–11.

Stubbs, Richard. 2011. 'The East Asian developmental state and the great recession: Evolving contesting coalitions', *Contemporary Politics* 17 (2): 151–66.

Sukekawa, Seiya. 2012. 'Higashi ajia keizaiken keisei to kigyo risuku bunsan' [The formation of an economic zone in East Asia and corporate risk diversification], *Ajia Kenkyojo Shirizu* 78: 251–73.

Sussangkarn, Chalongphob. 2010. 'The Chiang Mai initiative multilateralization: Origin, development and outlook', ADBI Working paper series 230 (July).
Sussangkarn, Chalongphob. 2011. 'Chiang Mai initiative multilateralization: Origin, development and outlook', *Asian Economic Policy Review* 6: 203–20.
Sutter, Robert. 2008. 'The United States in Asia', in David Shambaugh and Michael Yahuda (eds) *International Relations of Asia*. Lanham: Rowman & Littlefield.
Sutter, Robert and Huang, Chin-Hao. 2009. 'China-Southeast Asia relations: Ferment over the South China Sea', *Comparative Connections* (July). Available at: http://csis.org/files/publication/0902qchina_seasia.pdf.
Suzuki, Nobuhiro. 2008. 'Higashi ajia chiiki no shokuryo anzen hosho' [Food security in the East Asian region], *Nogyo to Keizai* 74 (14): 39–47.
Tabor, Steve R., Dillon, H. S. and Sawit, M. Husein. 1999. 'Understanding the 1998 food crisis: Supply, demand or policy failure?', Aciar Indonesia, Research Project Working Paper 99–13.
Takahashi, Wakana. 2000. 'Formation of an East Asian regime for acid rain control: The perspective of comparative regionalism', *International Review for Environmental Strategies* 1 (1): 97–117.
Takahashi, Wakana. 2002. 'Problems of environmental cooperation in Northeast Asia: The case of acid rain', in Paul G. Harris (ed.) *International Environmental Cooperation: Politics and Diplomacy in Pacific Asia*. Boulder, C.O.: University Press of Colorado.
Tanabe, Yasuo. 2004. 'Ajia enerugi patonashippu ni mukete' [Searching for energy partnership in Asia], in Yasuo Tanabe (ed.) *Ajia Enerugi Patonashippu* [*Energy Partnership in Asia*]. Tokyo: Enerugi Foramu.
Tanabe, Yasuo. 2011. 'Asian energy partnership: Opportunities and obstacles', in Elspeth Thomson, Youngho Chang, and Jae-Seung Lee (eds) *Energy Conservation in East Asia*. World Scientific: Singapore.
Taniguchi, Makoto. 2004. *Higashi Ajia Kyodotai* [*An East Asian Community*]. Tokyo: Iwanami Shoten.
Terada, Takashi. 2003. 'Constructing an "East Asian" concept and growing regional identity: From EAEC to ASEAN+3', *Pacific Review* 16 (2): 251–77.
Terada, Takashi. 2011. 'Nihon no APEC senryaku to TPP' [The TPP and Japan's APEC strategy], *Kaigai Jijo* 59 (9): 88–104.
Thelen, Kathleen. 1999. 'Historical institutionalism in comparative politics', *Annual Review of Political Science* 2: 369–404.
Toda, Eisaku. 2000. 'Higashi ajia sanseiu monitaringu nettowaku no keika to shorai' [The history and future of the Acid Deposition Monitoring Network in East Asia], *Shigen Kankyo Taisaku* 36 (10): 15–19.
Toyoda, Takashi. 2009. 'Higashi ajia fudo sekyuriti no chiiki kyoryoku' [Regional cooperation on food security in East Asia], in Hitoshi Hirakawa, Naoaki Kobayashi, and Akifumi Morimoto. (eds) *Higashi Ajia Chiiki Kyoryoku no Kyodo Sekkei* [*The Joint Design of an East Asian Regional Community*]. Tokyo: Nishida Shoten.
Van Evera, Stephen. 1997: *Guide to Methods for Students of Political Sciences*. Ithaca, N.Y.: Cornell University Press.
Verdun, Amy. 1999. 'The role of the Delors Committee in the creation of EMU: An epistemic community?', *Journal of European Public Policy* 6 (2): 308–28.
Vivoda, Vlado. 2012. 'Japan's energy security predicament post-Fukushima', *Energy Policy* 46: 135–43.
Walt, Stephen M. 1987. *The Origins of Alliances*. Ithaca, N.Y.: Cornell University Press.
Waltz, Kenneth N. 1979. *Theory of International Politics*. New York: McGraw-Hill.

Wang, Jianwei. 2005. 'China's multilateral diplomacy in the new millennium', in Yong Deng and Fei-Ling Wang (eds) *China Rising: Power and Motivation in Chinese Foreign Policy*. Lanham: Rowman & Littlefield.

Wangwongwatana, Supat. 2001. 'Step-by-step approach to establish Acid Deposition Monitoring Network in East Asia (EANET): Thailand's experiences', *Water, Air, and Soil Pollution* 130: 151–62.

Wangwongwatana, Supat. 2012. 'Instrument for strengthening the Acid Deposition Monitoring in East Asia (EANET)', presentation at Regional Cooperation Mechanisms for Air Quality Better Air Quality (BAQ) 2012 Conference December 5–7, Hong Kong.

Wendt, Alexander E. 2001. 'Driving with the rearview mirror: On the rational science of institutional design', *International Organization* 55 (4):1019–49.

Wilkening, Kenneth E. 2004. *Acid Rain Science and Politics in Japan: A History of Knowledge and Action toward Sustainability*. Cambridge: MIT Press.

Wong, Joseph. 2004. 'The adaptive developmental state in East Asia', *Journal of East Asian Studies* 4 (3): 345–62.

Wong, John. 2012. 'Think tanks in East Asia in need of more cooperation and more networking: NEAT after its ten years', *East Asian Policy: An International Quarterly* 4 (3): 91–96.

Yamada, Yasuhiro. 2002. 'Higashi ajia chiiki keizai togo to chugoku' [Regional economic integration in East Asia and China], *Chugoku Keizai* 438: 16–32.

Yamamoto, Yoshinobu. 2007. 'Chiiki togo riron to "higashi ajia kyodotai" ' [Regional integration theory and 'an East Asian community'], in Takehiko Yamamoto and Satoshi Amako (eds) *Higashi Ajia Kyodo tai no Kochiku: Aratana Chiiki Keisei* [*The Building of an East Asian Community: Forming a New Region*]. Tokyo: Iwanami Shoten.

Yamashita, Ken. 2009. 'Ajia chiiki ni okeru taiki kankyo seisaku ni kansuru kenkyu' [Research on atmospheric environmental policy in the Asian region]. Niigata Daigaku Daigakuin Gendai Shakai Bunka Kenkyuka. Available at http://dspace.lib.niigata-u.ac.jp:8080/dspace/bitstream/10191/8408/1/09_0008_YK.pdf.

Yang, Jian. 2009. 'China's competitive FTA strategy: Realism on a liberal slide', in Mireya Solís, Barbara Stallings, and Saori N. Katada (eds) *Competitive Regionalism: FTA Diffusion in the Pacific Rim*. Basingstoke: Palgrave Macmillan.

Yoon, Esook, 2006. 'South Korean environmental foreign policy', *Asia-Pacific Review* 13 (2): 74–96.

Yoshimatsu, Hidetaka. 2003. *Japan and East Asia in Transition: Trade Policy, Crisis and Evolution, and Regionalism*. Basingstoke: Palgrave Macmillan.

Yoshimatsu, Hidetaka. 2007. 'Regional integration and business interests: A comparative study of Europe and Southeast Asia', *European Journal of East Asian Studies* 6 (2): 217–43.

Yoshimatsu, Hidetaka. 2008. *The Political Economy of Regionalism in East Asia: Integrative Explanation for Dynamics and Challenges*. Basingstoke: Palgrave Macmillan.

Yoshimatsu, Hidetaka. 2012a. 'Japan, globalization, and East Asian dynamism', in Jan Nederveen Pieterse and Jongtae Kim (eds) *Globalization and Development in East Asia*. London: Routledge.

Yoshimatsu, Hidetaka. 2012b. 'Sino-Japanese energy relations: Processes and constraints', *Asian Journal of Political Science* 20 (2): 180–202.

Youngho, Chang and Koh, Collin. 2009. 'ASEAN petroleum security agreement: Sealed or leaking?', *RSIS Commentaries* 28/2009, March 16.

Yu, Hyun-Seok. 2003. 'Explaining the emergence of new East Asian regionalism: Beyond power and interest-based approaches', *Asian Perspective* 27 (1): 261–88.

Yuan, Wen Jin and Murphy, Melissa. 2010. 'Regional monetary cooperation in East Asia: Should the United States be concerned?', *Center for Strategic and International Studies* (November).

Zeng, Ka. 2010. 'Multilateral versus bilateral and regional trade liberalization: Explaining China's pursuit of free trade agreements (FTAs)', *Journal of Contemporary China* 19 (66): 635–52.

Zhang, Yungling and Shen, Minghui. 2013. 'Ajia taiheiyo ni okeru FTA: Chugoku no tenbo' [FTAs in the Asia-Pacific: The Chinese perspective], *Kokusai Mondai* 622: 41–50.

Zheng, Bijian. 2005. 'China's peaceful rise to the great power status', *Foreign Affairs* 84 (5): 18–24.

Zito, Anthony R. 2001a. 'Epistemic communities, collective entrepreneurship and European integration', *Journal of European Public Policy* 8 (4): 585–603.

Zito, Anthony R. 2001b. 'Epistemic communities, European Union governance and the public voice', *Science and Public Policy* 28 (6): 465–76.

Index

Printed and bound by CPI Group (UK) Ltd, Croydon, CR0 4YY